Qualitative Research in Context

Edited by

Laura Marks

Published by Admap
in conjunction with the
Association for Qualitative Research

First published 2000

Admap Publications
Farm Road, Henley-on-Thames
Oxfordshire RG9 1EJ, United Kingdom
Telephone: +44 (0) 1491 411000
Facsimile: +44 (0) 1491 571188
E-mail: admap@ntc.co.uk

A CIP catalogue record for this book is
available from the British Library

ISBN 1 84116 063 6

Typeset in 10/13pt Palatino by Marie Doherty
Printed and bound in Great Britain by Cromwell Press, Trowbridge

Contents

Introduction

Laura Marks

UNDERSTANDING PEOPLE: THE CONTEXT FOR GROWTH

The changing definition of consumerism

It is said that the consumer is king. The reality, as we all know from personal experience, is that the consumer has a degree of discretion or choice but in many cases the consumer choice is limited, and the extent of the choice varies hugely depending on the context. Often we are much more the pawn than the king. There are so many examples, commercial and otherwise.

We all have a vote but how many of us feel that political parties really care about us or understand our needs? Whilst we are told that we have a role to play in democracy, many of us feel that politicians have very little interest in normal people or what happens to them. I certainly do not believe that politicians take ordinary people seriously or understand their lifestyles, attitudes and priorities. As a result I am far from convinced that the choices they offer me (when they offer one at all) are for my benefit or indeed for the benefit of the community.

Secondly, I remember vividly as a student basically accepting that universities existed primarily for research. Inconsequential undergraduates like me had to take second place for our tutors. We certainly did not see ourselves as purchasers of academic services. The economic climate has changed, forcing universities to compete for students but few are equipped to deal with this challenge, which involves a major shift towards a consumer focused climate.

Again, I have often wondered how so many museums justified being so utterly dull and lifeless when I was growing up in London. This was the norm until recently when the arts establishments started to need to compete for public funds and, indeed, for audiences and visitors. We never challenged our rights to be treated seriously, never mind as 'king'.

The need to re-evaluate

The world has changed and much of this can be attributed to commercialisation and economic pressure on organisations. Whereas television producers were once able to feed us on a diet of programmes they thought interesting, artistic, innovative or funny, they have been challenged by a new marketplace where viewers have a wide choice. People can now access a vast range of programmes and makers have to fight for their audiences, their advertisers and, therefore, their income. While some may argue that this has reduced quality, it has certainly changed the rules of the game.

Similarly, the arts establishments now have to prove that they are worthy of funding and this is attached to a need to prove accessibility. They suddenly need to actively attract a broad range of people rather than a narrow band of loyal followers. Even the Church has woken up to the fact that people are finding alternative sources of spiritual sustenance and that, without action, the Church will find itself without a congregation.

Understanding the consumer context

In practically every aspect of our lives, providers of products or services are starting to recognise the need to understand people, to see their offering within the context of their 'customer'. In simple terms, this can be attributed to increasing consumer choice and the tightening of budgets.

Clearly, there are some 'industries' where the importance of the consumer context has been recognised for many years. Advertising has actively built the consumer into the process since the early 1950s and it is now a highly sophisticated process which is under constant scrutiny. Account planning was introduced into advertising agencies as they recognised the added value to the client which came with really understanding the target market. Better briefs were produced for the creative teams based on consumer, not just client insight.

For many industries, however, this is a major shift in emphasis, philosophy and working practice. The recognition that a better understanding of people can result in differentiation and a competitive edge has caused organisations and industries to rethink the way they operate and to embrace new techniques. These enable them to understand their consumers in meaningful ways.

This book is concerned with how and why specific industries have woken up to the need to understand people and the role of qualitative research in facilitating this process.

THE ROLE OF QUALITATIVE RESEARCH

What is qualitative research?

Qualitative research is described by many by what it is not. It is not quantified research. It does not enable the user to view the consumer world in terms of percentages or 'hard facts', such as 67% of all women in Hertfordshire buy this or 27% of all children under 8 years old eat that. Qualitative research is, however, a uniquely useful method of finding out about people, what they think, feel, hope, believe and understand. It enables us to explore beneath the surface and to consider why people do what they do, think how they think and, in some cases, behave the way they behave.

Qualitative research is more of an art than a science. It does not judge itself against the normal measurable standards of science or social science. It is measured, rather, by its usefulness in helping those that commission it. It provides insights into people and their motivations. In the commercial world this might illuminate purchasing behaviour, in the arts world, visiting patterns, in television, viewing patterns, and in the world of religion, it might shed light on people's affiliation or non-affiliation to a community or creed.

How is qualitative research conducted?

Qualitative research involves the interviewing of people, either in small groups or individually, by highly trained and experienced researchers. The aim is for the researcher to explore issues which underlie beliefs or behaviours, factors which will enable the researcher and, ultimately, the client to develop products, brands, services or communications with the public.

The research sample will be carefully chosen, not necessarily to be representative of the whole population but rather to represent a key element of that universe. For example, in order to help develop a new piece of advertising for a car, the researcher may choose to focus on people who are obsessed with their cars and who love advertising. The important factor in sampling is that the interviews are conducted amongst people who will enable the researcher and client to understand their audience better and to provide useful and unique insights.

Interviewing is also very different from traditional survey research in that there is no questionnaire or standard format for the interview. Instead, the researcher will prepare a topic guide, based on open ended questions and techniques which will enable him or her to explore the relevant issues in detail. The approach has several important functions:

- It allows respondents (those being interviewed) to talk in a way that is meaningful to themselves, in 'real' language, not that imposed by a questionnaire.
- It allows respondents to set the agenda themselves. Whilst it is important to measure responses or attitudes, in the early stages of the development of an idea it is extremely useful to allow respondents to tell you what matters to them, their own start point, their premises and their underlying beliefs.
- It encourages respondents to talk about things which they normally choose not to discuss or, indeed, are unable to easily discuss, such as their feelings about a brand or a market. People often think that they have no feelings or thoughts surrounding a topic but a skilled researcher can help them retrieve and express thoughts which lie beneath the surface.
- It enables the skilled researcher to watch the respondent as a whole, their language, facial expression, body language and so forth and, from this, to gain a much better understanding than via the use of a questionnaire alone.
- If conducted in groups the techniques can be very creative, enabling people to collectively develop and refine ideas which might be difficult individually.

Finally, qualitative analysis is very different from the analysis associated with a quantified survey. The researcher reviews the 'data' (what people said, how they responded, their body language, the silences, etc.) and comes to a view about what it all means. In particular, the researcher will advise the client not only on what was said (or expressed) but on what this means for the client and their market. The interpretation is based on data, an understanding of the client's industry or problem and a view of the consumers. This will be coloured and informed by the application of psychological, sociological or anthropological models on which the researcher might draw.

The theory of qualitative research is the subject of Chapter 1 as it sets the context for a discussion of the uses and applications of the methodology.

THE APPLICATIONS OF QUALITATIVE RESEARCH

Early applications

In its early days in the 1950s qualitative research was used primarily by commercial organisations and its aim was to gain insight into consumer behaviour, a process previously limited to quantitative techniques. This was a major breakthrough for business at the time and motivational research took off. Clients found great benefits in this new, deeper understanding of their consumers and in what drove people in a particular direction.

The importance of the advertising agencies

Gradually, qualitative research thinking and methodology started to be accepted in the broader business world. Advertising agencies recognised their value in enabling them to write better briefs and better inform their creative teams about the people the advertising targeted. This adoption of qualitative research enabled the UK to become a world leader in advertising in the 1970s and 1980s.

A perfect example might be the now world famous advertising for *The Economist*. I was lucky enough to work on this brand at AMV.BBDO for ten years during the development of the 'Red' campaign. Qualitative research helped us to understand the inherent prestige associated with the publication (at the time very understated), the quirkiness and readability attributed to it by its readers and the competitive, rather aggressive business environment of the late 1980s. All this led to a creative brief focusing on the emotional benefits of readership rather than product stories. The rest, as they say, is history…

The commercial world adopted qualitative research, recognising its limitations in terms of providing quantitative data but hooked on the unique way in which it illustrated the world, beliefs, attitudes and motivations of consumers. It allowed companies to better understand the way in which people might choose, buy and use products, brands, advertising and other forms of communication.

Recent converts

In recent years, other fields, not just those involved with the commercial world, have started to recognise that a better understanding of people is essential to their competitiveness or, indeed, their very survival. Many organisations have traditionally assumed that whatever they provided people would 'consume' or accept. They have been forced to question that belief. They saw that with a vast range of choices and options, people might opt out of needing them and certainly might switch their allegiance to competitors.

There is a new recognition that it is no longer sufficient to provide what the organisation wants to provide; the consumer context must be taken into account. Whilst the consumer is not necessarily considered the most important part of the mix, at least he or she now has a role in the future of a range of industries. Qualitative research is a key tool in assisting with defining and refining that role.

Resistance to qualitative research

Not all industries have accepted qualitative research as the appropriate tool. Resistance has been for cultural as well as practical reasons and these can only be broken down under the right set of circumstances. People used to setting their own agenda or people who are driven by a firm belief in a set of values have often found it very difficult to accommodate the view that the end users also have a valid role. This is particularly the case where there is no overt commercial relationship between the provider and user of a service and so the provider therefore feels no obligation to adapt to the needs of the public. Examples are found throughout this book.

AN INTRODUCTION TO THE BOOK

This book focuses on the context for qualitative research, the consumer and the context in which qualitative research is now being used. It considers the reasons why industries have had to face up to the need to understand their consumers. It also explores the issues and problems this has created when consumer input has not been welcomed or even accepted. The book considers what qualitative research can uniquely offer a given industry and the ways in which it can help move the industry forward. Finally, the practical implications of using qualitative research are explored with guidelines for practitioners and buyers alike.

The book is divided into chapters, each focusing on one field and written by a leading practitioner in that field. Each chapter has four main headings:

- *The context.* This explains the consumer context and why an understanding of the relevant public has become an essential.
- *The role for qualitative research.* This considers what qualitative research can and can't do in the given field.
- *Practicalities.* These consider what specific issues need to be considered when conducting research in a given field (not trying to cover the basics of how to conduct qualitative research per se).
- *The future* or a summary.

The choice of fields

I chose 13 different fields for this book. The list is by no means exhaustive. I know, for example, that the legal world has started using qualitative research to explore how juries are likely to react to particular topics or dilemmas. The medical world is using qualitative methodology in the field of new drug testing, recognising that the effectiveness of particular treatments will be influenced by how people feel about the drugs and their expectations and beliefs, and not just the potential chemical processes involved.

The aim here is to cover a range of ideas where qualitative research is well known and also those where it is new. In areas where it is well known the chapters focus more on new consumer issues and methodologies (such as advertising and design). In areas where qualitative research has not traditionally been used, such as broadcasting, the text focuses more on the problems associated with change and the difficulties of conducting research and making it acceptable within the industry.

Additionally, there are fields where marketing and the role of the customers or consumers has never been considered necessary or desirable but where it is now being demanded in the face of competition and the changing world. These include the arts, religion and higher education. Then there are fields which have recognised the need for insight but shunned qualitative approaches. The reasons why qualitative research has been introduced are discussed, along with the issues and problems it raises. These industries include television programme development, media research and direct marketing.

I have included two chapters on politics, one focusing on party politics and one on social policy. The chapters are very different from one another but discuss the need for consumer insight in the world of policy making and governance. Both explore the difficulties associated with researching this area and the controversial subject of a 'marketing' versus 'dogma' led approach to the development of government.

The book also covers the area of international research. Whilst not an industry per se, the issue of understanding consumers across continents and cultures is too important and too much a part of the future to leave it out. There is a degree of overlap between this chapter and the first chapter on the theory of research by Imms. This is inevitable given that international research is more of a methodology and philosophy than an industry. Those interested in theory would be advised to read both.

Finally, there is a chapter on the use of qualitative research in the field of innovation. In many ways this is the issue of the future for all the fields mentioned as everyone strives to differentiate themselves in a world where products and services can be rapidly copied and staying ahead in product or service terms is virtually impossible.

The start point

The book begins with an explanation by Mike Imms of the context in which qualitative research exists. Excellent books have been written on how to conduct research and on the practicalities and interpretation of the output.

These include two books by Wendy Gordon (one with Roy Langmaid) and one by Sue Robson and Angela Foster.

In the theory chapter we focus on the intellectual start point for qualitative research and consider how an understanding of the theories and philosophies of the discipline is the essential building block for practitioners. It is only by placing qualitative research in its academic and intellectual context that we can see how it can play a useful role in assisting industries to develop and grow.

The authors

Each author is a specialist practitioner. They are all well known as experts within their field and bring unique insight to the book. Most of the chapters also have a consultant author. The role of the consultant is to ensure that the chapter is grounded in reality, not purely in theory, to add a second view and to provide additional examples and illustrations to the chapter. In most cases the consultant author is also a practitioner in the field and not a researcher, though some also conduct research. To make life simple the chapter is attributed to the main author 'with' the consultant author.

I am eternally grateful to all these people who have given their time freely for this book. All have been motivated by a desire to further the cause of qualitative research and all have brought their intellect, experience and opinions to make the chapters live.

Using the book

Chapter 1 covers the theory underpinning qualitative research. Written by Mike Imms, it is an excellent start point for anyone entering the field, purchasing or using research or indeed for existing practitioners wishing to revisit old theories and learn about the new.

The book has been divided into sections by subject. We start the main body of the book with a section on broadcasting and the media. Chapters 2 and 3 are concerned with this area. First, Alastair Burns tackles the vast subject of the media and poses questions about how the changes brought about by technology will impact on broadcasting. Following on from this Tony Regan with David Brooke tackle the issue of the making of television programmes.

Chapters 4 to 7 cover the commercial worlds of advertising, direct mail, commercial media planning and design. Chris Forrest with Terry Prue, Tod Norman with Chris Barraclough, Will Collin and Jon Wilkins, and finally Jean Carr with Peter Wallis, look at the role of the consumer in the development of these specialist marketing services and the role of qualitative research in each (all quite different).

The next section covers more eclectic and unusual ground: Sue Robson with Angie Ballard on marketing higher education, Susie Fisher on the arts, Deborah Mattinson with Tim Bell on politics, Alan Hedges with Sue Duncan on social policy and John Griffiths with Bishop James Jones on religion. These are all fascinating chapters as they illustrate fields which have only recently begun to explore systematically their consumers and where qualitative research is a very new (and often controversial) tool.

Finally, Chapters 13 and 14 cover innovation, by David Spenser with Stephen Wells, and international research, by Peter Cooper. Neither of these is industries per se, but both illustrate advanced uses of qualitative research based on in depth understanding of consumer issues.

Each chapter starts with a short editor's introduction. The role of this is to help the reader understand the issues facing the industry and to put the chapter in its context within the book. Additionally, I have concluded each chapter with 'key ideas' to help consolidate the issues which are discussed in the text.

ACKNOWLEDGEMENTS

The contributors have worked unrewarded on this project with enthusiasm, diligence and professionalism. It is their book and their contribution is all. In turn, they have sought the advice, input and often the writing skills of the consultants who have brought new perspectives and ideas into qualitative research thinking, to the benefit of us all. In addition, a multitude of brains have been picked and opinions sought for each chapter and those experts add to our insight and knowledge.

Specifically I want to thank Matthew Coombes and Shahzia Chaudhri at NTC for endless patience, Rose Molloy for practical help, Louella Miles for reading the book and helping me focus and the AQR committee for support, reassurance and endurance.

Finally my wonderful family – tolerant children, believing husband, hardworking nanny, parents and parents-in-law.

FURTHER READING

Gordon, W. (1999) *Good Thinking – Guide to Qualitative Research*. NTC, Henley-on-Thames.
Gordon, W. & Langmaid, R. (1989) *Qualitative Market Research*. Gower, Aldershot.
Robson, S. & Foster, A. (1989) *Qualitative Research in Action*. Edward Arnold, London.

Contributors

Laura Marks

Laura's career started with a degree in psychology. She then trained as a teacher and spent a stress-free year in Canada as a Commonwealth Scholar. On her return, Laura decided to move into the commercial arena where she discovered qualitative research. She travelled the world conducting research for MBL before moving to advertising.

Laura spent ten years at Abbott Mead Vickers planning on a range of UK and international accounts including the famous Economist and Yellow Pages campaigns for which she won APG and IPA Effectiveness Awards.

Laura continued her deep interest in qualitative research and was elected chairman of the AQRP (now AQR) in 1994. She set up The Laura Marks Partnership in 1997, a planning and research consultancy. Laura spends much of her time in Los Angeles to fulfil multiple roles of wife, mum and planning consultant.

Angie Ballard

Angie Ballard entered social research after a degree in Geography from Sheffield. She started work with the Open University in the Institute of Educational Technology evaluating the new Community Education programme and other social outreach initiatives. In the late 1980s she moved to market research after completing an MSc in Survey Methods and the MRS Diploma. She was appointed Market Research Manager in 1988. Angie is a member of the MRS, SRA and AURA.

Chris Barraclough

A law graduate, Chris began his career at Smith Bundy. He moved on to DDM Advertising where he became Creative Director. In 1991 he became one of the founding partners of BHWG and the agency quickly found commercial success, handling the accounts of Alliance & Leicester, Volkswagen, BT, Barclaycard, Eastern Energy, Persil, Pedigree, PC World, Pizza Hut and the British Red Cross, among others. In June 1999, Chris was appointed Chairman of the company. He is also a noted industry speaker on creative matters and regularly writes for the trade press.

Tim Bell

Tim Bell is co-founder of Saatchi & Saatchi. As International Chairman, he was responsible for the company's development to become the world's leading agency by 1981. He joined Lowe Bell Howard Spink in 1985 and remained there until the formation of Chime Communications in 1989.

He ran successful PR campaigns for the Conservative Party in 1979, 1983 and 1987 and was awarded a knighthood by Lady Thatcher and a peerage by Tony Blair.

David Brook

David Brook is Director of Strategy and Development at Channel 4. He co-ordinates all of the channel's strategic and consumer marketing activities and has overall responsibility for the new digital and interactive services (including the FilmFour subscription channel). In David's previous role as Marketing Director of Channel 5, he masterminded the channel's highly successful and innovative launch. Prior to that he was Marketing Director of Guardian Media Group.

Alastair Burns

Alastair Burns is a qualitative research specialist with over 18 years' experience both as a user and practitioner of research. After reading English at Cambridge, Alastair spent eight years in advertising agencies, primarily with DMB&B. In 1988, he became a qualitative researcher with Reflexions Market Research before moving to Strategic Research Group. In 1991, he was appointed Managing Director of SRG, one of the top specialist research agencies in the UK. In 1995 he left SRG to set up his own qualitative research consultancy, Alastair Burns Research & Strategy.

Alastair has considerable experience of broadcasting through working with the BBC on a variety of qualitative research projects. He ran the research aspect of an internal training course for BBC Marketing. He is a full member of the Market Research Society and spent nine years as a committee member of the Association of Qualitative Research Practitioners.

Jean Carr

Jean Carr is a psychologist by training and has spent most of her working life exploring the attitudes, needs and aspirations of consumers, suppliers and organisations and advising on how these can be utilised for commercial benefit.

Jean started her career conducting research for the Unilever Board on models of consumer behaviour, in particular the diffusion of innovation and the effect of social change on consumer attitudes. In her work at SRU, she has built up specialist expertise in two closely related areas: the development of market led strategies and the internal imperatives required to implement these strategies – what is now fashionably called 'change management'. Jean has worked across a wide range of issues and sectors: retailing, packaging, the relationship between people and the built environment, the management of change in public sector institutions, and relationships between publicly quoted companies and the City. She has written for RIBA, the RSA and *The Observer*.

Will Collin

Will Collin learned his strategic craft at BMP DDB, which he joined as a trainee account planner in 1989 after graduating from Oxford with a degree in chemistry. During this time he was involved in advertising development and consumer research for brands such as Sony, Heinz and Alliance & Leicester, for which he won an IPA Advertising Effectiveness Award. Will joined New PHD as Communications Strategy Director in 1997. Since then he has worked on projects for a wide number of clients such as BBC Worldwide and BT, bringing the consumer-focused disciplines of account planning to the field of media strategy.

Peter Cooper

After graduating with a first class honours degree in psychology, Peter Cooper taught at Manchester University for ten years, first in experimental psychology and then in child psychology and psychodynamics. He has also held posts at universities in Oslo, Paris and London. Peter set up CRAM International in 1969, now one of the world's leading independent research agencies specialising in qualitative analysis of consumers, brands and social change.

Peter helped originate the qualitative paradigm in marketing, first in the UK and then globally. He developed the use of qualitative techniques, focus groups and extended creativity groups (ECGs™) and the use of psycho-drawing, collage, psycho-drama and other projective techniques for investigating emotional, social and cultural influences on consumer behaviour that can be applied to marketing strategy, branding and advertising.

Peter has contributed widely to Market Research Society, ESOMAR and ARF publications, and has published many papers over the years on the theory and practice of qualitative research.

Sue Duncan

Sue Duncan is Director of Policy Studies at the Centre for Management and Policy Studies in the Cabinet Office, where her responsibilities include encouraging the use of research in policy making. Prior to that, she was Chief Research Officer at the Department of Social Security, where she headed a unit responsible for commissioning and conducting research for the Department. Before that she worked for 12 years in the Department of the Environment (now Department of the Environment, Transport and the Regions).

Susie Fisher

Susie Fisher runs her own qualitative research agency, the Susie Fisher Group. With its roots in advertising and NPD, the agency specialises in research for museums and galleries. Her clients include the V&A, the Arts Council, the Science Museum and a host of local museums and galleries across the UK. Susie is a frequent speaker at arts and museums conferences. Her current research interests centre on interpreting the visual arts to the wider public and the primacy of objects in a world dominated by electronic media. Susie is a founder member of the UK Visitor Studies Group.

Chris Forrest

Chris started his career in 1982 at the Qualitative Research Centre. In 1985 he helped found the Strategic Research Group. In 1986 he joined Ogilvy & Mather's Planning Department and was promoted to the board in 1989, making him their youngest board director. In 1991 he joined Duckworth, Finn, Grubb, Waters as Planning Director and his work there with Daewoo won him success at the APG Creative Planning Awards and the IPA Effectiveness Awards. In 1997 Chris set up Forrest Associates to provide planning and research resources for advertising agencies and other marketing companies.

Chris was Vice-Chairman of the Account Planning Group until December 1997. He has lectured widely and has contributed to the IPA's book *Excellence in Advertising*.

John Griffiths

John Griffiths has worked as an account planner for a number of different agencies producing advertising, direct marketing, sales promotion and sponsorship. He is currently working at the advertising agency CDP. Throughout his career John has been involved in advertising campaigns to do with church collaboration. These include the 'There is Hope' campaign in Edinburgh, and more recently the 'Bad Hair Day' and 'Copyright' campaigns with Christians in Media on behalf of the Church Advertising Network.

Alan Hedges

Alan Hedges has worked in and around the worlds of social and market research for over 35 years. Since 1971 he has operated his own consultancy, advising on and carrying out research with a particular focus on qualitative methods. He has considerable experience of qualitative and quantitative research, mainly as a practitioner but also as a user and adviser, and has written and lectured widely on research methods and applications.

Mike Imms

After graduating in economics, Mike Imms spent four years as a researcher in the Special Studies Unit of the Price Commission. He moved to the private sector as a research buyer at Thorn EMI and Philips Consumer Electronics, before becoming an account planner at advertising agency Collett Dickenson Pearce. For the past decade he has run his own research and marketing consultancy and now concentrates on training and coaching core skills and personal and management development in the marketing services industries.

A long-standing member of the AQR Committee, Mike is a regular contributor to industry seminars and has presented papers at two conferences of the Market Research Society in 1998 and 1999.

James Jones

James Jones became Bishop of Liverpool in 1998 and prior to this he was Bishop of Hull. He was ordained in 1983 and served as a parish priest in Croydon. He has always taken an interest in the communication of the Christian faith using modern media, and has written and lectured on communications and produced materials for schools and churches. He is an author and broadcaster and a regular contributor to 'Thought for the Day' on the *Today* programme. He presented 'The Word on the Street', a series of seven programmes shown by the BBC.

Deborah Mattinson

After studying law at Bristol, Deborah Mattinson started her career in advertising working as an account director at McCann Erickson and Ayer Barker. In 1985 she set up Gould Mattinson, a specialist research-led consultancy to advise the Labour Party in all aspects of research and communications. Deborah has advised the Labour Party through general elections in 1987, 1992 and 1997. In 1992 she co-founded Opinion Leader Research which specialises in innovative social consultation and the monitoring of corporate reputations.

Tod Norman

Tod is a Strategic Partner at Zalpha, the strategic consultancy within WWAV Rapp Collins Group. Born and educated in the US, Tod has lived in the UK since 1984. He began his career in 1985 working for Research International in quantitative research. He then joined The Research Business, rising to become group head. In 1988, he joined GGK Advertising and was Senior Account Planner for IBM, Marriott Hotels EMEA, Alfa Romeo, Daihatsu and Swissair. In 1992 he joined Craton Lodge Knight (CLK) as a planning consultant, working on NPD, brand development, and strategic marketing projects, and rose to planning director. Tod moved to BHWG in 1997. His responsibilities included providing full-time planning support for clients such as Barclaycard, Volkswagen, PC World, The British Red Cross, Pizza Hut and Grattan/Look Again. He has developed and run numerous training sessions and internal programmes to inspire and get the best from staff. Tod has also written articles for *Campaign* and *Brand Strategy*.

Terry Prue

Since 1993, Terry has been a Senior Partner at The HPI Research Group. He heads the Quantitative Unit and specialises in brand and advertising research. Prior to joining HPI, he worked on the client side for Gillette and Southern TV, and as a senior account planner for J Walter Thompson. Terry has written three winning papers for the IPA Advertising Effectiveness Awards, and in 2000 returns as a member of the judging panel.

Tony Regan

Tony Regan is Managing Partner and joint founder of Michaelides & Bednash. He has led the company's pioneering work in fusing the account planning discipline with media planning, in particular through the use of qualitative research for the development of consumer-led, insight-based media strategies for advertisers. M&B's media clients have included Channel 4, Channel 5's launch, Flextech Television, BBC Worldwide (beeb.com). Prior to the creation of M&B in 1994, Tony worked as an account planner at Cogent and in media strategy at HHCL. He has spoken at AQR meetings on the use of qualitative research in media and at the AQR's Annual Trends Conference in 1997 on the subject of qualitative research in television.

Sue Robson

Sue Robson has a degree in Psychology and Physiology from Oxford University and, after a spell in postgraduate research, began her market research career at BMRB. She also worked at RI and MBL, where she was promoted to Managing Director in 1980, before setting up her own agency, The Qualitative Consultancy, in 1982.

Sue has considerable qualitative research experience, with a particular interest in services rather than product research, and she is a Fellow of the Market Research Society, in recognition of her academic and professional contribution to the industry.

David Spenser

After brief spells in the crime and education businesses, David entered qualitative research in the early 1980s. His company, Direct Dialogue, is based in Suffolk and specialises in development programmes of brands, communications, corporate image and identity and new products. David pioneered the use of integrated client–consumer dialogue groups and ideas workshops. He works primarily on issues requiring innovation or strategic development, both in Britain and internationally. He also tutors the Brand Managers' Development Programme at Ashridge Management College.

Peter Wallis

Peter Wallis has two parallel careers – as a management consultant and an author/broadcaster – and two names.

As **Peter Wallis** he was the co-founder, with Dennis (now Lord) Stevenson, of the management consultancy SRU Ltd, and during the 1980s developed the SRU Group of nine specialist business consultancies.

In addition to a wide ranging experience advising major corporates, Government departments and institutions in many sectors, Peter's particular specialism has been the commercial exploitation of cultural change and 'brand rehabilitation' – the redevelopment of brands and businesses that have lost positioning focus.

Under his other name of **Peter York**, author, broadcaster and journalist, he is known as a commentator on 'lifestyle' and social change. He was Style Editor of *Harpers & Queen* for ten years. With Ann Barr, he co-authored the *Sloane Ranger Handbook* – the UK's biggest selling trade book of the 1980s. He has written five other books on social/style/social change, and wrote and presented 'Peter York's 80s', a BBC series shown in 1996. He is a member of the Channel 4 'Power Commission' which nominated the 300 most powerful people in the UK in 1998 and 1999, and is a columnist for *The Independent on Sunday* and for *Management Today*.

Stephen Wells

Following a botany degree from London University, Stephen Wells joined Unilever as a graduate trainee, before moving on to Beechams as a research executive. He moved into brand management at Beechams, before returning to research as Director of a newly formed company, Food and Drink Research. There, Stephen worked extensively on new product development projects, mainly for major food manufacturers.

In 1978, he co-founded The Consumer Connection Ltd which developed into The Connexions Group. In 1991 Stephen formed Wells and Company where he focuses on broad-based projects, understanding and evolving the culture of organisations to encourage customer-led innovation.

Jon Wilkins

After starting his career at Granada TV, MTV Europe and Disney, Jon Wilkins joined DMP DDB as Media Research Manager, ultimately being promoted to Director of Media Strategy.

At BMP Jon worked on 'full service' accounts including VW, Scottish Courage, Sony, Thomson Holidays as well as media specialist accounts. While at BMP Jon founded the industry-leading ROAR research project into the youth market.

In 1996 he joined New PHD as Creative Communications Director, where he has a brief to work across all business with a view to providing a better consumer understanding, and a more creative approach to media solutions. In October 1999 he was promoted to Joint Managing Director.

Chapter 1

The Theory of Qualitative Market Research

Mike Imms
Proprietor, Mike Imms Marketing Planning & Research

Editor's introduction

Qualitative research enables us to explore the consumer context surrounding the numerous industries mentioned in this book. However, in order to put qualitative research into context we need to understand the theory underpinning the practice. This chapter is therefore concerned with the theoretical framework in which qualitative research operates. The area to be covered is vast and could clearly fill many books. However, Mike Imms has prepared this chapter to cover the essentials, the key concepts, the major theories and how this translates into qualitative research practice.

The reader will gain an understanding of the psychological, sociological and anthropological basis of the discipline of qualitative research. Mike reveals the importance of theoretical constructs and of thorough analysis of qualitative data. While this should not deter the newcomer, it should equally clearly demonstrate that the role of the researcher is much more than listening to people talking and passing on to the client what was said.

The value of qualitative research in any field is in the interpretation, a process which starts with the client briefing and ends with the debrief. This value depends upon the clarity and quality of the thinking and this chapter focuses on that.

Mike has recently evolved from research practitioner into research tutor. His practical knowledge ensures that even this theoretical chapter will be useful and stimulating for practitioners as well as furthering their knowledge base.

THE CONTEXT: THE NATURE OF QUALITATIVE RESEARCH

It is increasingly the case that the decision-making of all organisations needs to take into account the wants and needs of customers – not just buyers of goods and services but also staff, colleagues, stakeholders, ratepayers, voters, congregations, passengers, communities, inmates – the length and diversity of this list is boundless.

Moreover, it is self-evident that people, their motivations and behaviour are complex, multi-faceted and often downright contradictory. If we wish to achieve true *understanding* of people we need a discipline that can analyse and interpret such complexity in a meaningful, valid and, above all, *useful* way. This is the purpose and unique contribution of qualitative research.

The four key components of qualitative market research

We can think of qualitative market research as comprising four interlinked elements that combine to create the discipline. The important facets of these elements are explained more fully below, but it is useful to start with a brief overview of the constituent elements of qualitative market research.

Exploring 'qualitative' issues

This starts from the premise that understanding people, their motivations and desires is *not simply* a matter of 'hard facts'. Qualitative research acknowledges the importance of influences beyond the conscious, and the logical and rational. It aims to identify and understand such issues as pre-conscious and unconscious influences, feelings, emotions, etc. – all of which are powerful influences on consumer beliefs and actions. As such, it aims to give a more complete understanding of motivations, needs and wants.

In addition, qualitative market research aims to understand and explain *why* people do, think and feel as they do, and not simply to state *what* they do, think and feel. As such, it is a powerful diagnostic tool for decision-makers.

The use of concepts, philosophies and theories as the basis for enquiry

Without a conceptual framework for enquiry and analysis, findings would be little more than reportage, for example, 'some people said this, others said that'. The dominant concepts and theories underpinning qualitative market research come from psychology, and increasingly from social sciences of cultural study, such as social anthropology.

Non-statistical qualitative methods of enquiry

Specifically, this includes the use of non-directive questioning techniques via group discussions and in-depth interviews, but can also include observation, etc. There is of course a link between theory and method of enquiry in the sense that the nature and content of enquiry is predicated by the 'terms of reference' and information requirements of the proposed analytical framework.

Presenting findings in a non-statistical, discursive way

This does not really relate to any theory of research, but an important facet of qualitative market research is how findings are presented as a discursive, non-statistical description. At a practical level, many clients find this more accessible and understandable. In addition, the qualitative market researcher has spoken to and understood both clients (and their decision-making requirements) and respondents (and their wants and needs), and this means that the presentation of findings forms an interrogatory 'triangulated discourse', with the researcher linking both client and respondents.

The first three of these four elements warrant further explanation.

SOME BASIC CONCEPTS OF QUALITATIVE RESEARCH

Exploring beyond the conscious, public factors

To understand people fully, their motivations, wants and needs, we need to explore beyond hard facts, beyond the conscious issues people are willing and able to express. Thus we need research methods and techniques that go beyond what people can and will say in response to simple, direct questions.

Interpersonal communication

One of the simpler ways of considering this is embodied in the Johari Window (Figure 1) – a conceptual model for describing, evaluating and predicting aspects of interpersonal communication (for example, as in our case, a market research interview). The axes of this model distinguish between those factors which people are or are not aware of about themselves, and the feelings they will and will not express.

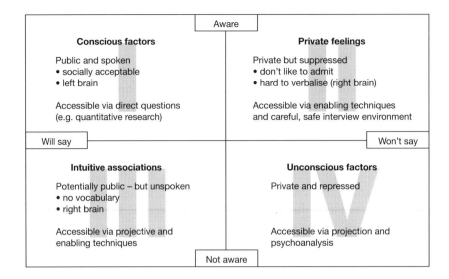

Figure 1 The Johari Window.

Conscious factors

It is useful to start with some observations about the top left-hand quadrant 'Aware + will say'. This is very much the domain of conventional survey research; for example, ask a direct question and elicit a direct response.

The dilemma is that people will tend to express views that are:

1 Socially acceptable. These include views they do not share but feel are 'the right thing to say'.
   • e.g. 'we only watch nature documentaries on TV.'
   Moreover, it excludes things they do mean but believe are unacceptable to say.
   • e.g. 'I chose this car because I loved the statement it makes about me.'

2 'Left-brain' mental processes. Seminal work by Sperry in 1968 demonstrated that the left and right hemispheres of the brain process different sorts of thoughts. The left hemisphere concerns *verbal* processes – and market research interviewing is of course predominantly a verbal medium. This gives it an inherent bias to the left-brain mental processes which, as well as being verbal, include analytic processes of rationality, logic and deduction. In contrast, right-brain mental processes exhibit two important and different characteristics:
   • They are non-verbal – and this means we often do not have the words to express right-brain thoughts however powerful and influential these thoughts may be.

- They include feelings, emotions and intuitive associations. Thus exploration of such factors perforce means developing techniques to elicit right-brain, non-verbal mental processes.

While the 'Aware + will say' is of course a wholly legitimate area of enquiry for research, the importance of the Johari Window is that it maps out important dimensions *beyond* the 'aware + will say' and clarifies the nature of the task for exploring this broader territory.

Unconscious factors – the private and repressed – are not generally regarded as a legitimate area for market research, but qualitative market research methods and techniques are designed to go beyond conscious factors and to explore the two further quadrants of the Johari Window: private feelings and intuitive associations.

Private feelings

Qualitative researchers need to create an interview environment and adopt techniques that encourage respondents to feel safe and comfortable enough to reveal *private feelings* (top right quadrant 'aware + won't say').

Intuitive associations

Qualitative researchers need to adopt interview styles and methodologies that allow respondents to express *intuitive associations* – things they may never have thought about before, and things they have no vocabulary to express in words (bottom left quadrant – 'will say but not aware').

As we will discuss below, the key techniques in exploring both quadrants concern:

- non-directive, open question techniques
- active listening
- projective and enabling techniques.

Concepts, philosophies and theories of human behaviour

The legacy of psychology

While it would be wrong to describe most qualitative market researchers as psychologists, the dominant concepts and theories behind qualitative market research arise directly from the discipline of psychology – specifically post-Freudian, humanistic psychology (the so-called Third Force in psychology that began to emerge in the 1940s and dominated psychology in the 1960s and 1970s).

Humanistic psychology

The distinction between humanistic phenomenological psychology and earlier schools of psychology is important here.

First, the humanistic principle that people (therapy patients and respondents in research alike) have within them everything they need to self-direct means that the purpose of the interview is to enable them to express and explain *themselves*. This represented a major shift from the earlier Freudian psychoanalytic belief that patients/interviewees are unable to interpret and understand their own motivation, and that true meaning can only be understood by the psychoanalyst. (Clearly a qualitative market research industry which demanded that all practitioners were psycho-analysts would be untenable.)

Second, whereas the Freudian psychoanalytic movement concerned itself solely with the psychology of the individual, the humanistic movement asserts that the individual is a function of his or her own personality and sociocultural context. This impacts directly on the type and style of questions for research and also the relevance and legitimacy of *the group discussion* as a technique for exploring shared sociocultural meanings and values, as well as individual wants and needs. In this respect, related *disciplines* of social sciences, such as social anthropology, are also relevant sources of theory in qualitative market research.

Third, humanistic psychology acknowledges that people don't simply passively respond (in the way that behavioural psychologists saw stimulus–response), but they *interact* with the stimuli. As such, the work of qualitative market research concerns the exploration of relationships (between consumers and organisations, brands, advertising, services, etc.) in order to understand the nature of this interaction.

The key psychological concepts

An essential part of the qualitative inheritance from psychology includes a variety of models and concepts that provide a framework for understanding what makes consumers tick.

The nature of cognition and perception

Cognition concerns the mental process of knowing, perceiving and judging – processes which enable individuals to interpret the world around them. Perception concerns the *content* of that interpretation.

Learning theories

Notably the concept of stimulus–response, which explores the relationships between environmental/operant stimuli and the respondent behaviour/ response triggered by those stimuli.

Models of motivation and the nature of needs

Notably Maslow's hierarchy of needs, which provides a framework for assessing motivations and needs in terms of various types of physical and psychological needs, including higher order needs concerned with realising one's own potential.

Models of human interaction and communication

Notably transactional analysis, which provides a framework for understanding the influence of parent, adult and child ego states in determining the nature and effectiveness of interpersonal relationships and communications.

Theories of personality

Notably Jung, in particular descriptions of personality in terms of four 'pairs' of temperament types and the importance of emotions, feelings, intuition and perceiving in determining human behaviour.

Significantly, these models and concepts have been augmented over the past 40 years as other schools of thinking in psychology have emerged; for example, neuro-linguistic programming, which concerns the interpretation of language (verbal and non-verbal body language) to give insights into subconscious thoughts and feelings.

Other disciplines of cultural study

While the dominant influences on qualitative market research have come from psychology, other disciplines also provide qualitative researchers with theories and frameworks for exploring consumer understanding.

Specifically, there has been a persistent and growing acknowledgement of the importance of sociocultural influences on the actions, thoughts and feelings of individuals – and with this has come an increasing use of methods, techniques and thinkings from various disciplines of cultural analysis. There follow two examples.

Anthropology

Anthropology is the study of mankind, in terms of institutions, beliefs and relationships. It is a recurring influence on qualitative market research; for example:

- researchers often refer to myths and rituals in interpreting consumer motivations and attitudes – and myths and rituals are at the core of social anthropology
- the growth of international qualitative research brings with it a shift in emphasis towards understanding similarities and differences in the cultural context for client activities.

Moreover, anthropology introduces alternative methodologies to group discussions and interviews – specifically ethnography or observational studies. This in turn introduces qualitative methods for exploring *behaviour* (including unconscious, ritualistic and culturally derived patterns of behaviour) in a context where conventional interview-based qualitative methodologies at best explore only *claimed* behaviour.

Semiotics

Semiotics concerns the cultural meaning of signs and symbols – and semiotic methods include:

- understanding and making explicit shared meanings – often including meanings that are never commented upon because they are taken for granted
- understanding the cultural and symbolic significance of those meanings
- determining trends in such meanings (emerging, residual and dominant 'codes' of meaning and significance).

THE PRACTICALITIES OF QUALITATIVE RESEARCH

Gathering qualitative information

Most qualitative market research consists of group discussions or in-depth interviews led by a qualitative researcher or moderator – and the purpose and nature of these groups or in-depth interviews are summarised in Table 1.

Working with a discussion guide of key topics and issues (not verbatim, standardised questions), the principal roles of the researcher at this stage are threefold.

Table 1 Purpose of interviews.

	Group discussion or in-depth interview
Purpose	Exploration
Moderator's task	To explore anything respondents feel is relevant to the topic at hand
	To manage group dynamics (prevent domination by the noisy and elicit comments from the quiet)
	To encourage debate
Questioning technique	Non-directive questioning
	Open, probing
Themes	Speculation, ideas and comments, including the totally unpredictable
	Breadth and depth, or range of response
Output	Understanding

Source: Goodyear (1996)

1 *To be aware of the client's objectives* in carrying out the research and ensure the discussion includes relevant debate to enable the researcher to reach an informed insight into respondents' perspectives on these issues. Importantly, this is not to say that the qualitative researcher – or indeed the client – delegates decision-making responsibility or judgment to the respondents in the group or interviews. Rather, the aim is to assess *response* – to ideas, plans, options, etc. – and then to decide whether or not this response helps achieve organisational objectives. (And, if not, how those ideas, plans, options could be adapted to improve their effectiveness in meeting organisational objectives.)

2 *To manage the process of the group or interview* – specifically to manage group dynamics, prevent domination by the noisy and elicit comments from the quiet. A variety of techniques are used by moderators but as these are inevitably situation and circumstance specific (rather than prescriptive and mechanistic), they are difficult to describe in a general book of this nature. Suffice it to say that these techniques concern sensitive use of such things as body language cues; changing pace and state; and conversation 'closure' or opening techniques – either away from the dominant or towards the quiet as the situation demands.

3 *To get beyond the conscious public factors* and explore the broader range of influences on motivations, wants and needs (as described above) by using appropriate questioning and elicitation techniques.

Non-directive, open question techniques

Non-directive open question techniques were first described by the psychologist Carl Rogers in 1945. He devised non-directive interviewing procedures for counselling and psychotherapy, and commented later that these were useful in research interviewing as a means of avoiding biased response. In essence, the counsellor (or moderator in qualitative market research) retains the initiative regarding the course of the interview, but respondents are encouraged to freely relate their experience and reveal their attitudes and opinions as they see fit, with as little direction as possible from the interviewer.

Three key principles

This psychotherapeutic model of interviewing embraces three key principles that inform the main element of 'best practice' for qualitative market research moderators.

1 'Transparency', including genuineness, authenticity and congruence.
2 Unconditional positive regard, and acceptance of interviewees in a non-judgmental way.

These first two principles have underpinned key aspects of 'best practice' in moderating qualitative market research, i.e.

- non-judgmental
- not to give opinion
- not to answer questions
- not to proffer information
- using open questions.

Open questions usually begin: what; where; when; how; why; who...? In contrast, closed questions typically begin 'can you?', 'is it?' 'Don't you think?'

These two principles are still very much in evidence today, although alternative models of moderation are beginning to be used – e.g. moderator as 'team leader', with respondents as 'problem solvers' given as much inside information as they need.

3 Empathetic understanding via attentive listening. This includes restating what interviewees say as a way of clarifying its emotional significance, and sensitivity to meanings that are just below the level of awareness.
   Specifically, this introduces a fundamental requirement to create within the interview or group an atmosphere where respondents feel safe, respected and trustful (i.e. the so-called 'warm up' at the start of groups and interviews is a profoundly important part of the process).

It also introduces the need for *specific* skills and techniques, notably:

- the use of probing (e.g. 'why do you say that?');
- active listening skills (including sensitivity to non-verbal communication) and summarising restating skills;
- a requirement to *understand* the nature and expression of emotional responses and alertness to the pre-conscious.

Projective and enabling techniques

Earlier in this chapter we discussed the importance of exploring private feelings, and the need to overcome the limitations of a purely verbal medium. Projective and enabling techniques are key tools in these types of exploration.

Projection

Projection involves getting respondents to reveal private feelings comfortably by 'projecting' their own views onto another person or object; for example, at a simple level the question 'why do so many people enjoy watching soap operas?' allows them to fully express their reasons without admitting to being addicted to EastEnders!

Enabling

Enabling techniques seek to help respondents reveal things they find hard to say (either because they are not socially comfortable or because they can't find the right words).

Projective and enabling techniques commonly used in qualitative market research include:

- collage, picture sorts and drawing (visual imagery and associations)
- word association
- sentence completion
- analogy and metaphor
- bubble drawings (thematic apperception tests)
- story-telling
- guided dreams/visualisation.

Different techniques generate different types of information, and their relevance depends on the objectives of the research.

Observational techniques

Group discussions and in-depth interviews are powerful ways of exploring beliefs, attitudes and feelings; however, it has to be recognised that they do not accurately assess *behaviour*. Importantly, most people are not consciously aware of patterns of behaviour that are habitual, unconscious or culturally driven, for example:

- Think how often you complete a familiar journey but cannot recall it – you undoubtedly stopped at red traffic lights, took the right route, (probably) observed the speed limit – but you couldn't *describe* all those actions with any accuracy.
- Think how people behave on a crowded train, in a crowded pub – the subtle protocols to avoid collisions, aggression, etc. We do all this intuitively – we couldn't *describe* our behaviour in these circumstances.
- People's description of their behaviour reflects their self-image, perceived or desired behaviour – for example, they may like to think they should buy the *Big Issue* every week or take a bath every day and may therefore claim they do so, irrespective of whether they actually do.

For these reasons, observational techniques are sometimes used whereby researchers accompany respondents, say, to stores, pubs, on journeys, etc., and observe and then interview them about *actual* behavioural patterns.

Analysis and interpretation

The 'output' from qualitative research fieldwork (groups, interviews or observation) represents the 'data', and this needs to be analysed formally as part of the project.

As we have discussed, this is not simply a matter of 'reporting what people said'. Analysis and interpretation are integral to the progression of a qualitative market research study, and cannot really be divorced from the fieldwork stages. Analysis and interpretation concern the continuous development, evolution, refinement (and often rejection) of hypotheses. The theories and concepts discussed in this chapter continue to play a major role at this stage of the research process – along with an understanding of the client's requirements.

In process terms, analysis typically involves four distinct stages:

- A functional analysis of *content* – a matter of giving order and structure to the mass of input from the groups or interviews by sifting, differentiating, separating and sorting responses to different topics by different respondents/types of respondents.

- Interpretation – level 1: What do respondents feel and mean?
- Interpretation – level 2: What patterns emerge – and what do they mean?
- Interpretation – level 3: What are the implications for the client?

(Source: Glenn, 1997)

The reliability of qualitative market research

As a non-statistical exercise, based on relatively small numbers of respondents, it is important to consider the reliability of qualitative market research findings.

Qualitative market research is in no sense 'statistically valid', but it is none the less valid – within the framework of a rather different concept of validity. There are five key facets to the concept of validity in qualitative market research:

(1) Validity can be checked empirically, via *internal* consistency within the project – i.e. consistency of findings in different interviews/groups with similar types of respondent. This highlights the importance of ensuring that the project is large enough to enable such checks.
(2) Validity can be checked empirically via *external* consistency with knowledge from other information sources.
(3) Validity can be *maximised* by reliable sample selection and recruitment.
(4) The nature of validity is quite different when exploring *shared* values and beliefs rather than personal preferences (for example, the essence of 'Fairy Liquid-ness' has a shared meaning which all 'normative' respondents can describe, whereas the validity of specific individual likes/dislikes about Fairy Liquid is dependent upon a 'representative' spread of opinions).
(5) In a rather different way, some things *just are* – and, once they have been revealed, their validity is self-evident. As Chris Barnham asked at an AQRP Seminar in 1995:

> 'How many times would you see *King Lear* in order to make sure that Cordelia dies? The question when framed in this way is clearly nonsensical. We are much more interested in understanding the significance of her death within the context of the play – and this is the qualitative question.'

Certain topics do not lend themselves to reliable assessment via qualitative market research.

- The issue of actual behaviour versus claimed behaviour, in groups or in-depth interviews, has already been discussed.
- Price is a complex issue. While qualitative research is reliable in exploring price perceptions, components of value for money and psychological price

points, it is less reliable in assessing price sensitivity, price elasticity and predicting propensity to buy.

CONCLUSIONS

Qualitative market research enables us to understand people better. This is increasingly the starting point for the development of companies, brands and organisations in our competitive world. It enables them to relate to their consumers by knowing them and their context better.

The discipline embraces a wide variety of well-documented, tried and tested techniques, methods and procedures that enable qualitative researchers to reliably explore, beyond conscious, public factors, the deeper levels of motivation and true meaning. Qualitative market research offers a unique route to providing more profound insights into the true wants and needs of people (customers or consumers, however defined).

KEY IDEAS

- Qualitative research exists to help us understand the complexity of human motivations and behaviour in a useful way.
- The aim of qualitative research is to act as a diagnostic tool for decision-makers.
- Qualitative research recognises that there are more than just 'hard facts' in this process and that there is a need to consider influences beyond the conscious, the logical and the rational.
- While some opinions and attitudes are easily and readily communicated, others are private or even intuitive and much less easily accessed by researchers.
- Key theories and philosophies underpin qualitative research. While rooted in humanistic psychology, these also include anthropology (the study of mankind in terms of institutions, beliefs and relationships) and semiotics (the cultural meaning of signs and symbols).
- Qualitative research is deliberately non-statistical in terms of its gathering and presenting of information.
- Most qualitative research is conducted in discussion groups or in-depth interviews and the moderator plays a key role in ensuring that respondents are able to express all relevant views, in managing the group dynamics and in encouraging debate and exploration.

- Qualitative interviewing is based on non-directive, open questioning techniques, projective and enabling techniques, and observation.
- Analysis and interpretation is ongoing throughout the project. It is based on an understanding of the marketing issues and concerns the continuous development, evolution and refinement of hypotheses.

REFERENCES

Barnham, C. (1995) Does size count? AQRP Seminar, December 1995.

Glen, R. (1997) Analysis and interpretation in qualitative research, in *Excellence in Advertising* (Leslie Butterfield, ed). Butterworth Heinemann, London.

Goodyear, M. (1996) Divided by a common language. MRS Conference Paper, 1996.

Sampson, P. (1967/1996) Commonsense in qualitative research. *Journal of the Market Research Society*, October. First printed 1967.

Schlackman, W. (1984) A discussion of the use of sensitivity panels in market research. MRS Conference, 1984.

FURTHER READING

Callingham, M. (1991) The role of qualitative notions in company decision-making. *Journal of the Market Research Society*, January.

Chandler, J. & Owen, M. (1989) Genesis to Revelations – the evolution of qualitative philosophy. MRS Conference Papers.

Cooper, P. & Lannon, J. (1983) Humanistic advertising: a holistic cultural perspective. *International Journal of Advertising*, Vol. 2.

Gordon, W. (1999) *Good Thinking – A Guide to Qualitative Research*. NTC, Henley.

Gordon, W. & Langmaid, R. (1985) *Qualitative Market Research*. Gower, Aldershot.

Robson, S. & Hedges, A. (1993) Analysis and interpretation of qualitative findings. *Journal of the Market Research Society*, January.

Chapter 2

Qualitative Research in the New Broadcasting Age

Alastair Burns
Consultant, Alastair Burns Research & Strategy

Editor's introduction

Much is spoken about the broadcast revolution, the explosion in choice, digital TV and so on. It is a rapidly changing, complex world which leaves many, particularly older people, way behind and totally in the dark. The strange thing about this revolution, as Alastair points out, is that it was not consumer driven. It came about because the technology became available for it to happen. No one asked for 300 television channels and no one knows how people will use them.

In this chapter, Alastair Burns outlines the changes taking place in the world of broadcasting. He then goes on to pose questions about how these changes will impact on television programme-makers, broadcasters themselves and, in particular, the brands that operate in this arena. He discusses the changing role of brands and how these will depend for their future on a deep understanding of their particular consumers, why and how they differ from competitors' target markets and in what ways they must be understood. Qualitative research is now widely used in this field as broadcasters struggle with the changes they face and their need to segment their audiences in meaningful ways.

The future in broadcasting is far from clear and broadcasters have no option but to evolve their brands rapidly. They must stay one step ahead, as must those researchers who will be of real value to them.

I recommend reading this chapter before those on television programmes and commercial media, as it illustrates the context for all of these areas. For me, this is the Wild West of qualitative research, the biggest challenge and the great unknown. Qualitative researchers have the ability to shape the way in which we communicate with one another if they can rise to the challenge.

Alastair has conducted extensive research among a wealth of experienced practitioners and thinkers in the field to write this chapter. I hope he has made some great contacts through his extensive efforts!

THE CONTEXT: THE WORLD OF BROADCASTING

'Broadcasting is undergoing a revolution that is going to change it more than it has ever changed before. It's more than the change from black and white. What we'll see is audiences fragmenting, and consumer behaviour changing in terms of how they will view, listen and use our programmes and services.'

(Cary Wakefield,
Head of Marketing for Digital Services, BBC Brand Marketing)

The changes taking place in TV

The launch of digital TV in autumn 1998 marked a watershed in the history of British broadcasting. If we are to believe the broadcasters and pundits, we are on the brink of a revolution which will re-invent the structure of the industry, transform the role and importance of brands, and alter forever the relationship between audiences and the box in the corner of the living room.

Revolution is probably too strong a word, at least in these early stages. The British public has shown itself to be somewhat sceptical about the merits of multi-channel, paid-for TV – only 25% of us had signed up prior to the launch of digital although, in some groups (for example, young men following sports) the penetration is close to 50%. Going digital does not necessarily change all this overnight.

However, there is something inexorable about the march to telly nirvana. Fifteen years ago there were just four TV channels. At the launch of digital there were some 130. By 2002 it is predicted that there will be 300 or more. Given that the government will switch off analogue at some point, we will all end up as multi-channel households in the not-too-distant future.

Interactivity will become a much more viable proposition through digital TV (particularly when cable goes digital), and services such as banking, e-mail and shopping are being introduced by the main digital broadcasters. The blurring of edges that we have seen in fields such as financial services, supermarket retailing and telecoms has now hit the shores of broadcasting. On the principle that change is always good for the market research industry – after all, it is our livelihood – this development must augur well.

Understanding the implications of these changes will be vitally important to broadcasters and advertisers. At this stage nobody really knows how people will behave, so the issues facing broadcasters tend to take the form of a list of questions.

How will people react to the choice now available to them?

There are a number of theories knocking about. One school of thought takes the view that choice of any kind *has* to be a good thing. Choice creates competition and competition means greater efforts to respond to consumer needs. Choice puts consumers in control of what they watch and when they want to watch it (rather than being at the mercy of benevolent schedulers and network strategists). This is where Sky is coming from, with its 130-channel range and aspirations to offer more.

The industry's detractors paint a rather bleaker picture of a nation of channel hoppers suffering Acute Attention Deficiency Syndrome. As Bill Bryson puts it in *Notes from a Big Country*, 'You're not watching to see what's on, you're watching to see what *else* is on.'

To counter this, it is interesting to note that in the USA, where they have enjoyed multi-channel TV for longer, it is still the case that 65% of prime-time viewing is with the four main channels. Furthermore, it seems that, despite greater choice, TV viewing is in decline. We must remember that consumers did not ask for 200 channels or for digital.

How people will make their viewing choices is, of course, one of the big questions facing the industry. When you have 200-plus channels, the conventional TV guide will look like a telephone directory. The Electronic Programme Guides (EPGs) developed by Sky Digital and OnDigital are designed to address this, by giving current and forthcoming menu choices on screen.

This will help to manage the data, but how do people want to organise their decisions? Will they choose by channel brand, by genre (documentary, sport, news, drama, film and so on), by mood state (such as relaxing, inspiring, reflective, escapist) or by programme?

The chances are that it will be a combination of all these factors. Understanding the complex decision-making process and how to position broadcasting brands in order to maximise the chances of audiences finding them is a critical area for the future. (For example, is it best to position *Top of the Pops* under a general BBC channel umbrella, a genre 'music' brand or as a channel in its own right?)

Added to this, there is the issue of cost. Most viewers are still unused to having to pay directly for the channels they watch. This is changing, and considerations such as value for money – a basic element of marketing in most other categories – are becoming increasingly relevant in audience decision-making.

What will happen to scheduling?

In the current broadcasting environment, a lot of effort goes into holding on to an audience once you have got it. (The fuss about *News at Ten* was partly about this issue.) Increasingly, broadcasters have been looking to create 'zones' which echo our mood states across the week and across the day. 'Drive-time' radio is an obvious example. BBC Radio 1 introduced Friday's *Dance Zone* to chime with young people's needs for music to get them in the mood for clubbing. BBC2 and Channel 4 have both identified Friday night as a time for switching off the 'work' persona and revving up for the weekend. They have reflected this in their escapist, upbeat scheduling. Likewise, Sunday nights tend to be more reflective and mellow.

Understanding the ebb and flow of mood states for different target audiences, and the potential role of media within them, has obviously been an important factor in scheduling the traditional 'linear' channels. However, in the new environment we will have the power to select the programming we want to watch at the time we want to watch it. We can, in effect, become self-scheduling. Does this signal the end of scheduling, perhaps even the end of linear channels serving up a menu of consecutive programmes to maintain our interest? As A.A. Gill pointed out in *The Sunday Times*, 'You won't be part of a mass audience patronisingly bussed from soap opera to sitcom to news night after night.'

Again, there are different schools of thought. Some believe that technology will enable us to develop 'customised channels' in which each member of the household could have their own menu. A smart card could even 'learn' your preferences and pre-select programming that reflects your individual tastes.

If this is the model, then it would favour the development of 'thematic' brands delivering a particular style of product across the day to meet a particular need state. (It is no accident that Sky has developed this parallel structure of specialist channels in preference to the linear variety of traditional, generalist terrestrial TV stations.)

Others are more sceptical, believing that part of the pleasure of the broadcasting experience is the sense of being swept along on a wave of programming designed to pace and vary our enjoyment. If viewing is governed by past preferences and patterns, where is the opportunity for being surprised and challenged by material you would not normally watch? This model would suggest sticking with linear, general channel brands that people will trust to provide an evening's entertainment.

Commercial necessity will also drive scheduling. With so much airtime to fill, and so little new programming to fill it, broadcasters will aim to maximise the leverage of their 'beacon' programme brands to attract the big advertisers and signal to audiences where and when to find them.

For example, in the US, NBC has achieved success with a strategy of showing all its block-buster soaps in one 'must see TV' Thursday night. Audiences know where to find *ER*, *Friends* and *Frasier*. Advertisers know where to find the audiences.

What will happen to the viewing experience?

One of the benefits often quoted about broadcasting, and particularly public service broadcasting, is its capability of 'unifying the nation'. Watching TV used to be a shared experience for families and peer groups. Everyone used to be able to replay Monty Python jokes in the playground or discuss the soaps in the pub.

This has, to some extent, already fragmented, through the increased penetration of multiple TV ownership and the growth of multi-channel pay TV. The chances are that this individualisation will accelerate, so is this the end of pub conversation as we know it?

What are the implications for broadcasting brands?

It will not have escaped anyone's notice that, over the past five years or so, broadcasters have woken up to the concept of brands. In the old days, sitting on virtual monopolies, what mattered was the content, not the 'corporate' brand. Now you only have to look at the amount of airtime given to 'idents' and brand messages to realise their importance.

Broadcasting is becoming more like a retail environment in which you not only have to have the right product, but you've got to signal that you are there on the shelf and generate expectations that will motivate people to find you rather than someone else. If you can develop a relationship between your brand and the audience, it follows that it will be more likely to seek you out.

However, it is not just about *branding* in the sense of giving channels and programmes a consistent identity. The role and nature of brands in this marketplace is moving from network brands ('you are watching this or that channel') to 'thematic' brands ('you are watching so and so's sport' or FilmFour).

The subject of branding is particularly complex in broadcasting because there are so many levels operating simultaneously. Few markets have such a complex brand hierarchy. Take *Match of the Day*, which has at least four levels of brand in operation, namely:

- the programme brand (*Match of the Day*)
- the genre brand (BBC Sport)

- the channel brand (BBC 1)
- the broadcaster/corporate brand (BBC).

One might even have added the 'presenter brand' – Des Lynam – if he had not moved to ITV!

Understanding the interrelationship between these brands, how they motivate audiences and influence decisions, is a critical issue for broadcasters. Questions of brand hierarchy become very important here: What does one brand give to (or take from) the other? For example, your view on the demise of *News at Ten* will depend on whether the most important trigger for you was *News at Ten*, ITN or Trevor MacDonald.

Having established a brand the next question is: How should it be used? Broadcasters are increasingly interested in understanding how they can maximise the value of their brands by stretching them across other fields. Taking another BBC example, can *Top of the Pops* be used as a credible platform for thematic development? Could we have *TotP* documentaries, comedy, music videos, CDs and an internet site? Channel 4's launch of FilmFour was a good example of using the existing channel brand strengths (film) as a platform for a thematic digital brand. We will no doubt see many more of these brand extensions.

Of course, this desire to maximise brand values is not unique to the broadcasters. Other (non-broadcast) brands are looking at how they can stretch their offer across media. Take National Geographic, which is now available as a magazine, TV channel, CD Rom and online.

All this suggests that broadcasting is now moving into an extremely complex and sophisticated stage of brand development which, a few years ago, would have been unheard of.

Looking a little further into the future, we are about to be hit by even bigger changes in broadcasting, again brought about by the technology. One of the main drivers of this will be the convergence of the various media. In the near future we will see TVs that can behave like PCs, connecting us to the internet and other online services (or perhaps PCs that behave like TVs). There is even talk of microwaves and washing machines with internet connections!

How will developments in technology affect us in the future?

When all of this comes to pass, the choices facing audiences will go beyond *what* they want to watch and *when* they want to watch it, to *where* and *how* they want to interact with the brand or programme. The choice may be between watching *Match of the Day* highlights on TV with your mates in the living room or taking part in an interactive discussion session over the internet (also sponsored by *MotD*) from your bedroom PC.

The blurring of borders affects radio as well. The BBC is testing digital radios which can also show text and pictures. The potential for an explosion in the number of channels exists on radio as well, with similar consequences for broadcasting brands.

Broadcasters are also recognising that the internet and online represent another, more diverse and open broadcasting channel which they cannot ignore if they want to maintain and develop the relationship of audiences with their brands. A whole new area of broadcasting is opening up, as recognised by the BBC with its investment in its 'Third Service' – BBC Online and beeb.

THE ROLE FOR QUALITATIVE RESEARCH

What does all the change mean for qualitative research?

These changes mean that, now more than ever, broadcasters need to understand people in order to make the right decisions for their brands.

Quantifying the audience has always been important to broadcasters who, to a large extent, have been judged and rewarded by the ratings they achieve. Quantitative audience research has been the trade currency since commercial television and radio began.

As one of the last 'production-led' cultures, broadcasters in the past have been wary of using qualitative research as a tool to develop their offer, preferring to trust their own creative judgment and the ratings figures.

This is changing. Until recently, broadcasters were to some extent insulated from the raw energy of consumer power by the monopolistic way in which the industry has been organised. With limited choice and 'linear' channels, audiences were to some extent served what broadcasters believed they should get.

In the new broadcasting age the risks are higher, the unknowns are greater and the audiences have much more power. As the market fragments and many more channels compete for the dwindling audience, the broadcasters who survive and win will be those who best understand their audiences and deliver the products that are most attuned to their lifestyles and media needs.

As David Kogan, former Director of Channels at Granada and now a broadcasting business strategist, told me: 'The power is shifting from broadcasters to audiences. There has been a fundamental shift. Until five to seven years ago, the commercial broadcasters didn't need to think about audience research because they all ran monopolies.' In this context, qualitative research is becoming increasingly important as a tool in broadcast marketing.

How can qualitative research contribute?

There are a number of areas in which qualitative research can make a particularly strong contribution and, one hopes, shine a torch in some of these dark corners. There are also areas in which qualitative researchers, like everyone else, need to develop new tools to meet the particular challenges of this marketplace.

This section looks at where qualitative research can, or will be required to, make an input:

- in understanding internal brand relationships;
- in identifying and providing insights into target groups;
- in deepening understanding and aiding the application of segmentation studies;
- in developing and monitoring brand–audience relationships;
- in assessing the impact of new technologies and guiding their application.

Understanding brands

Qualitative research is needed to unravel the complexities of multi-layered brand relationships. As I pointed out above, the brand hierarchies and interrelationships operating in broadcasting are much more complex than in most markets. There are a variety of routes by which audiences can navigate to your door. Finding the optimum balance of influences for a particular type of broadcasting brand requires a sensitive, exploratory approach which can isolate the gravitational pull of the various elements.

Qualitative research is well placed to handle this sort of task because of its flexibility and ability to deconstruct complicated decision-making processes. It is very difficult to pin down these relationships quantitatively because it involves probing so many scenarios and sets of brand associations.

The changing nature of brand–audience relationships in broadcasting will also have a knock-on effect on advertisers. When there is a fragmented market, advertisers will pay even more attention to the brand context in which they are placing *their* brand. The context and the 'rub-off' effect of the media brand on the advertiser's brand will become the key issue, rather than 'ratings' alone.

Identifying and understanding specific audiences

As the market fragments, broadcasters will no longer be able to rely on the mass-market audiences which tune in for peak-time viewing. They will need to go in search of the pockets of interest which can sustain a channel or a programme brand. The day may come when getting audiences of a million will be regarded as doing well, rather than the ten million-plus we see today. 'Broadcasting' may actually become a thing of the past, to be replaced by 'narrowcasting' (a view being supported in media departments which now see 'outdoor' as the only remaining broadcast medium).

Given the level of investment involved in building brands and the cost of producing programming, the pressure to get this aspect of targeting right will be enormous. Broadcasting used to be about how *many* people you speak to in an audience. Increasingly, it is becoming about talking to the *right* people. Understanding the nature of communities of interest will become more useful than demographics.

Complementing new segmentation studies

The changes in the market have also given birth to a new generation of segmentation studies, driven by the need to find ways of identifying audiences which provide more meaningful communities of interest than traditional demographic typologies.

Clearly, these are based largely on quantitative analysis but, increasingly, broadcasters are turning to qualitative research to help them 'flesh out' their clusters and provide the insights which bring them alive (or, if necessary, kill them off). The highest profile of these has been the BBC's '100 Tribes' work, a study which aims to understand the needs and behaviour of different communities of interest which the BBC, as a public service broadcaster, must cater for.

The benefit, from the audience's point of view, is that there will be much more opportunity to cater for minority interests and groups which, in the world of massive, general broadcasters, have had little hope of enjoying material specifically for themselves. Cultural and religious groups, minority sports and leisure activities will all do well out of this.

Of course, quantitative research is going to be essential in identifying and establishing the viability of these niches. But what use is it to discover that there are one million people expressing a passionate interest in clog-dancing and dry stone walling if, when it comes down to it, they actually want to buy a partwork about it and not watch a TV documentary or indulge in online shopping?

Qualitative research skills will become increasingly important to broadcasters because they will need to understand exactly what makes these people tick, what binds them as an interest group and what part their interest plays in their lives. The more they can understand the nature of their target group and how a media brand *could* relate to their lives, the more likely they are to identify the 'hot spots' that lead to commercial success. Qualitative researchers, in essence, will need to be the prospectors searching for those little glints of gold in the sieve.

Brand–audience relationships

Having established this relationship between the specific community of interest and the brand, there is an ongoing need to keep tabs on two moving targets: the brand and the audience.

In this sense, qualitative research in broadcasting will become more like NPD research. Quantitative research will be used to identify the priority areas and uncover gaps or opportunities. Qualitative research will provide the understanding and insights that illuminate the ideas. As Mark Ellis, former head of research at the BBC, said: 'There's a demand for research which is less about testing and more about inspiring.'

The impact of new technologies

The final, and most difficult, area in which qualitative research has a particular role is in understanding the impact of the new technologies on people. This is the area in which market research, in general, has difficulty, because our raw materials – the public – are simply not very good at telling us about what they will think or how they will behave in the future. Added to this, the territory we are entering is so new that people have few if any reference points to draw upon. Trying to get a handle on how people will interpret and understand the new broadcasting environment as it unfolds is a critical issue for the main broadcasting organisations.

The issue is that the technology being developed is well ahead of consumer 'need'. Audiences are being given the *capability* of enormous power, but there is no guarantee that they will actually want to use it. After all, we have the power to time-shift programmes on old-fashioned VHS videos, but very few of us actually use them in this way.

For broadcasters, therefore, it is critical that they do not just develop what the technology *allows* them to develop. They need to turn this technological capability into consumer benefits.

Cary Wakefield, Head of Digital Marketing at the BBC, is very conscious of this issue:

> 'The technology is driving a lot of this and we can see many things that will be possible over the next two to 15 years. Now, whether they can be turned into benefits which consumers want is a completely different thing.'

So questions such as 'What should an EPG look like?' were difficult to answer before an EPG – or even digital TV – existed. Similarly, researchers are being called upon to help broadcasters understand a raft of fundamental questions, such as:

- how audiences will make decisions between channels in the new environment;
- how they might react to e-mail via the TV;
- how they might assimilate digital radio into their media consumption;
- how consuming programmes via a PC might differ from consuming them on TV;
- how they would handle the software for interactive programmes.

Clearly, qualitative research has its limitations when it comes to futurology but, for all this, it still offers us the best chance we can get of early guidance in these sorts of areas.

PRACTICALITIES

Thus far I have described the unique nature of broadcasting brands, how things might change as we enter the new broadcasting age and the increasing importance of understanding people through applying qualitative research techniques. All of this presents enormous challenges to the qualitative research practitioner. How to tackle some of these challenges is the subject of this section.

The issues facing practitioners differ according to the type of broadcasting issue we are discussing:

- researching 'traditional' linear channel brands;
- researching audiences in the new broadcasting age;
- researching new technology.

Researching 'traditional' channel brands

Traditional channel broadcasting brands are notoriously difficult to research because, unlike most brands, they are extremely malleable and fragmented entities. All brands change or evolve over time but not usually on a daily or weekly basis, as do these brands. (Newspapers are probably the closest parallel.)

The key research issues relate to:

- who we speak to;
- overcoming the historical baggage of brands;
- the role of the researcher.

Who we speak to

Trying to pin down the brand values of a channel can be very difficult, because the view of any one person is going to be influenced by a wide variety of factors:

- their level of exposure;
- their 'point of entry';
- their historical experience;
- who they are in terms of interests, tastes, passions;
- misattribution (people are rather bad at telling you which programmes belong on which channels).

As a starting point, we have to be as clear as we can which 'entry point' or facet of the brand we are accessing. If we do not, there is a danger of recruiting people with such disparate experiences of the brand that it is harder to interpret any pattern. (For instance, people who watch BBC2 for Friday night comedy will have a very different perception of the brand from those who watch it the rest of the week.)

Historical baggage

Second, we need to overcome the 'dead weight' of the baggage which established channels tend to carry around with them. It is so difficult for people to hold such disparate, often contradictory, brands in their heads that they tend to draw on highly distilled historical versions built up over the years. This makes it difficult to focus on how the brand is *now* and how to understand the impact of any recent changes in style, approach or identity.

A related issue is that everyone – well-informed or not – has an opinion on broadcasting and broadcasters. It is all too easy to end up with people in groups who can talk for an hour about the BBC or Channel 4 who, in fact, hardly watch either channel at all nowadays.

Ways to address this include:

- encouraging people to fill in 'media diaries' prior to attending interviews, to help focus attention on more recent brand experience and its role in their lives;
- using techniques which encourage people to 'dump' their historical memories or images early in the session and talk about how things have changed;
- getting people to watch/listen/use the channel intensively prior to the interviews, to ensure that they have a clearer, common 'snapshot' of how it is now;

- alternatively, it can be useful in some circumstances to deprive people of the use of their channel. For example, if you were exploring the role of a radio channel in people's lives it may be instructive to see how they cope without it for a while. People tend to claim that they do not listen to radio much, or use it as audio wallpaper. Depriving them of it can dramatise all the subtle roles radio channels can fulfil;
- showing an amalgam of clips from the channel(s) in question can also help because it stimulates recall of a richer seam of brand identity (although, obviously, one has to be very careful about the balance of such montages and when they are used).

The researcher's role

Another implication for researchers in this field is that we need to be consumers ourselves. The brands are so diverse and changeable that, in this field more than most, it seems important that researchers are themselves immersed in the output. If we are not, there is a danger that we will not recognise the significance of telling comments or lack the product knowledge to interpret how different access points to the brand affect perceptions.

This is a difficult one because, I suspect, qualitative researchers are likely to be one of the lightest TV viewing (and heaviest radio listening) groups in the country by virtue of their out-of-hours lifestyle. Perhaps the old adage should operate in reverse: we ought to get *in* more.

Researching audiences in the new broadcasting age

Up to this point, the qualitative research issues discussed have related primarily to 'traditional' broadcasting brands. What challenges will qualitative research have to meet in the 'new' broadcasting age?

As the audience fragments, it will become increasingly important for broadcasters to identify viable niches and understand the 'communities of interest' which can spark a channel or programme identity. The better qualitative research is at bringing to life these target groups and at understanding the 'glue' that holds different (perhaps disparate) audiences together, the more useful we will be to broadcasters.

'Doing this better', in my view, will involve moving closer than before to people's experiences. We need to abandon some of the measured objectivity of old and become more involved with audiences as partners rather than as passive respondents. Research, like music and media, needs to become more 'ambient'.

This could mean a number of things, such as:

- Leaving the controlled environment of studios and front rooms to encounter and experience the experience of others closer at hand. If it happens to be clog-dancing or drystone walling, then go out there and join them.
- Incorporating more observational techniques into our methods (observation of both the activities and the role of different media in people's lives).
- Using research environments more relevant to the interests of those taking part.
- Talking to people in groups which share a common interest and who interact socially in 'real life' (as opposed to people who are strangers to each other).
- Taking the same group of people through a learning experience with us, revisiting them for their views and guidance as we go through the development process.

Researching new technologies

The final, and most difficult challenge is to help broadcasters develop the services and technologies which will shape our future media consumption. This is the area in which broadcasters – as in any area of innovation – find it hardest to use and trust conventional research. The problem is that the field is *so* new and is developing *so* fast that there are no 'consumers' or 'audiences' who can offer a credible view.

Marc Sands, Marketing Director of ONdigital, admits that, prior to their launch, there was little that research could do to help them. The major development decisions were made primarily on judgment rather than by reference to what consumers may or may not have thought of the ideas:

> 'Digital is a totally new category that is extremely difficult to research. Applying a lot of existing methodology actually doesn't get you very far ... because people have no idea what you are talking about. In a totally new category, it's a real challenge for research to add meaningfully to what you are doing. It tends to be used as a check and a balance rather than as a developmental tool.'

However, difficult or not, Cary Wakefield at the BBC feels that getting a handle on what lies around the corner is vital:

> 'The offerings are so vastly different from what people are used to, but we do need to start looking around the corner because if we don't, we're in danger of just delivering things that are driven by the technological capabilities and aren't really turning them into benefits that people really want.'

So, how can we rise to this challenge? There seem to be a number of areas to think about in terms of:

- the people we consult;
- the way we gather our information;
- the role of the researcher.

The people we consult

Clearly, finding the *right* people is the key to all of this. To most of the population, multi-channel TV is now fairly familiar but digital is still only known about by a few (the 100,000 or so digital early adopters must be the most researched group in the UK). But even digital TV users will not help us with forthcoming services which will represent much more of a leap forward – such as interactive TV, TV/PC convergence or radio with text and pictures.

The problem has been to find 'leading edge' technologically sophisticated consumers who understand what exists now and can imagine a different reality. For example, in their digital radio development work, the BBC sought out consumers who were advanced in equivalent areas – in this case using mobile phones for text messaging and news/information services (a fairly small category).

Having found these sorts of people, it seems sensible not to let them go too quickly. Recruiting 'leading edge' respondents as a panel, to take through the development process with you, may be appropriate for some studies (especially where a lot of time has been spent giving them a vision of what is possible in the future).

At the other end of the spectrum it is just as important to keep tabs on what 'ordinary' consumers (not just 'propeller heads') are thinking and doing. ONdigital, for example, commissioned a programme of rolling qualitative groups with a watching brief on their broad target audience to monitor attitudes to themselves and the market in general.

> 'Things are changing week by week in this category, so every month we do a series of groups ... I need to feed in what people are thinking.' (Marc Sands)

The way we gather our information

Observation is another methodology that is becoming increasingly important to complement qualitative research techniques. Broadcasters are keen to understand in greater depth not just what people *think* of the new media possibilities, but also how they behave. What *actually* happens when people use an EPG? How in fact do people cope with the additional capabilities of a digital radio or an online service?

Faced with these questions, the BBC commissioned experimental psychologists to partner qualitative researchers when developing some of these new services, to gain a deeper understanding of whether (and how) people might actually use them.

In this area, the issue of stimulus material is also critical. Marc Sands again:

> 'You're only as good as your stimulus material – it was ever thus. It's very difficult to make good stimulus material in a category nobody knows about.'

Poly board concepts are simply not adequate when the products are so unfamiliar and complex. People do not have the reference points with which to decode them.

The approach taken by the BBC has been to get as close as possible to 'live' stimulus by setting up rooms with all the necessary equipment. They believe the only way to discover whether the technology will have a viable place in people's lives is by letting them try it out. Their emphasis is on getting people to actually *use* the kit (wherever possible), rather than comment on demonstrations. Sometimes this involves in-home placement, such as giving people a digital radio to play with for a month or two.

The researcher's role

Finally, broadcasters are making increasing demands on researchers and it may be that a specialism will develop. Meeting the challenges of this marketplace will require researchers who are themselves at the 'leading edge' and can grasp the possibilities. To explore these new areas the researcher needs to become part of the stimulus material, explaining, inspiring and developing the vision of how things could be.

I finish with a challenge from Cary Wakefield. She believes such researchers are hard to find and thinks the qualitative research industry needs to develop the skills that are needed to help marketers working in these areas.

> 'We're looking for people who can provide that understanding. One of the difficulties is that people may be good at whatever they do in the current world of broadcasting, but understanding what it means in tomorrow's world is a completely different thing. So we are looking for people who can understand tomorrow's technology as well as being good researchers.'

What all of this demonstrates, I hope, is that there is a huge opportunity for qualitative research to make a unique contribution to the development of the new broadcasting age. At the same time, qualitative research will have to evolve to meet the challenges it presents and develop new tools.

I am also painfully conscious that change is happening so fast in this area that the situation as described here may well alter completely in just a few months. So, like every Hollywood movie these days, I leave this with an ending which contains the potential – if the box office justifies it – for a sequel.

Hold on to your hats, everyone, and good luck.

ACKNOWLEDGEMENTS

In writing this chapter, I am deeply indebted to a number of people who were willing to succumb to my interrogation and give me the benefit of their own vision and great experience of the broadcasting world.

David Docherty, Deputy Head of TV, with overall responsibility for new channels at the BBC; Mark Ellis, formerly Head of Research for BBC, now running his own planning consultancy, The Knowledge Agency; David Kogan, formerly Head of Channels for Granada, now broadcasting business strategist with his own consultancy, Reel Enterprises; Sara Munds of Reel Enterprises; Marc Sands, Marketing Director of ONDigital; Paul Twivy, Founding Partner of Circus Communications, formerly Marketing Adviser to the BBC; Cary Wakefield, Head of Marketing, Digital Services in BBC Brand Marketing; Andrew Ingram, Head of Planning for the Radio Advertising Bureau.

KEY IDEAS

- British broadcasting has undergone a revolution from four channels 15 years ago to over 300 by 2002.
- This fragmentation means that the way in which people choose what to watch and the way broadcasters schedule will never be the same again.
- As a result, broadcasters are having to rethink the role of their brands; not just the corporate brand, but also channel, genre and programme brands. Brands may also expand to cover film and even retailing opportunities.
- In this new climate of more channels and dwindling audiences, the survivors will be those who best understand and serve their public.
- Qualitative research can be used to understand these complex branding issues, to pinpoint and understand key target audiences and to help develop the relationship between the brands and their audiences.
- The role for qualitative research is broad. It can help in a better understanding of traditional linear channels but must deal with the historical baggage associated with them.
- Research can also help broadcasters understand what would glue disparate audiences together so that they might become viable 'communities of interest'.

- A challenge for qualitative research is to help understand the likely impact of new technologies, particularly as these are developing ahead of any consumer need or demand.
- Only researchers who are themselves 'leading edge' will be able to meet this challenge.

FURTHER READING

Dixon, P. (1999) *Futurewise: Six Faces of Global Change.* HarperCollins, London.
Gates, B. (1995) *The Road Ahead.* Viking. Revised Penguin, Harmondsworth, 1996.
Gates, B. (1999) *Business at the Speed of Thought.* Penguin, Harmondsworth.
Henning, K. (1998) *The Digital Enterprise.* Century Business Books, London.
Levinson, P. (1997) *The Soft Edge.* Routledge, London.
Negroponte, N. (1995) *Being Digital.* Hodder and Stoughton, London.
Tapscott, D. (1998) *Growing up Digital: The Rise of the Net Generation.* McGraw-Hill, Maidenhead.

Chapter 3
Developing Television Programmes

Tony Regan
Managing Partner, Michaelides & Bednash

with

David Brook
Director of Strategy & Development, Channel Four

Editor's introduction

The explosion in TV channels has brought with it the need for a parallel explosion in the production of programming. This programming will need to be innovative, budgeted and targeted at specific segments of the population if a channel is to succeed in a highly competitive marketplace.

This chapter explores the wary relationship between programme-makers and their viewers and explores the reluctance of makers to listen to viewers.

The changing nature of the TV marketplace is discussed to provide a context, but the emphasis of the chapter is on developing the programmes themselves. Above all, it argues for greater creativity and innovation if programmes are to win audiences. This will be based partly on creative research approaches to obtain unique insights into the audiences. To do this, Tony Regan argues that the creative process and the research associated with it must evolve and develop and the programmers must put their viewers at the heart of the development process.

Tony's work has been guided by the expertise of a highly experienced broadcaster, David Brook, who adds the perspective of someone who champions a consumer-led programme-making ethos within a large broadcast organisation.

THE CONTEXT: UNDERSTANDING THE TV CONSUMER

'We're challenging the previous underlying assumption in UK broadcasting that giving the public what they want is "bad". The reality is that people – viewers – are getting better at knowing what they like, and at talking about it.' (David Brook, Channel Four)

Mummy, where do programme ideas come from?

In the first episode of the hit series *I'm Alan Partridge*, we learn that Alan's chat show has been dropped and he's currently working at Radio Norwich, trying to find his way back into TV. In this scene, Steve Coogan presents Alan as the enthusiastic and increasingly desperate programme-maker pitching ideas to a commissioning editor:

Scene: BBC restaurant, lunchtime

Tony (the Commissioning Editor): Please, don't hesitate, if you have any other ideas, I'd be very interested.

Alan: (reaching down to pull folder out of briefcase) Got them here, got them here (he starts to read from the pile). Right, OK. Shoestring, Taggart, Spender, Bergerac, Morse. What does that say to you about regional detective series?

Tony: There's too many of them?

Alan: That's one way of looking at it. Another way of looking at it – is, people like them, let's make some more of them. Er… a detective series based in Norwich, called Swallow. Swallow is a detective who tackles vandalism. Bit of a maverick. Not afraid to break the law if he thinks it's necessary – he's not a criminal, but you know, he will perhaps travel at 80 miles an hour on the motorway if, for example, he wants to get somewhere quickly. Think about it. No one had heard of Oxford before *Inspector Morse*. This'll put Norwich on the map.

Tony: Why would I want to do that?

Alan: Yeah, fair point. Anyway, right…(flicks through pages). *Alan Attack*. Like the *Cook Report*, only with a more slapstick approach.

Tony: No.

Alan: Erm, *Arm Wrestling with Chas and Dave*.

Tony: I don't think so.

Alan: Pity. Because they were very keen on that one.

Tony: (shakes head)

Alan: *Inner City Sumo*.

Tony: What's that?

Alan: We take fat people from the inner cities, put them in big nappies and then get them to throw each other out of a circle that we draw with chalk on the ground.
Tony: No.

While this is of course an exaggeration, there's something well observed about the way programme ideas have traditionally been invented without involving or consulting consumers or even seeking to meet their needs.

There's an urgent need for these attitudes to change, and new ideas about creativity and innovation are beginning to emerge. Writing in the BBC's house journal *Ariel*, Jane Root, Controller of BBC2, calls for programme-makers to be less concerned about peer group approval, and to place more emphasis on a vivid understanding of the reality of viewers' broad lifestyles and leisure choices (Root, 1999):

> 'We can't just be the hothouse of creativity for our own sake, satisfying our own need to express ourselves in new ways. We have to compete with all the other things which are vying for the attention of our audience – not just the other television channels, but the Internet, a mushrooming news-stand of papers, magazines and books; jobs which take up increasing amounts of the days, nights and weekends of an increasingly cash rich, time poor society; parents who have homes and children to look after, children who have Playstations.'

The reality of television in a broader leisure context is the real new competition that television faces – when viewing hours are declining while channels and choices multiply, and when the internet is already slashing US TV-viewing hours *in half* for established net-users. This is why the TV industry needs to make viewers into active partners in the creative development process, rather than involving them just to tweak existing programmes or not consulting them at all.

Television meets the people

The organisers of the 1998 Edinburgh Television Festival chose as its theme the phrase *Television v. The People*. Real viewers, in the form of the 'People's Jury', were invited to Edinburgh to take part in the proceedings – normally an event populated only by television professionals.

Every year at Edinburgh, a prominent speaker is invited to give the James McTaggart Memorial Lecture. Previous speakers have been John Birt, Rupert Murdoch, David Elstein and Janet Street Porter. In 1998 the speaker was Peter Bazalgette, independent programme-maker and creator of the hit series *Changing Rooms*, *Ground Force* and *Ready, Steady, Cook*. He closed his lecture by twisting the conference theme from *Television v. The People* to *Television AND the People*, based on his strong conviction that the future of television is about a much more level partnership between programme-makers and viewers.

Of course, the use of the word 'versus' as a conference theme was there to provoke discussion and debate, but it reflects the hot topic in programming and broadcasting circles of the pressure to become 'audience led'. To many people in television this phrase is deeply concerning, apparently working against the grain of such ambitions and values as innovation, experimentalism and risk-taking. In the minds of many programme-makers and schedulers in the broadcast world, being 'audience led' reduces the scope for creativity, and conjures up formulaic, lowest-common-denominator programming.

Television's attitude to the people

When you remember the paternalistic public service origins of TV, it's easy to understand the tension there has always been between striving for popularity and seeking to be inventive, challenging and risk-taking to exploit the full cultural potential of the medium.

The assumption is somehow that *good* programming and *popular* programming would naturally gravitate to the opposite ends of an imaginary spectrum, and it has therefore been the continuous challenge for enlightened broadcasters to 'make the popular good, and the good popular'. British television has always prided itself on the way it has achieved this balance, something which many programme-makers and broadcasters would say has been achieved by relying on their artistic and professional judgment, and not particularly by consulting viewers. Geoff Mulgan (1990) described this notion as 'producer sovereignty':

> 'The most eloquent representatives of British television, brought up within this tradition of professional autonomy, argue that producer sovereignty has produced the best television in the world, simultaneously innovative, challenging and popular.'

So programme-makers have largely avoided being led by audience taste, and seen it as their role to provide for viewers without asking them what they want.

Peter Bazalgette, in the role of 'McTaggart' speaker, warned the industry about 'a revolution in TV that will take power away from broadcasters and give it to the viewers.... A profound change which the UK's television industry is completely unprepared for.'

Viewing by numbers

'The stale debate is between a crude populism ("ten million viewers can't be wrong") and an equally crude elitism ("ten million viewers will almost certainly be wrong"). (Mulgan 1990)

Most of what programme-makers know about their viewers is provided by the quantitative measures prevalent in the industry – providing estimates of audience size and the percentage share of viewing audience achieved by a particular programme.

This has been the primary means of feedback from viewers to programme-makers, and reflects the needs of the key broadcasters in the broadcasting landscape of the past few decades. The BBC has needed audience size, share and 'reach' to demonstrate that it is fulfilling its public service obligations and justifying a universal licence fee. ITV has needed to provide audiences of a size and profile that its advertisers want to reach, and also to be seen to be competing against the BBC for viewers. Channel Four has had to show that it is fulfilling its regulatory remit to provide for minority tastes and audiences. So for different but related reasons, quantitative measures have had great significance inside the cultures of broadcast organisations, and thus have continued to dominate programme-makers' thinking.

Other means of feedback between audience and programme-makers have been limited. While *Points of View* and *Right to Reply* might suggest that there is some dialogue between viewers and programmers, very few viewers actually volunteer any feedback. There is a survey of audience reaction in the form of the Appreciation Index, or AI, which measures how much people enjoyed what they watched. But this is of limited use to programme-makers, being a single 'score' that tends to be quite high (you mainly watch something only if you're enjoying it), and fluctuates within quite a narrow band of scores.

The impact of the digital age on programme-makers

For *viewers*, digital broadcasting will have wide-ranging effects on their experience of television – a massive expansion of choice, and an enhanced capability to choose, control and schedule their own viewing. The implications of this are covered in detail by Alastair Burns in Chapter 2, this volume.

For *programme-makers*, the digital age will have four fundamental and related implications.

The demand for programming

One implication is the huge expansion in demand for programming because of the enormous growth in available airtime through many new channels. While access to archive material can partially fulfil this need (as UK Gold has shown with great success), there will be an explosion in the need for a great deal of high-volume, low-cost programming. Granada, historically a broadcaster and producer within ITV only, is gearing its programme production arm to seize the business opportunities being presented by the new era: 'the explosion in the number of channels triggered by digital will create an enormous demand for new, original, high volume, low cost programming.' (Granada Group plc Annual Report 1998)

Innovation and creativity

The second is the pressure for innovation and creativity, which can only gain in importance in a more competitive environment, with viewers ever more demanding and looking for distinctive, original programming. This isn't necessarily about landmark high-status material, but also about the spark of imagination that would differentiate one 'budget' programme from another.

The role of the brand

Third is that programmes will be increasingly brand led in the sense that they'll be created to actively build the relationship between the viewer and the 'provider' brand. The link that now exists between the programme and the broadcast channel (as the point of access) will loosen as technology allows consumers to select their viewing via electronic programme guides. But even when people don't need to get to a programme by knowing which channel it's on, they will still need to be guided by clues to the 'quality' or likely editorial perspective of a programme by knowing its brand origins. What this means for programmers is that they'll increasingly see briefs for programmes where the 'brand positioning' requirement is clear.

Pay-TV

Fourth is the growth of pay-TV. As early as 2001, revenues from pay-TV (at £2.5bn) are expected to overtake those of the licence fee, and to reach £3.5bn by 2007 (Figure 1).

With digital technology paving the way for pay-per-view and programming on demand, broadcasters can charge the viewer for watching particular programmes (as opposed to accessing a whole channel via a

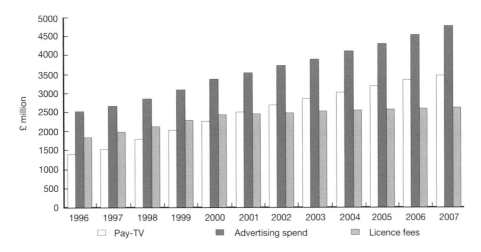

Figure 1 Pay-TV revenue overtakes licence fee.

monthly subscription). In BSkyB's Annual Report 1998 the need for a focus on perceived value is already clear:

> 'we recognise that our biggest challenge is to give people the things they value most and are willing to pay to get. The best way for our company to grow and provide value to our stakeholders is to provide value to our customers. '

While the obvious 'high-value' programming will continue to be the 'events' of movies, sport and first-run imports like *Friends*, broadcasters will also be interested in attracting pay-TV revenue beyond these categories with programmes that have high value for particular audiences. Once again, getting this right will demand much closer involvement with viewers in conceiving and developing the programmes they'll pay for.

The stakes are high. The safety net is no longer there of a guaranteed audience in a limited channel line-up. Broadcasters and production organisations will increasingly need to begin their investment in creative development with an intimate knowledge of the viewers' needs and interests. Only then can they reduce risk, maximise revenue and audiences, build their creative reputations, and also create distinctive, relevant, enduring programming in the high-volume low-cost category.

Dumbing down? Or a new hunger for innovation?

All these developments ridicule the notion that television is 'dumbing down'. Clearly the key to success in the new landscape of television is ever more innovation and creativity from UK programme producers – as Michael Jackson, Chief Executive of Channel Four, writes in their company report:

'Channel Four's success is based on its continued ability to provide distinctive and innovative programmes....But there has not been enough drama or entertainment that can match the appeal – or indeed the distinctiveness – of such American shows as ER, Frasier, Friends and King of the Hill. One of our key tasks for the future is to develop more home grown programmes that can match their combination of popularity and originality.'

The BBC is also vociferous about this in its own *Commissioning Guides for Independent Producers*:

'from daytime to late peak we require innovation and invention, programmes that will stop a popular audience in their tracks or have them switch across to BBC One at key points every day.' (Peter Salmon, Controller, BBC1)

'Innovation has never been more important. Now more than ever, BBC Two has to be the channel with the power to surprise....It's one of the few places in a crowded television world where audiences positively want to be stretched by experiences they've never had before.' (Jane Root, Controller, BBC2)

THE ROLE OF QUALITATIVE RESEARCH

'Too often research is used simply to justify programming or scheduling decisions, or to make minor tweaks to something. Not enough of the time is it used as a framework for better understanding of viewers, which can then be the foundation for ideas.' (David Brook)

Qualitative research – gaining momentum in programme development

Qualitative research is not new in programme development. Insiders can give examples of where it was being used more than a decade ago to help develop programmes, and, although not in widespread use, it was being positively received by those involved in it.

There has been a growing acceptance of qualitative research among programming people. In the early days, programmers were understandably wary about a discipline that was alien to their culture, and qualitative researchers were often not sufficiently sensitive to this to build relationships with programmers. Over the past ten years, research has succeeded in proving its relevance to programme-makers, many of whom now see a real value in it:

'Part of the progress is in attitudes among programme people; that there's no need to be scared of viewers, or of viewer research – they can't make you do things.... A couple of years ago only a handful of commissioning editors were seeking out research; now they're genuinely interested in what consumers have to say.' (Claire Grimmond, Market Research, Channel Four)

'People like programme commissioning editors are aware that qualitative research can help them. They have more confidence than they perhaps used to have because they see it happening. It used to be that research was merely a disaster check, or a ratification of a programmer's decision. Now it has a value of its own, that commissioning editors appreciate.' (Jon Priest, Simons Priest)

Qualitative research is clearly adding value at the programme level. Its roles already encompass the following:

- regenerating long-running programmes;
- development of programmes from concept stage.

The following focuses on the contribution of qualitative research to these two aims.

The role of research in regenerating long-running programmes

For broadcasters, these programmes function like strong brands. Viewers have a well-developed relationship with the programme, incorporating many levels of connection; for example, how it fits into their viewing routine, their typical frame of mind when viewing, their relationship with the characters, the way the programme might work as conversational currency with their friends or work colleagues. This familiarity works for both broadcaster and consumer, providing viewers with landmarks in their viewing routines that don't involve much decision making, and giving the broadcaster confidence about the likely audience such a programme will attract week in, week out.

The value of a programme

When a programme brand such as this, drawing many millions of viewers in peak time, suffers an audience decline, the broadcasters are understandably keen to tackle the situation. For them, this loss of audience threatens their highly treasured 'share of viewing' position against other broadcasters. All this, combined with the cost (in risk, effort, investment) of finding a replacement programme, makes it extremely viable to use research as a diagnostic tool – to identify why viewers are losing interest in the programme, and to develop improvements that will turn it around. It's critical not to lose the value of a programme that's already established in people's viewing routines.

For the likes of Granada and Carlton TV, which are looking to develop their businesses beyond their ITV broadcasting base and into programme production, these programme brands are of critical commercial importance.

Coronation Street *and* **The Bill**

Coronation Street and *The Bill* have both been reinvigorated by a process involving qualitative research to identify reasons for weaknesses and provide guidance for rebuilding ratings performance. David Liddiment, Programming Head of ITV, describes these programmes as 'extremely strong brands' – but both brands had problems that qualitative research could help address. *Coronation Street* was beginning to struggle against a strong *EastEnders*, and *The Bill* had declined long term, never recapturing the audience levels or appreciation of its early days and going through various unsuccessful changes over the years. After a review process that has involved qualitative research, both programmes are performing better, and *Coronation Street* has achieved the important double of improving both its audience profile and its audience size.

Peak Practice

Peak Practice is another long-running programme that has used qualitative research to maintain its success. With runs of 26 weeks, this is a programme that's important both to viewers and to ITV, and lucrative for Carlton, who proudly describe it as 'the largest drama commission ever made by ITV'.

News at Ten

Probably the most famous recent example of consulting viewers in research about a long-running programme was ITV's change to the scheduling of *News at Ten*. In its current slot, this news programme was a weakness for ITV:

- it had fewer viewers than the 9 p.m. dramas that typically preceded it in the schedule;
- it was an easy target for competitors to schedule against (C4 in particular had exploited this over the years with strong programmes in a variety of genres);
- it made it difficult for ITV to schedule peak-time feature films or longer dramas without breaking for the news.

Qualitative research was critical to get to viewers' real views about a topic that was being widely speculated about in the media, setting the agenda for viewer reactions. The symbolic status of the programme, the fact that it had been running for so long in that slot, and that ITV was being 'ratings driven' and commercial at the expense of its public duties were the kinds of arguments in circulation. Research had to get beyond these superficial responses and really understand the changes in viewers' needs from TV news, their experiences of accessing the news via more channels, including 24-hour news providers like Sky News and the BBC's News 24, and other sources such as the increased number of radio stations. It had to explore their desire for non-news programming in that time slot, and the way such a landmark programme had 'timetabled' their evenings and bedtimes for so many years. What became clear from the qualitative research was that viewers were more open-minded about a change than their initial reactions would suggest.

The role of research in creating new ideas for programmes

While qualitative research will continue to provide understanding about the nature of viewing, and to help broadcasters revive long-running programmes, it's in the development of ideas from the earliest stages that its biggest opportunity lies.

The two examples that follow (*This Life* and *Ground Force*) show how qualitative research has been involved – not in the role of tweaking, checking, adapting a programme but in helping the early ideas form into programmes that viewers would truly engage with and value. These case histories start to show the way in which qualitative research can be active in the process of innovation in the years to come. In each case qualitative research generated some key insights which fundamentally affected the way in which the programme was developed and taken forward.

This Life

Research was used in the earliest stages of the creative development of *This Life*. Unlike *Ground Force*, however, research was not used in the same way and consumers were not approached initially for insights that could lead to programme ideas.

For new drama, there is a different balance between the creative impetus and the potential guidance that research can provide. In the case of *This Life*, the team was creatively ambitious, and wanted the programme to operate outside the normal conventions and parameters of the drama genre. The first step was spotting the opportunity for an innovative drama. This came from Michael Jackson, then Controller of BBC2, as described by Katherine Viner in *The Guardian*:

> '*This Life* began as an attempt by Michael Jackson … to attract younger viewers: 'Young people think and feel very differently than they did ten, even five years ago,' says Jackson. 'There's this tribe, in this case 20-somethings who used to be called 'yuppies' and TV drama has never really tapped into what different tribes think and feel. *This Life* is a window into a world that hasn't been seen on TV before.'

Executive Producer Tony Garnett conceived the idea for a programme to meet this brief. He imagined a drama concerned with people's everyday lives, and the interaction between them. It would have strong story lines but no dominant plot full of cliff-hanging climaxes. Instead, the programme would be developed to draw viewers into the lives of the characters.

The initiative for research came from the BBC themselves, but (critically) was welcomed by Garnett, who was happy to take guidance from what consumers had to say. He had already involved a young team of writers in the creative process to access their 'first-hand' experience of being in the 20-something cohort and his attitude to research was very positive: 'I will listen to the audience's response wherever I can get it', he said.

The early stage research took the form of workshops, where respondents were not asked to sit in judgement on the appeal of the programme concept but to be active participants in its development. This innovative approach has since become much more common in the development of drama.

Respondents worked with a range of stimulus material: 'blurbs' describing key elements of the show; detailed descriptions of the role and personalities of key characters; and a huge selection of photographs for respondents to embellish their sense of the characters' personalities. Based on that material, respondents explored the potential interplay between the characters, imagined how those characters might behave, and discussed the plausibility of possible story lines.

The research provided early guidance about those issues, as well as endorsing the production team's creative instinct about the ways in which they were challenging the drama genre. Research was involved again before transmission, when rough-cuts of the first two episodes were available. At this point, the production team was concerned about whether the first two programmes were giving viewers a clear enough sense of the characters or an incentive to watch later episodes. Research showed that respondents understood the character-led concept, but after seeing the rough-cuts were frustrated that the first episode did not give them enough knowledge of or intimacy with the key characters. This confirmed the team's suspicions, and they went on to restructure the first two episodes and re-edit them into one.

The programme went on to be a resounding success, with audiences for the first series building via word of mouth. The commitment to research continued, with more at the end of the first series amongst viewers of the show, designed to identify any issues for the second series.

Audiences built and articles on the show appeared in the newspapers. The series had created a buzz amongst its audience and journalists were impressed by how well-observed it was. Later, writers such as Katherine Viner began to investigate why the programme had seemed so intuitive in its handling of relationships, and identified the significance of qualitative research in its development.

Ground Force

For Peter Bazalgette, research at concept stage has provided important learning in the development of successful programmes. His production company is the creator of *Changing Rooms, Ready, Steady, Cook* and *Ground Force*. According to him, it's critical to identify a key insight into the lives and experiences of the target audience for a programme, and then make sure the show is structured consistently around that insight. The insight for *Ready, Steady, Cook* was that most women have to prepare an evening meal in under half an hour – so that becomes the challenge within the show. Research can tell you at a very early stage how well the programme idea exploits the insight.

Ground Force, currently the highest-rating programme on BBC1 after *EastEnders*, is achieving audiences of 10 to 12 million viewers: an audience size, and with a young profile, that was previously believed impossible for a gardening programme. Bazalgette thinks a key reason for the success of the programme was the early refinements that were made to the concept through qualitative research. Originally the insight was 'suburban rivalry':

> 'like the old Qualcast ad with the two neighbours competing for the stripiest lawn. We called it *Over the Garden Wall* and put it into focus group research, where it got a very lukewarm response. More importantly, the groups helped us see beyond the suburban rivalry idea: that in fact when young homemakers think about the garden, they think about it as an extra room in the house. And that when they think about gardening, it's about instant solutions for time-poor lifestyles, not about an expert saying "this weekend you'd better be doing the pruning". So we were able to develop the programme around these insights, into what you see on screen, which is a gardening show on BBC1 in primetime, with 12 million viewers.'

These examples show how qualitative research can add enormous value by being incorporated into the creative development of programme ideas at the earliest possible stage. We'll have to see whether the systematic incorporation of qualitative research will ever become commonplace in the industry (as it has in advertising). But it's difficult to argue against its potential to grow, or against the importance of building it in at the beginning of the creative process.

PRACTICALITIES – FOSTERING INNOVATION AND CREATIVITY IN PROGRAMME DEVELOPMENT

> 'Here at Channel Four we're determined to make sure that research is an enabler of creativity; that it works effectively to fuse commercial and creative skills, and becomes a way of encouraging more risk-taking, not less. It mustn't be a device,

as it has often been in the United States, for taking the rough edges out.' (David Brook, Channel Four)

We saw at the start of this chapter that greater creativity and innovation in programming are key to the TV industry's future. It needs innovation to satisfy a number of goals:

- to provide high-volume, low-cost programming with high perceived value for viewers;
- to nourish channel brands, which in an EPG context become 'provider' (broadcaster or producer) brands;
- to deliver real value to viewers who will increasingly access programming on a 'pay as you go' basis;
- to expand its creative and cultural importance in the life of the nation, and the world's TV industry.

In the next section we saw qualitative research becoming more established and accepted in the industry. *This Life* and *Ground Force* were two examples of programmes where qualitative research played a pivotal role in their early development and eventual success.

In this final section we'll consider how the evolution of qualitative research is critical to the TV industry's ability to face the digital future with confidence, and to the development of a new mindset in the industry about how creativity happens, and how creative ideas can be sensitively developed.

For qualitative research to seize this opportunity, two things need to happen.

- *Research must emphasise its own creativity*, drawing attention to its ability to perform an enabling role in the creative process. This means dissemination of best practice in qualitative research applied to programme-making, and a continuous process of reassessment and development of the discipline to meet the needs of programme-makers.
- Qualitative research must be both the catalyst and the beneficiary of a change in the culture of the TV industry that is just beginning to see the fundamental importance of *putting the viewer at the start of the creative development process*.

Increasing the creativity of qualitative research itself

Qualitative research is already developing methodologies and techniques in an effort to achieve fresher, better insights that drive creativity. Just as in advertising, where qualitative research has been incorporated into the discipline of account planning, the mindset should be that qualitative research is a means to an end, working towards an ultimate goal of programmes that stimulate and engage the viewer:

> 'Our mental attitude should be that we're working in television, not so much in market research. The industry shouldn't be defensive and bleat against criticism of focus groups. If there are issues about the shortcomings of techniques and methodologies, then it's up to us to invent new ones, not spend time defending the inadequate ones.' (Nino Cirone, Broadcast Research)

Research can work harder to emphasise its own creativity, and tailor its methodologies and output to the particular needs of programme-makers and the reality of viewers' experience of television. I've highlighted a few examples of how research is already taking steps in this direction.

Applying creativity to sampling and recruitment

Television is less and less the collective cultural experience it was when there were only a handful of channels. With the viewing audience now fragmented across many channels and programmes, it's getting more and more difficult to gather together for research a group of people who all watch the same programmes.

This is a particular problem for smaller channels, which may attract only a few thousand viewers a month across the whole country. With the geographical clustering that's necessary for standard methods such as focus groups, it's clear that a bigger toolbox of methods is needed. This demands a particular creativity in designing methodologies and sample, but one which pays back in the richness of the insights that can emerge and therefore the credibility of research in the minds of creative people.

Ways of overcoming this will continue to be important as audiences continue to fragment across more and more channels. For example:

- recruiting people who have an affinity with the kind of programming you want to talk about;
- asking people to watch the channel for a week so they can comment with some intensity;
- recruiting via the channel itself: 'call this number if you'd be interested in taking part in viewer research';
- qualitative panels, and recalled groups.

The very early development of ITV's *Cadfael* drama provides a good role model for the first of these. Qualitative researcher Terry Watkins exploited an imaginative way of defining the potential audience, not just on their viewing habits but also their reading habits:

'We gathered together people who were readers of the *Cadfael* books, and also people who watched 'whodunnits' on TV. They helped us clarify things like the kind of Middle Ages imagery they saw being most appropriate: you know, Maypoles or Black Death.'

Many smaller channels want to steal viewers from each other or from the main channels. David Brennan, at Flextech, describes these viewers as 'floating voters' – they're not loyal to a channel or even regular viewers, but they might be attracted by the right programming and marketing. He says, 'it's about gaining knowledge about how to attract people to your programmes and channels, rather than preaching to the converted'.

Creativity in the development of stimulus material for research

Stimulus material plays an important role in attempting to replicate how we, as viewers, weigh up our decisions about which programmes to watch.

A commonly used approach when researching new programme ideas is to describe them to respondents in a TV listings style, incorporating stars' names, a plot synopsis and so on. This has been used very successfully in concept development research, particularly if respondents are invited to construct their own evening or week of viewing from these programmes. Experience has also shown that it helps to 'disguise' established programmes in these synopses, so that new ideas can be judged on a par with established ones.

The TV Times/schedule construction approach is well established in concept development research, but Claire Grimmond talks about the need for lots of stimulus material beyond simple listings-style descriptions: 'You need an awful lot of stimulus material, to give tangibility and a flavour to what the programme would actually be like; so you need pictures of presenters, the on-screen look, the tone, the running order.'

The ideal if possible is for a pilot programme to which potential viewers can give detailed reactions. Not surprisingly, the cost of producing a pilot makes it inappropriate in many cases, so other kinds of stimulus material continue to be important. But the key advantage is in how well a pilot helps viewers to gauge their interest in a programme in the 'real world', as Claire Grimmond describes:

'Getting those first five minutes of a programme right is critical, and developing a pilot to help with that is invaluable. You have to remember that consumers make very quick decisions about programmes, based on a lot of clues that set expectations for them: partly the channel, but also presenters, tone, studio, music, titles and so on.'

Interpretation is an act of creativity

This is true of course of all research, but particularly so in the creative context of programmes and even more so at the concept stage. This is about introducing opinion and judgment and going beyond the literal:

> 'It's easy to find examples of where a literal interpretation of research would have been unhelpful. In the case of the *Big Breakfast* at the outset, research did say that it was going to be successful – for the viewer segment who understood Channel Four. When you looked at the research results across the population as a whole then it was heavily negative. But the programme wasn't setting out to appeal to the whole population.' (Nino Cirone, Broadcast Research)

> 'There are dangers in looking for consensus in a qualitative research group. You run the risk of lowest common denominator acceptability, when polarisation in a group often signals a potent creative idea that will have saliency and strong appeal to an important segment of the population.' (Jon Priest, Simons Priest)

Commissioners of research, such as Louise Dickens (Sky), Pascale Woltho (ITV Network Centre) and Claire Grimmond (C4), all emphasise the importance of interpretation that is both cautious and bold. Not surprisingly, this creates a situation where particular individual researchers build experience and reputations, and therefore very strong relationships, with the broadcast companies' heads of research.

Understanding the viewer at the start of the creative process

David Brook's comment at the beginning of this section emphasises the potential for qualitative research to build on its expanding role as an important tool in developing programmes, and to progress to a bigger strategic influence in broadcast organisations. David Brennan, at Flextech, sees this strategic opportunity for research:

> 'It's about making the organisation better informed: balancing innovation with consumer insight. It's not about making creative people dependent on research; but it must help to create a climate or organisational culture that's more aware of what works and what doesn't and where audiences can be pushed or not.'

Qualitative research will grow in influence by capitalising on changes that are already happening in television, but also by stimulating and accelerating those changes. In particular, research needs to continue to encourage programme-makers to think about some key strategic issues:

- new ways of thinking about target audiences;
- more imaginative thinking about programme briefs;
- linking research with the creative process.

New ways of thinking about audiences

It's clear that broadcasters are already moving in this direction by thinking of fresh ways to define audiences (rather than the clichéd demographic categories) and then using these to familiarise programming people with the reality of viewers' lives. David Brook says, 'it's critical to think of the audience in new ways', and admires the work David Docherty has done at the BBC in identifying the many *Tribes of Britain*.

The BBC's 100 Tribes of Britain

This is a wonderful example of how a new understanding of audiences can be driven by an organisation, developed primarily through quantitative analysis, and then go on to stimulate a climate of thinking about viewers whereby qualitative research can add value.[1]

As a public service broadcaster, it's crucial for the BBC to provide for (and be seen to be providing for) every segment of the population. It has recognised that satisfying this need is not simply about appealing to upmarket and downmarket, young and old – because these definitions are too crude in representing the reality of people's lives. The initiative for *100 Tribes* was an attempt to classify the population into many more groups, partly to get beyond the limitations of demographic analysis and partly to make sure that the BBC was seen to be catering for every segment of the population.

David Docherty, architect of the project, has talked about the limitations of demographic analysis which fails to take account of social changes that emerge from a more knowledge-based economy, the decline of manufacturing industries and an expanding 'middle class':

> 'The reason the ABC1/C2DE thing is not useful for a public broadcaster is that really it's a classification system for selling audiences to advertisers. It never really was that sensible. An 'A' can be a 73-year old judge or a 22-year old office worker – what do they have in common?'

The exercise has identified particular segments where the BBC has been underperforming, often because rival broadcasters are meeting audience needs better. Examples include:

- less well-off mothers and fathers under the age of 25 (6.3 million people);
- those on the lowest incomes (13 million people earn or receive under £7,800 per year), including young unemployed, single parents and state pensioners;
- those belonging to ethnic groups (2.8 million people).

As an example, this last group (according to Docherty) is much more likely to subscribe to cable and satellite than the UK average: 'This may be driven by a feeling that terrestrial TV isn't representative of their lives. We need to find ways of making a better connection with Asian and African-Caribbean audiences.'

The work is already being credited with encouraging programme-makers to think beyond simplistic definitions such as ABC1, which lead to unhelpful assumptions and stereotypes and run the risk of misleading producers rather than guiding them.

It also has implications for marketing: 'If you suddenly spot a group that doesn't think that much of you, then you can bring in your marketing toolkit and ask yourself if you should make more programmes for them, send them different messages or launch new services for them,' says Docherty.

The BBC's ultimate objective is to make sure that it's meeting the needs of the whole population, and not failing in particular areas. Docherty describes this as 'tribe busting': 'The great danger of all segmentations is that you end up stereotyping and this should be anti-stereotyping. By all means segment, but don't stereotype.'

The impact on commissioning briefs

This new definition of the audience is designed to be a stimulant to the creativity of programme-makers – and is therefore being incorporated into the BBC's commissioning briefs provided to independent production companies. The BBC's summary of this work is inspiring reading for anyone who wants programmes to be influenced by, and made for, real people:

> 'The lives of our audiences are constantly changing and we have recognised that simple segmentation tools like the ABC1/C2DE classification system are not nearly sophisticated enough to understand the myriad of audience groups and their complex lives.... It is our collective responsibility as broadcasters and programme-makers to try to take the lid off the UK and understand better the different ways in which people lead their lives today. By doing this we have a better chance of not only delivering them the sorts of programmes they know they want to watch (and without "dumbing down") but also those that they cannot even envisage. We have the most amazing opportunity to surprise and delight and to match the passions and enthusiasms of programme-makers with the aspirations of the audiences.' (BBC Commissioning Guide 2000–2001)

In the competitive landscape, Channel Four's focus takes account of new ways of thinking about audiences, but without some of the motivations that influence the BBC. Here's David Brook:

> 'because of our remit, our history and our culture at Channel Four, we don't have to achieve the universality that is the BBC's remit, and which makes it important for them to cater for the many Tribes that exist in the UK population. Instead we

can identify a particular audience, one that appreciates innovation, and build our reputation amongst that set of people.'

More imaginative briefing

Linked to the stimulation for programme-makers that comes from new ways of thinking about viewers is the notion that briefs can become more imaginative. This creativity at the briefing stage is fundamentally rooted in a desire to cater for the needs of particular audience segments, instead of looking for an idea that is a new version of an old programme (thinking back to the Alan Partridge examples).

In this context, it's easy to see the advantages of a brief based on accurate insights into the audience's viewing routine and preferences. Michael Jackson in particular has been admired for his ability to conceive a programme brief in such a way that it creates a 'real springboard to creativity'. The programming breakthrough of *This Life*, which we saw earlier, and genre-busting innovations such as *Ready, Steady, Cook* were both based on briefs from Michael Jackson during his time at BBC2. Here, Peter Bazalgette talks about the briefing stage origins of *Ready, Steady, Cook*:

> 'This was developed in response to a brief from Michael Jackson when he was at BBC2 in 1994. He's very good at coming up with briefs that are informed by schedules; he saw the demographic watching *Countdown* and *15 to 1* [on C4], and he thought 'food plus entertainment'. It's become an archetype for us – the first leisure-based game show – and a real step on from the 'how to...' approach that dominated before.'

Linking research with the creative process

Even with better ways of defining and understanding audiences, and greater discipline about creativity in programme briefs, many programmes will continue to emerge the 'old way'. Yet all the demands and pressures of the new digital era make it necessary to rethink assumptions about creativity.

Back to Edinburgh and the McTaggart Lecture, where Peter Bazalgette expressed serious concerns about the ability of the business as it's currently structured to meet the industry's new challenges:

> 'In the world of advertising it's axiomatic that creativity happens – on cue – in response to a brief. That is their discipline and it's taught right from the start.... In the softer climate of British television we've never had the same disciplines. We teach people to edit videotape but we don't teach them how to answer a specific brief with a creative scheduling solution addressing the intended audience. We hope to have the ideas by accident. We're going to have to change.'

He calls for a thorough rethink of the creative process in TV production. At the heart of his thinking is a stronger bond between 'creative' people and audience research along similar lines to the combination of creative team and account planner in an advertising agency.

Here he describes what he has done to redirect his organisation and emphasise the critical importance of audience research:

> 'We've had a think about what it means to be in business as an independent producer. And it's to create intellectual property: the more we invent, the more value we have as a business – so it's critical we have a process for having ideas. We have reorganised our company more along the lines of an advertising agency and I've given myself the title of Creative Director and I've set up the office with Head of Research.'

Bazalgette has seen beyond the prevailing view (television versus the people; research versus creativity) to a productive partnership between research and innovation: 'I firmly believe that research is an aid, not a hindrance, to the creative process. In fact, it's now crucial, and the only way to survive'.

Whatever the success of qualitative research in achieving a more influential role within large broadcast companies, it has a golden opportunity to add enormous value in the independent production sector.

THE FUTURE

Research and creativity in the independent sector

We will close this chapter by looking at a particular trend in the business that could expand the opportunity for qualitative research. While research has primarily been commissioned by broadcasters, even in those examples where the programme idea is originated by an independent producer, the independent sector could potentially create significant demand for qualitative research. This will happen rapidly if the independent sector is successful in its lobbying for significant regulatory change.

The independent sector has a real axe to grind. The complaint is that, in spite of their flair, innovation, entrepreneurialism and success, most production companies are very small, perhaps only gaining one programme or series commission per year (80% of the 714 independents who worked for C4 in 1997 received less than £250,000 in payments, and 65% received less than £100,000). The cost of research is something that these businesses' narrow margins don't allow for, so when it happens it's usually the broadcaster who pays.

The trade organisation (PACT – Producers Alliance for Cinema and Television) that supports the independent sector is now busy lobbying the government for major changes to the way the sector is regulated. In its document *The Courage to Compete* PACT argues that, despite a strong track record of programme successes through the 1980s and 1990s, few independent production companies have increased in size or value as businesses. Their criticism is that regulations have limited the sector's access to the secondary or tertiary rights or the spin-offs of merchandising and foreign sales that can dramatically increase their profit margins. In most cases these rights are retained by the broadcasters.

As production companies look to mature as businesses they see their opportunity as specialists in creativity, while broadcasters' businesses are increasingly focused on assembling content: distribution, marketing, publishing, and, for the next decade, investment in digital technology. Only by building the independents' strengths as businesses that can plough back profits to allow for more risk taking will they be able fully to develop the processes that would incorporate qualitative research and the benefits to the programmes produced.

This is why PACT's lobbying campaign could potentially open up a parallel opportunity for qualitative research in programme development within the independent production sector. As well as taking an increasingly strategic position in broadcast companies, research has the potential to achieve perhaps its most hands-on, creative origination role within the most dynamic independent production companies.

The challenge

Qualitative research faces many challenges in expanding its role in programme making. However, I hope I've shown that the opportunities are certainly there too – even if the television industry at large is only just beginning to become aware of how much it's going to need qualitative research as a creative discipline.

The transformation in the viewing experience of multi-channel and digital TV drives much of the necessity for change in the attitudes and practices of programme-makers.

ACKNOWLEDGEMENTS

In particular, to David Brook for direction and early input, and also to Claire Grimmond at Channel Four. Also to Peter Bazalgette at GMG Endemol Entertainment for his stimulation and encouragement. To Tony Garrett, Executive Producer of *This Life*. To the Heads of Research whom I consulted in other broadcast companies: David Brennan and Kate Hornby at Flextech Television, Pascale Waltho at ITV Network Centre, and Louise Dickens at Sky. To qualitative market researchers specialising in broadcast and programming research, in particular for the guidance and input of Terry

Watkins at Terry Watkins Research, Jon Priest at Simons Priest, and Nino Cirone at Broadcast Research. Also, for their comments, Anne-Marie Sweeney at Sweeney Pinedo, Mike Donovan at One World, and Michael Edison at National Research Group. To Shaun Williams at PACT, Tim Dams at Broadcast Magazine. To Laura Marks for keeping me on track, and making sure my writing made sense. Finally, huge thanks to my business partners Graham Bednash and George Michaelides, and especially to my wife, Kathleen, who encouraged me in taking on the task of writing this chapter, and who supported me throughout.

KEY IDEAS

- TV has always seen creativity in programme making as something best achieved by the instincts of the producer rather than the viewers' preferences.
- The information about audiences that is generally available to programme-makers provides little insight, as it largely comes from insensitive quantitative measures.
- With the massive expansion of programming time resulting from the arrival of digital broadcasting, there will be a need for a vastly increased volume of programming, often at lower cost than has been typical in the industry.
- Yet the programming produced will need to compete for the attention and respect of demanding consumers experiencing hugely increased choice.
- The risks associated with the high cost of producing programmes can be reduced via a better understanding of viewers, and an ability to innovate and so meet their changing needs.
- Qualitative research will be key in helping programme-makers adapt their creative instincts to meet these particular challenges. Examples are beginning to emerge of programmes developed via positive collaboration between research and the creative instincts of producers.
- In order to help make TV become more consumer led yet still creative, qualitative research in the field needs, in itself, to be more creative – in how it thinks about the target market, in helping to create more imaginative programme briefs and in building itself more effectively into the early stages of the creative process.
- Key consumer insights must form the basis for this creativity and they can be provided via imaginative, sensitive qualitative research.

- The cultures within large, traditional broadcast organisations are becoming more positive towards qualitative research, and the potential is clear for research to be integrated into the creative process (as in advertising). The independent production sector may also prove to offer a particular opportunity for research to be built into creative development

NOTE

1 This section is based partly on an article published in *Broadcast* magazine, 'Television's tribal gatherings', by David Wood and Peter Keighron.

REFERENCES

Mulgan, G. (1990) 'Television's Holy Grail: seven types of quality', in *The Question of Quality*, BFI, London.
Root, J. (1999) *Ariel*, 16 March 1999.

FURTHER READING

Barwise, P. & Ehrenberg, A.S.C. (1988) *Television and Its Audience*. Sage, London.
Peak, S. & Fisher, P. (eds) (1998) *The Media Guide*. Fourth Estate, London.
Creative Industries Mapping Document (1998) Department for Culture, Media and Sport, London.
PACT (1998) *The Courage to Compete*. Producers Alliance for Cinema and Television, London.

Chapter 4
Advertising Research

Chris Forrest
Director, Forrest Associates

with

Terry Prue
Senior Partner, The HPI Research Group

Editor's introduction

Advertising is probably the most established use of qualitative research nowadays. Advertising agencies in the UK and increasingly elsewhere have not just research departments but an account planning function. This exists to ensure that the advertising meets the human and not just the client need. Working as a planner for many years, I never questioned the viability of this role.

Whilst advocating the need for consumer input, Chris Forrest demonstrates that even in advertising, the acceptance of research input is not universal and in the 'Creative as King' culture, its role is by no means unquestioned.

In this chapter, Chris Forrest and Terry Prue outline much of the theory that underlies advertising research. They demonstrate that the very nature of advertising makes the role of consumer input complex and not always useful unless carefully constructed and interpreted. They go on to show, largely by case study, how consumer insight and qualitative research can continue hugly to the advertising process at many different stages of the development process.

THE CONTEXT – ADVERTISING TODAY

How advertising works

If you were to stop a random sample of passers-by and ask them how advertising works, they would probably say something like 'It makes people buy things'. If you ask them how it does this, they might say something like 'It makes things desirable so you want to buy them', but they would also be quite likely to joke that 'It brainwashes us, doesn't it?'.

The man in the street, the chairman of Megacorp, the EC commissioner and the academic critic all assume advertising is more powerful and sophisticated than it is. The people who work in and closely around advertising know how unpowerful it is, but of course we have our own reasons for not spreading too much alarm and despondency.

The true power of advertising

Anyone who believes in advertising's power to make people do things they didn't want to do has never sat in a focus group discussion listening to people ripping apart the strategy behind an advertisement, identifying what the ad is trying to say to them, explaining why it doesn't work for them and suggesting improvements.

Implicit in the academic critiques of advertising is a condescending view of human gullibility. Our moral guardians and legislators have always implied that, although advertising has never made clever people like them buy anything, less intelligent people might be taken in by it. The truth of the matter is that they have probably been influenced more than they would admit and the general public has been influenced less than they might fear. People aren't stupid. David Ogilvy's (1973) dictum, 'the consumer is not a moron she is your wife' jars on modern ears with its apparent sexism, but it needed saying in mid-1960s America. It is still good advice today to think in terms of how you would convince your best friend rather than some imaginary moronic consumer out there. Ads don't work on passive economic agents. People aren't programmable worker ants.

We seem to have a real dichotomy here. On one side we have a body of people involved in advertising who want it to be regarded as a 'profession', who spend many millions of other people's money and who want this to be seen as a hard-nosed business investment. It is right and proper that company finance directors will operate at the macro level and will want to know what they are likely to get in terms of extra sales or extra profit from an advertising budget.

On the other side, when we look at the micro level, the world becomes less certain. Advertisers are not all-powerful – all power resides with the people watching or ignoring advertisements. How can we produce any certainty for the finance director on whether the advertising will 'work' – let alone predict exactly what the financial return will be? The best we can do is to marshal our resources in a way that gives us the best opportunity for success.

Advertising works on people, not on sales

It's easy to forget this. We analyse how much advertising investment we made in a brand last year and how many sales this produced and we can quickly shorthand the advertising process into how advertising generates sales.

A statement such as 'Advertising's primary role is to generate and maintain sales' sounds irrefutably sensible, and to disagree with it sounds irresponsible, even heretical, but I disagree. I believe that 'Advertising's primary role is to generate and maintain *customers.*' As Charles Channon put it, 'Advertising is not there to create sales, it is there to create profitable, protected sales... Advertising and marketing help companies stay profitable by creating and keeping customers' (Channon 1993).

Advertising doesn't even work directly on customers in the sense of 'see ad, buy product'. This model fits direct response and classified advertising, but for most display advertising the advertisements work on people through influencing an intermediary construct: the brand.

Long-term, repeat sales arise from customers' relationships with brands. Which would you rather invest in:

- Advertising that produces a sale?
  or
- Advertising that produces a stronger brand which can command sale after sale after sale?

How do people use advertising?

The subtleties involved in looking at how advertising works on people to build stronger brands can be usefully approached by turning the question around.

None of us can avoid being subjected to large amounts of advertising. Someone estimated that we come across upwards of 3000 commercial messages a day. We cope with it all by ignoring most of it. To be more precise, we register its existence at a pre-attentive level but only 'click in' and pay real attention to those messages that do something for us. There are two routes to avoid screening out.

- We register the message as personally relevant (e.g. an ad for a 4% mortgage when we are just about to buy a house).
- We see an ad that is creatively stimulating (e.g. the latest Guinness TV ad or Eva Herzigova calling 'Hello Boys' from a hoarding).

Once a person engages in an advertisement the next big question is whether it will communicate anything at either a rational or emotional level that can influence our relationship with the brand. Here the response could be anything from simply reminding us that the brand exists through to changing the way we feel about it. This range of responses must also encompass those which have little or no basis in rationality (e.g. advertising that simply makes us feel good about the brand or which suggests it is popular or modern). The response to this type of advertising is often entirely driven by 'style' rather than 'content'.

Where does research fit in?

We have said that we want our ad to engage people and to communicate something that will enhance perceived brand values. But how? And what has research got to do with it?

The most common process by which advertising is now produced dates back to 1968 when changes were made (almost simultaneously) in the structure of two London-based advertising agencies: J. Walter Thompson and Boase Massimi Pollitt. In both cases a department was set up to be the intellectual driving force behind the 'process' of advertising creation. Its importance for us is that it was to use research in a systematic way at every stage of this process. Thanks to Stephen King (at JWT) the department was given the name 'Account Planning'.

Both Stephen and Stanley Pollitt (at BMP) thought in terms of 'a planning cycle' of advertising. Broadly, this had three parts arranged in a continuous loop (Figure 1).

Research needs and methodologies differ at each of these stages.

Strategy development

This stage is both exploratory and developmental. Research of all kinds will be used to identify problems and opportunities for the brand that could conceivably be influenced by advertising.

Creative development

Once we know where we want to take the brand this stage investigates ways of getting there. It is the arena in which qualitative research is most important and it is central to the main philosophical underpinning of account planning. As Stanley Pollitt said of successful account planning:

> 'It requires a total agency commitment to getting the advertising content right at all costs.... It means a commitment and a belief that you can only make thoroughly professional judgements about advertising content with some *early indication* of

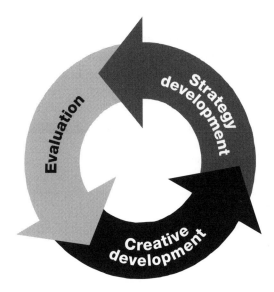

Figure 1 Planning cycle.

consumer response…. If advertising is to be rejected or modified it is better if this should be the result of response from the target market than the second guessing of account men or clients.' (Pollitt 2000)

Evaluation

After the advertising has run, we need to evaluate what happened. Most important will be to see how this advertising affected people's knowledge or feelings about the brand. Research into the advertising itself helps us to understand why the intended brand responses did or did not move according to plan. The results then naturally feed back into the next stage of strategy development.

More about measuring the effect of advertising: macro level

After the advertising has run its course, the managing director, finance director and marketing director all want to know how well it has done. At this macro level a primary interest is often sales performance, and they may well use econometric modelling to try and estimate the contribution of advertising after the influences of price, distribution, weather, competitive activity, etc. have been removed.

The modelling of post-exposure advertising effects is difficult and often concentrates only upon short-term benefits, i.e. month-to-month changes as a result of promotion rather than the long-term contribution of advertising to the dominance of, say, Tetley and PG Tips over Quick Brew or Sony

Television over Ferguson (remember them?). Where modelling is not undertaken, effectiveness is often judged on whatever quantitative research measures are to hand: notably campaign recall (I'll come back to this later).

More about measuring the effect of advertising: micro level

None of these macro, 'after the event' techniques is of any value when we are trying to use the results to feed back into *predicting* the effect of advertising. The clients of advertising agencies can be exasperated by what they see as a failure of the industry to find a 'black box' that can predict what the next ad campaign will do. It would be an ideal answer if we could type in the media budget figures, distribution, price, some assumptions about competitive activity, external influences such as the weather and consumer spending power, insert a tape of the ad and get the answer.

The missing link for advertising is, of course, that you cannot insert a tape of the ad and hope the computer measures its effectiveness. You have to involve people in watching the ad and assess their reactions. This is the really tricky bit, as we will see below.

I wish we did have a black box. If we could show advertisers how effective an advertising investment could be, budgets would double. Ferrari days would be here again. Advertising is one of the best investments a business can ever make. The IPA Effectiveness Awards in the UK and the similar 'Effies' in the USA have produced hundreds of cases showing astonishing payback from successful advertising. Payback is not easy to prove in hindsight and is well nigh impossible to predict in advance. If you think this sounds defeatist, I agree. Surely there must be someone out there who has cracked it. Unfortunately, even the leading firms of management consultants haven't reached that point. According to McKinsey's (Admap, 1996): 'In our experience, advertising objectives can rarely be set in terms of sales results; instead they must focus on what advertising can reasonably hope to achieve for the brand.'

(If anybody reading this thinks they have got a scientific model which can forecast the sales effects of advertising, they should sell it to McKinsey's for no less than £10 million.)

The lack of predictable payback doesn't mean we should stop advertising.

Uncertainty and advertising

The key to reducing uncertainty about the potential effectiveness of advertising is to return to the planning cycle.

At the strategic development stage the research input should be extensive and eclectic. It can involve everything from the 'Sherlock Holmes' approach of sifting through libraries of data to the spark of inspiration (often helped by listening to consumers in focus groups) that has, for example, turned Lucozade into an energy drink and the Co-op into the ethical bank. The questions to ask at this stage are of the kind discussed in David Cowan's article 'Why can't big companies grow?' (*Market Leader* 1999/2000):

(1) How can the organic growth rate be doubled?
(2) What are the root causes of sales decline and what can be done about them?
(3) What do we have to do to get new users?
(4) Why is the customer base not buying more from us and what do we have to do to change this situation?

There is no excuse for not having done everything possible to button down the advertising strategy. If advertising could change or enhance certain brand values, then to know that there are indeed values which are important to a sizeable proportion of the target group is key.

When we move to the creative development stage and the need to bring strategy to life, the uncertainty returns. The advertising business, especially on this side of the Atlantic, has become more 'uncertainty tolerant' over time, more likely to accept that advertising is an art, not a science. Many of today's more successful advertisers are successful because they are relaxed about embracing uncertainty and, with their advertising, as with other aspects of their business, promote a corporate culture that rewards experimentation rather than punishes failure.

Agencies chose to get around the unpredictability issue by embracing it and reinterpreting it as sexy radicalism: 'Rule number one. There are no rules.' If it's an art, not a science, there must be some guidelines: 'People don't buy from clowns', 'Long copy doesn't sell', etc. Ogilvy arose alongside a star system of creative directors, which is still with us today. The advertising business has tried to reduce uncertainty, to inspire confidence by elevating creative directors as the men who know. 'I can't tell what will make for great advertising but I know a man who can.' Every week the advertising trade paper *Campaign* attempts to analyse the latest ads. How do they do this? They ask a creative director to give his 'Private View'.

For some advertisers this is good enough. It is not uncommon for very successful advertising campaigns to be launched without any research, and simply to be based on the gut feel of the agency and the advertiser. For others, however, confidence requires something more: back to Stanley Pollitt's philosophy of getting an early indication of consumer response. This may be with a view to developing the advertising to make it better or simply to provide reassurance to support judgment. Either way, it is the subject of the remainder of this chapter.

Its place in the advertising process

Quantitative research is essential for strategy development. It is the natural starting point for the broad questions:

- Who buys my brand?
- How often versus competitors?
- What are the barriers to buying at all or buying more?, and so on.

Similarly, it has a natural role in the process of post-campaign evaluation. Quantitative tracking, whether conducted continuously, in the manner pioneered by Millward Brown or on an *ad hoc* pre/post-exposure basis, is normal for most advertisers. More contentious is the role of quantitative research in campaign development.

Quantitative campaign development research – the early years and models of advertising

By the 1920s American advertising men believed they had solved that infamous grumble attributed to Lord Leverhulme (among others) that he knew that half the money he spent on advertising was wasted but he didn't know which half. They had adapted Henry Ford's car production processes to advertising. Daniel Starch claimed that advertising had now become a science. The theories and techniques of behavioural psychology and its work with laboratory rats were gleefully adopted for advertising measurement. The claims of 'motivational research' practitioners drove Vance Packard's *The Hidden Persuaders* (1960) to be a bestseller in the paranoid 1950s. Packard was saying, 'Look out world, the marketing men can manipulate us now. Isn't this scary?' It would have been if the claims were true, but most of it was over-claim.

Two philosophies of advertising grew up. 'Persuasion', based on a belief that advertising works by effecting a measurable shift in people's attitudes at the time of viewing the advertisement. 'Recall', based on a belief that people see ads, remember something claimed about the brand and, the next time they encounter the brand, decide to see if the claim is true.

Both of these philosophies of advertising involved a sequential view of how advertising works: DAGMAR and AIDA belong to the persuasion school, AIETA to the recall school (Figure 2).

For most of the pre and postwar period persuasion held sway. It felt right. Its practitioners exuded certainty and made confident assertions about the validity of their techniques. Unfortunately, too much of the validation of quantitative research at the time was based on new products. When a product is launched, sales can only go up.

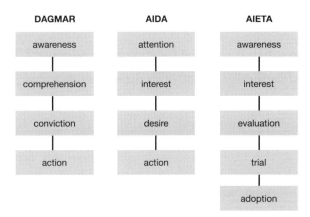

Figure 2 Models of advertising.

Persuasion shift measurements developed where people were asked their brand preferences and were shown a programme with a commercial break in the middle including the test commercial. The interviewer would then come back in and say 'I'm very sorry but we've lost the questionnaires you filled in before the programme. Please could you fill them out again', and look for a shift in brand preferences.

The validity of the persuasion shift technique remains a live issue of debate today. It still has adherents (particularly from American multi-nationals) and has been strongly advocated by one impartial academic (John Philip Jones). From the other side, doubts have been expressed about its accuracy and relevance (particularly in the UK from Simon Broadbent and Andrew Ehrenberg).

The generally held view in the UK is that a persuasion shift technique may have some relevance for the particular type of advertising that presents 'new news'. Beyond this application it has few advocates and, since few brands have genuine functional advantages, the focus has shifted to new concepts like brand personality which require a different type of research.

An American adman called Rosser Reeves used 'recall' research to prove that people who bought his clients' products were much more likely to have noticed advertising for it; therefore the advertising must have worked. Unfortunately, all the other agencies were able to show the same thing and, once the hype had died down, someone pointed out that Rosser had confused cause and effect. The truth is that people who use a brand are much more likely to also pay attention to its advertising. They're interested in it. They already have a relationship with it. This confusion of cause and effect still crops up today and is known as 'the Rosser Reeves fallacy'.

To understand and therefore produce more effective advertising you have to think more deeply about things, even though this often seems wimpish behaviour. It was against this background that qualitative research started to play a greater role in advertising.

Quantitative campaign development research today

Outside of persuasion testing, quantitative research has become much more sensitive and useful, largely due to the influence of qualitative research. Gordon Brown, founder of Millward Brown, did much to raise the game in the UK and wean his clients on to more useful measures. He argued against persuasion and for recall on the basis that recall better fits how people talk about advertising in qualitative research.

Mike Hall and Doug Maclay's framework model (1991) and, more recently, Terry Prue's alphabet model (1998) both codify the different ways in which advertising seems to work and adjust their quantitative research accordingly. Both of these models also owe most of their philosophical development to insights gained from qualitative research. The advertising industry today is much better served by quantitative research because it approaches its subject less as behavioural scientists looking to measure and experiment and more as humanistic pollsters, looking to take qualitative insights and enumerate them. There is more stress on the diagnostic elements of quantitative research and less on the normative yardsticks.

THE ROLE OF QUALITATIVE RESEARCH

Early qualitative research

Qualitative research is so much a central part of the creative development research process in the UK that it is easy to forget that in the 1960s and 1970s it was still fighting hard for acceptance.

We can note the start of the serious battle with the formation of the first two account planning departments in London in 1968. The sure sign of acceptance by the advertising establishment would be a decade later in 1978 when there were enough account planners to form a trade body, the Account Planning Group. In between these two events lay the publication of the first truly seminal description of the role and power of qualitative research for advertising creative development.

The paper in question was by Alan Hedges, and was entitled 'Testing to destruction' (1974). Originally published by the Institute of Practitioners in Advertising, it continues to be available from the IPA with much of the original text unchanged and largely unchallenged.

Alan Hedges codified a growing understanding about brands and brand values – i.e. that they had a component which went beyond the rational and functional. Just like people, brands have 'personality', and it was only through the subtle and more free-flowing use of qualitative research that these personalities were researched.

I have quoted below a short extract from a speech Stephen King made to the Advertising Association in 1970 entitled 'What is a brand?'. It is fascinating today to think that 30 years ago you had to try and prove the existence of brand personalities. It is also fascinating to read the transcripts and gain an insight into how people lived and talked a generation ago. This is one of the great benefits of qualitative research: the insights it gives you into social trends, and the vocabulary surrounding brands. Just as we think we know certain markets, qualitative research brings them into sharper focus. The following brings the late 1960s more vividly to life.

Interviewer: What would Mrs Fairy Snow do in the evenings?
Housewife: Well, just sort of sit by the fire and watch television.
Interviewer: And what about Tide? What sort of personality would Tide have?
Housewife: A very gruff old man, very fierce. Ex-army type.
Interviewer: What about Tide, if Tide became a person?
Housewife: A little nearer a Mrs Ariel sort of person. She would be a little more with it, more mini-skirted, more Americanised, I would think. The sort of person who tends to buy the frozen foods and have a rather flashy car. It matters to her – social things matter to her, I would think, rather than with Mrs Surf. I don't think it matters too much if she doesn't keep up with the Joneses.

Qualitative research may not have changed that much, but the brands have gone own-label and, most interestingly, reading between the lines, British society and speech patterns have changed. Frozen foods are no longer considered go-ahead and people don't sit by the fire to watch television. This is one of the great utilities of qualitative research: the lifting of the veil, the insights into behaviour. It is often the quotes from research, the revealing little soundbites, that inspire effective advertising as much as the formal, overt, research objectives and findings. You'd be surprised how many brand managers come away with better understanding of their brands as a result of soundbites too.

The validity of qualitative research

Qualitative research has wonderful utility. It also has what Charles Channon called 'operational validity'. Companies find research methods that seem to work for them and keep doing them. Creativity doesn't have any scientific validity either, and surely that should be our point of reference. After all, creativity is the advertising industry's core competence, its reason to exist.

Qualitative research today operates best when it provides insights which act as a creative springboard. It is uniquely able to delve into the life and motivations of people and to offer the creative team stimulating glimpses into the people and the brands. The industry isn't choosy. It'll use whatever works to produce effective advertising. Most practitioners believe they are more likely to generate effective advertising as a result of a process that prioritises insights and enlightenment rather than assessment and measurement. Indeed, Peter Field's analysis of the IPA Effectiveness Awards seems to bear out the view that qualitative development of advertising is more useful in developing effective advertising than any other methodology.

Qualitative research today

Qualitative research can be valuable at all stages of the planning cycle for advertising.

Strategy development

To help give *colour* to the problems and opportunities for a brand. Qualitative research can extend understanding of the underlying dynamics behind the quantitative market data. This is particularly true of the 'softer' elements of, for example, brand personality and user image. Qualitative research is particularly suited to the early stages of exploration of brand positioning routes, i.e. *realistically*, what could the brand be made to stand for? Here one may be exploring different brand positionings from both the points of view of whether it could have a beneficial effect on brand standing and of the size of the task which would be needed to make the positioning 'stick'.

Creative development

There is a spectrum of relevant topics for qualitative research from the exploration of broad advertising strategic directions through to final advertising executions. It is part of the iterative process where ideas are checked for what Stanley Pollitt was quoted earlier as calling an 'early indication of consumer response'.

In the early stages of creative development it may be that the brand advertising direction is known, but that the specific way to bring it to life is still being sought. It can be immensely valuable to listen to the reactions of target group respondents:

- when they talk about the way they use the brand;
- when they talk about their feelings about brand users versus competitor users;

- when they respond to initial creative ideas;
- when users try to 'sell' the benefits to non-users, and so on.

Pre-exposure evaluation

This is a subset of creative development, and can involve both qualitative and quantitative methodologies. One advantage of qualitative investigation is that it can more easily distinguish between reactions to the core creative idea from those to the executional detail. If combined with quantitative methods, it will give more of a diagnostic understanding of why certain aspects are working better than others.

Post-exposure evaluation

As we intimated earlier, this is predominantly the territory of the quantitative advertising tracker but, again, an element of qualitative techniques can add to a diagnostic understanding of the interactions that lie beneath the results.

PRACTICALITIES: METHODOLOGICAL CONSIDERATIONS

Groups versus depths

Group discussions (or focus groups) remain the most widely used methodology for advertising research. Do groups smother individual responses? There's not as much written about this as one might expect. Criticisms levelled at group discussions are that they are an unreal way of studying responses to advertisements. People don't generally sit at home discussing TV adverts in depth with seven strangers. Moreover, some individuals' responses can be smothered by noisier respondents.

I think the counter-argument to this is to look at groups as teamworking exercises. Just as in many other walks of life, teamworking, interaction with others, is the way to move a project forward, so in advertising research it can be more useful, more enlightening, to conduct a teamworking exercise with members of the target audience. It is impossible to truly replicate the real-life environment in which TV ads are consumed while slumped on a sofa for the evening. As long as teamwork never becomes dictatorship by the noisiest individual, groups work. The benefits of a group discussion, people building on or disagreeing with others' comments, generally make for richer research data than individual interviews where the respondent can feel a little inhibited or intimidated by the one-to-one situation which they probably last experienced when applying for a job or visiting the doctor.

Most researchers use a variety of techniques that allow the individual response to come through in a group situation. Examples include:

- simple questionnaires;
- bubble drawings (i.e. cartoons showing relevant situations but with empty speech bubbles for respondents to fill in);
- immersion exercises before the group begins, where respondents may, for example, be asked to keep a personal diary.

Beyond this, it is important to remember the golden rule of group discussions: we don't expect group members to give us the answer; it is for the moderator to interpret the answers by using respondent comments as a catalyst and support.

Going beyond what was 'said' in group discussions

People's familiarity with advertising has big implications (pros and cons) for the research. On the one hand it's great, because they'll talk fluently about strategy; on the other it can be a problem because they're stuck on their understanding of how the strategy works, and they're not always right! It takes clever researchers who understand how people respond to a range of types of advertising to allow people their own language to discuss the strategy, but to make allowances for it in the interpretation.

We need to help people talk about brands and advertising by suggesting frameworks (e.g. which one did you prefer, what made it seem effective, etc.), and by using some projective techniques to help people articulate things they don't often think or talk about but where there's a tension. Some researchers claim to go well beyond this and to conduct deep psychologically based tests to uncover the unsaid Freudian and Jungian roots of advertising responses.

As a research user, one has to decide how far one is happy to go in this claimed cross-over between 'hidden' advertising responses and psycho-therapy. The latter route is particularly fashionable in other markets (e.g. France), but my personal view is that the more we try to develop artificial, often embarrassing tasks for people, the more we get away from the commonsense roots of just asking people questions and so we reinvent all the foolishly artificial structures of behaviourist quantitative research. This is one of the reasons 'Keep it simple, stupid' applies to advertising research as much as to most aspects of brand communications.

Stimulus

To help with the creative development of advertising, stimulus for research is generally best in either very raw or very finished format.

Raw 'artist's roughs' or TV scripts make it clear to respondents that they are being asked to comment on the underlying ideas. Finished materials obviously provide the closest to a real-life test. Problems are more likely to arise when the material is a halfway house. For example, animatics (where drawings of the potential ad are filmed and a basic soundtrack is added) or storyboards of a TV commercial where respondents get hung up on the way a particular character has been drawn or who come up with the dreaded comment, 'Will it be a cartoon when they make it then? My kids love cartoons.'

In addition, contributing to the idea by using the imagination gets respondents into a positive frame of mind that encourages them to help make the idea work for them. Great for creative development; dangerous (but not impossible) for genuine pre-testing.

'Going live'

There is something unnecessarily static and cosy about many people's idea of qualitative research. Clearly, there is no reason why it has to take place in suburban living rooms. Several research companies, like HPI, make a point of going 'live' whenever possible – this means talking to beer drinkers in the pub, grocery buyers while in the supermarket, and so on. It all adds to a more dynamic interchange, and because respondents are talking while doing rather than thinking about it several days later, the insights they provide are both richer and more relevant.

Who should conduct the research?

Qualitative advertising research is conducted by both agency planners and independent researchers. Sometimes the work is best carried out by someone who is very close to the issues; sometimes an outsider's fresh perspective is more useful. Bringing in an outside researcher also introduces a fresh set of questions that the agency needs to deal with in order to provide the most effective research. Some of these questions can be difficult to answer. In *Excellence in Advertising* (Butterfield 1999), Roddy Glen writes:

> 'Of particular importance in creative development work is the need to understand not only what the proto-advertising is trying to communicate (per strategy and brief) but how it seeks to go about this, in terms of the creative structures it employs. This is a question which unfortunately too few agencies are ready to answer at the briefing.'

Agencies would agree with this as good practice, but it is more honoured in the breach than the observance.

QUALITATIVE RESEARCH AND THE CREATIVE DEPARTMENT

Should the creative department be involved?

It's worth picking up on this point because I think there's a big issue lurking in here somewhere. It touches on the perspective of the creative people as end users of the research. Creatives' involvement with qualitative research is not thought about as much as it should be, given their central role in the advertising process.

Advertising people talk about the importance of advertising that contains a big idea, but they are not good at articulating those big ideas. They tend to fall back on executional elements rather than the structural components that researchers like Roddy (and clients who are being asked to buy the advertising) quite rightly ask us to identify.

To understand why this is so it's worth starting at the beginning. The act of creation is very different from the act of analysis.

Just as we need to get inside people's heads to understand how brands work, we must now take a detour into the heads of the typical advertising agency creative team: the land where the wild things live. Everyone who works in advertising or marketing should go on a role reversal course at some point.

Writing advertising

Writing an ad is a process of having bits of ideas, playing with them for a while to see if they'll work, sensing that those ideas aren't the best possible, putting them aside, having other ideas, interspersed with huge periods of doodling, daydreaming, playing around, waiting for inspiration to strike. This will be interrupted by the agency creative director ruthlessly rejecting some ideas as not good enough, but telling you to look again at one of your earliest ideas and marry it up with another new thought. Elation and despair are present in rapid succession. Giving birth to advertising ideas is a very messy, bloody process.

Before I entered advertising I discovered a wonderful book called *Decoding Advertisements* (1978). The author, Judith Williamson, applied structuralist art criticism to advertising, pointing out (sometimes with echoes of Vance Packard) the language of advertisements. The following is typical of her style: 'This is the hidden visual reference that the advertiser is using, this is the sign, this is the signifier and this is what is signified.' I was overawed. I thought creatives were omniscient manipulators.

As with other forms of human endeavour, the conspiracy theory is usually less likely than the cock-up theory. People aren't smart enough to conspire to the degree that those outside assume they have done. Creatives don't consciously do any multi-layered manipulating; they study ads all the time, work out what feels right, and just do it.

I have tried to persuade creatives to read *Decoding Advertisements* or other academic analyses, but they generally throw them aside in disgust. Not only do they not like it, but it usually makes them angry. Jeremy Bullmore once wrote an article entitled 'Decoding Judith Williamson'.

The importance of the idea

Inside agencies, everyone talks about the importance of the idea but creative work is rarely sold into clients in terms of the idea it employs because creative people are not skilled at articulating these ideas in clinical terms. They talk instead about the way they put the ad together, the chronological sequence of ideas they had. 'We started out by thinking in terms of what our mums do with this stuff and we wanted to keep the dancing parrot from your previous campaign. We tried coming at it from the parrot angle but everything we came up with was terrible and we were getting nowhere. We were over in the pub last Tuesday evening and I was telling Steve about my old Maths teacher and his catch phrase and that gave Steve an idea for a great endline and it reminded us of a sequence from a film that we want to use.'

Creatives are brilliant at picking up on popular culture and playing it back to people. They know when an ad feels right but aren't good at pulling apart the constituent components.

Creative people generally aren't very good at analysing their work. When you see an artist profiled, for example, on television programmes such as *The South Bank Show*, the artist generally talks in terms of what was going on in their lives and how they were feeling when they created this work. They talk more about their subjective, emotional perspectives than about the external meaning of the text and how other 'readers' will interpret it.

> 'I think I've got phenomenal ability to base very important decisions totally on emotion. If it feels right, 100%, I don't ask myself why. I wouldn't be able to find out the answers, and I think that's why a lot of people get stuck. If it feels right I just do it.' (Damien Hirst, *Observer*, 14 February 1999)

It is the art critic who is typically more illuminating about why the work has such merit. Just as the art market needs critics to explain what people are buying, so the advertising business needs qualitative research to illuminate what its clients are buying.

The research 'critic'

The research 'critic' needn't be entirely divorced from the process. It can be helpful for a researcher to play back some of these 'cultural hunches' to the team. There's a big role for a form of 'applied semiotics' that explains how certain symbols or codes in advertising generate the responses they do. When I worked for Roddy Glen he used to put this in terms of 'Creatives write the ads in horizontal leaps. Our job is to slice the ads up vertically. To pull out the underlying structures.'

Clients are often surprised that creatives don't attend more group discussions or qualitative debriefs. Creatives often find the experience uncomfortable and invent excuses to be elsewhere. Again, agencies can feel awkward about this and aren't good at explaining the creatives' absence.

I suggest one way to understand this is to imagine you are a creative who has just sweated blood to produce some precious embryonic advertising ideas. Research can be like a case conference of medical people examining your babies, holding them upside-down, making them cry, weighing them, drawing blood by pricking their toes. It's upsetting to behold, and the analysis can be brutally dispassionate. You may hear the consultants predicting that three of the four babies are perfect specimens and are going to grow up to lead wonderfully fulfilling lives, but one is hopelessly under-branded and doesn't have long to live. The experts know that three out of four is an extremely good ratio in this field and want to congratulate you on your output, but all you can hear is a voice inside screaming 'MY BABY'S GONNA DIE!!'

There's no easy solution to this natural discomfort between creative teams and qualitative researchers. All one can hope for is to have 'grown-up' creatives and then to choose sensitive and specialist qualitative researchers.

SOME EXAMPLES

Qualitative research at the strategy development stage

HEA Drugs Education Campaign

The Grand Prix winner from the IPA Advertising Effectiveness Awards of 1998 concerns the print campaign to advise children and younger adults on the dangers of using recreational drugs. Qualitative research provided the strategic insight that all previous campaigns had got it wrong because they misunderstood the way young people are first introduced to drugs. The new strategy succeeded because it was honest and informative – presenting the health risk without scare tactics and seemingly allowing users to make up their own minds.

BT 'It's Good to Talk'

The brief for the Bob Hoskins campaign originated from a detailed qualitative investigation of barriers to people making more calls or spending longer on them. The key strategic insight involved the role of men both because they use the phone less and because they act as 'gatekeepers' to restrict use by other members of the family. The final campaign therefore decided to target males and their attitudes towards the telephone, even though the resulting increase in usage would be found to come from males and females alike.

Qualitative research at the creative development stage

BUPA

When O&M was pitching for the BUPA campaign it wanted to talk about BUPA as the healthcare experts, but was told by the client to come up with 'positive health' messages. 'We feared we were in the area of vitamin supplements, low-fat spreads and even yoghurts.' Their breakthrough came when one respondent said: 'It's like cars and it depends on how much you value them. If you've got a BMW or Merc you take it to an expert whereas if you've got an old Skoda or something then the bloke under the arches will do.' The agency realised they needed to get people to value their bodies more, to appreciate the complex, precious, amazing nature of their bodies as machines.

Polaroid

Polaroid had been in decline for years and was seen as naff. BBH gave respondents a Polaroid camera to carry around with them for a week. When they reconvened the sample, people reported back on how embarrassed they had felt being seen with a naff Polaroid. They also asked people to take both a conventional camera and a Polaroid camera to various social events and to photograph people. When they analysed the photographs it was clear that, whereas people compose themselves formally for a conventional camera, they pull faces and act up for a Polaroid because it's not to be taken too seriously (the flip side of naffness). This gave the agency an insight into the true role of Polaroid as a social lubricant, a way of getting people going.

This example of advertising research also shows how agencies can often be very innovative users of research. Researchers are generally encouraged to be objective, to tell it how it is, impartially and without any spin. Researchers still get paid if they say, 'Sorry, but people think your brand's naff'. Agencies only get paid if they can demonstrate a potential for advertising to make a difference and be a worthwhile investment. Agencies are often desperately searching for an 'angle', an insight that can get them to a more powerful proposition. Since necessity is the mother of invention, they can be pretty inventive.

KEY IDEAS

- Advertising is not all-powerful. The power lies with people watching or ignoring the advertising.
- Advertising is not there to create sales but to generate and maintain customers, so ensuring long-term commercial success.
- Research fits in at all three stages in the advertising planning process: strategy development, creative development and final evaluation.
- Predicting the effect of advertising is a complex issue – market modelling may help at the 'macro' level but not at the 'micro' level.
- Many excellent campaigns have been launched based on the gut feel of creative directors, but both qualitative and quantitative methods exist to provide reassurance and insights into consumer response and motivation.
- The best quantitative methodologies have borrowed heavily from qualitative research as it approaches its subject less as behavioural scientists and more as humanistic pollsters looking for insights.
- Qualitative research acts best as a creative springboard able to offer the planners and the creative team stimulating glimpses into people and brands.
- While great store is placed on the creative idea, creative teams do not come up with ideas in such a structured way. Qualitative research can help unravel the thinking and define the idea retrospectively.

REFERENCES

Butterfield, L. (ed.) (1999) *Excellence in Advertising*, Butterworth Heinemann, London.
Channon, C. (1993) *The Charles Channon Papers*, IPA, London.
Cowan, D. (1999/2000) Why can't big companies grow?, *Market Leader*, Winter.
Hall, M. & Maclay, D. (1991) Market Research Society Conference Papers.
Hedges, A. (1974) *Testing to Destruction*, IPA, London.
King, S. (1970) *What is a Brand?*, JWT, London.
Ogilvy, D. (1973) *Ogilvy on Advertising*, Pan Books, London.
Packard, V. (1960) *The Hidden Persuaders*, Penguin Books, Harmondsworth.
Pollitt, S. (2000) *Pollitt on Planning*, Admap Publications, Henley-on-Thames.
Prue, T. (1998) An all-embracing theory of how advertising works?, *Admap*, February.
Williamson, J. (1978) *Decoding Advertisements*, Marion Boyars, London.

FURTHER READING

Broadbent, S. (1997) *Accountable Advertising*, Admap Publications, Henley-on-Thames.

Bullmore, J. (1991) *Behind the Scenes in Advertising*, NTC, Henley-on-Thames.

Cooper, A. (ed.) (1997) *How to Plan Advertising*, Cassell, London.

Field, P. (1997) Admap Conference, 'Researching Creativity', October.

Franzen, G. (1994) *Advertising Effectiveness*, NTC, Henley-on-Thames.

Kendal, N. (199) *Advertising Works 10*, IPA and Admap Publications, Henley-on-Thames.

McDonald, C. (1972) *How Advertising Works: A Review of Current Thinking*, The Advertising Association and NTC, London.

Chapter 5

Qualitative Research and Direct Marketing

Tod Norman
Planning Director, BHWG

Chris Barraclough
Chairman, BHWG

Editor's introduction

Coming from an advertising background, I had always assumed that direct marketing would use many of the same planning tools, including qualitative research. In fact, this is far from the case.

Historically, the essential factor in the evaluation of direct marketing has always been response. Indeed, as Tod Norman explains in this chapter, qualitative research was actively rejected by the industry as embarrassed respondents notoriously lied in groups about 'junk mail', all claiming they never look at it.

The breakthrough came when direct marketers realised that they needed to better understand their customers, not simply to predict response rates but rather to build better relationships. Understanding would lead to better and more appropriate creative work, and even more relevant offers.

This crucial concept – relationship marketing – has fuelled a new era of investment in direct marketing. Whether the contact with an existing customer be via mail, magazine, telephone or the internet, our industry is focused now not just on direct selling but direct relationships, where the customer and the company are not separated by an intermediary such as a retailer or agent. One of the fastest growing and most influential trends of marketing today – customer relationship management (CRM) – is based purely on this concept. While direct mail examples have been used in this chapter, the principles discussed do, however, relate to all aspects of direct marketing.

Tod and Chris Barraclough explain how the industry woke up to the need to understand the consumer and how qualitative research is now adding value in the field. Tod is one of the rare breed of direct marketing planners, a specialist in the field and ideal as primary author. I have been lucky to work with Chris and know him as one of the great creatives in the field.

THE CONTEXT: THE EVOLUTION OF DIRECT MARKETING

Junk mail

Direct marketing is often dismissed as junk mail. Many people see it as a humble, old-fashioned marketing technique with little creativity or importance. But this condemnation ignores the important role of direct marketing in oiling – indeed driving – the wheels of commerce.

Born of the printing press, direct marketing – or, at its most basic, direct sales – has played a massive role in the success of capitalism. Without it, our ancestors would never have had the ability to buy anything that wasn't for sale in their locality.

Luckily for us, manufacturers in the early eighteenth century came to realise that unless they found ways of selling their wares beyond the limited coverage of existing shops and field sales staff, their growth would be restricted. Early newspapers, and eventually catalogues, allowed companies to reach those far-flung customers beyond the reach of other channels. If it was Sears Roebuck that brought civilisation to the great American West, it was direct marketing – through the company's catalogue – that was the main tool in this process.

Direct marketing went from strength to strength throughout the early twentieth century. By the 1960s it was a global industry worth tens of billions of dollars selling millions of products and employing hundreds of thousands of people – all without a single focus group.

Direct mail as a science

By the end of the 1970s direct mail was a science. Direct marketing agencies could predict to two decimal points the exact ratio of letters to responses, responses to sales, and sales to profit once the costs had been subtracted. Because the measurement of success was empirical, based purely on response, the practitioners developed 'golden rules'. These rules were hard-and-fast guides to success; every seminar and conference featured some guru with his particular formula.

The statistical validity of the formulae was based on the massive scale of the mailings. In this period before databases and segmentation, the basis of the industry was to mail millions of people with the same message, and to reach cost-effectiveness (and establish scientific proof) through the scale of the response. On these sort of equations, if a campaign pulled a 1.5% response, it was a success. Therefore, all the focus and energy of the agency and client were spent in either raising it to 1.6% or achieving 1.5% for less cost. What happened to the other 98.5% was irrelevant.

The dogma included 'leverage percentage points for success'. For example, one formula listed the importance of the list of names used for a mailing as responsible for 50% of the campaign's success, the incentive as 25%, creative 15%, and 10% mailing format.

Creative freedom at this time was oxymoronic. Creative teams were expected to understand and adhere to the definitive code of practices. A yellow envelope would pull more responses than a white one. Seven individual elements in a pack would draw more response than five. Free prize draws would enhance response by $X\%$ if the first prize was worth so much, and by $Y\%$ if it was worth so much. The amount of space allocated on a page to any product was determined not by its creative insight, but by an index of its expected profit per square inch. 'Involvement' was the core of any creative idea; the more items there were to see, rip open and play with, the higher the response.

Given such science, 'fuzzy' investigation through things like market research was eschewed. This was particularly true of any research aimed at providing customer understanding to be fed into the creative work; why worry if the creative treatment had such a small impact on the return on investment?

By the mid-1980s, however, some agencies were looking for new ideas that would help them improve response rates and attract a new, more brand-literate form of client. Qualitative research was one such idea.

THE ROLE OF QUALITATIVE RESEARCH IN DIRECT MARKETING

The problems of using qualitative research

The image of qualitative research

Every time qualitative research was used in the early days it ran up against a familiar and somewhat basic problem. It got the answers to the key questions wrong. When a facilitator asked a group of housewives in

Nottingham or New York whether they looked at direct mail, the answer would be no.

Perhaps more importantly, when he asked whether they would be more likely to respond to pack A or pack B, the response would be the reverse of the truth. If the research suggested that people liked pack B much more than pack A, a test programme would show that A out-pulled B by a huge margin. I personally recall with chagrin the experience of being shown to be wrong both definitively and very, very publicly. The less said the better.

The general interpretation of this fact was that when surrounded by seven of their peers, people lied. Direct mail had a terrible reputation based on the very aspects that had driven its success. Mass mailings, regardless of the appropriateness of the message, and 'tacky' executions, which got response but lacked the entertainment values that TV advertising was deploying so well, had created a social outcast. No one wanted to admit they read direct mail (much less created it). Thus like body odour or haemorrhoids, it was an inappropriate topic to be discussed with strangers in public.

A more generous interpretation of the findings was that qualitative research, by the nature of its small samples, was simply an inappropriate tool to examine direct response marketing. After all, a good response rate to a mailing might be 1%. A standard qualitative research project of six groups (or 42 people) might not have anyone in it who was likely to respond. Thus the research findings were based on the opinions of people who would never actually respond anyway.

The most sophisticated explanation of the failure of qualitative research was that most of us are more likely to articulate what others would approve of us doing ('I'll always get three insurance quotes') rather than admitting to what we will actually do (renew the old policy automatically). Even when asked to recall past behaviour, our memory becomes 'selective': we will admit to what is deemed socially acceptable ('I never open junk mail') rather than confess to what actually happened ('Yes, I bought this shirt through a catalogue').

We have seen this last behaviour time and time again. We recently witnessed a group of people who owned a certain product only available through direct mail wherein one of the respondents admitted having the product, but was 100% convinced that he never, ever opened junk mail. This posed another problem; once committed, he couldn't back down, and was thus embarrassed when the truth came out. He could never rejoin the group emotionally after this.

Causality

Perhaps the most important reason behind the failure of qualitative research was that we, as researchers, fundamentally assumed that there was a direct, causal link between what people like and feel comfortable with and their propensity to act.

To a qualitative researcher, particularly one trained in brand development, this link seemed like common sense; people will buy from companies they respect and will respond to advertising they identify with. It's a simple principle, and lies at the foundation of most modern advertising.

However, the motivations for actual buying are a little more complex. Successful selling is not just about being likeable; ask any successful salesman. Executions that were liked and appreciated in research often lacked both the impact to cut through and the motivational hook to generate a response. They were likeable because they made no demands. Nothing was expected of you. No decision had to be made. No action was required.

But selling is the opposite; it lives only by the successful 'close', where the customer is called upon to act – to reach into his or her pocket and do something. It is often an uncomfortable moment; forking out money, even for something you want, is seldom carefree. Sometimes, the more at ease you feel with someone, the more difficult it is to actually give them money.

This, we believe, is the main reason why qualitative research so often fails to accurately predict response. Successful direct response ads are usually intrusive, pushy and loud. They say, 'Buy Me Now!' This very fact makes them less than appreciated in qualitative discussions.

The role for qualitative research

Thus qualitative research, with all the tremendous value it adds to understanding the softer emotional elements of a brand and the relationships a customer has with it, is simply inappropriate and ineffective at predicting response. If direct marketing was still only used for direct selling, qualitative research would still have little or no role to play.

However, the industry has changed. While the direct sales market is still large and growing (one third of all computers sold in the UK today, for example, are bought off the page or over the internet), there have been three key trends that have changed our industry forever.

Branding

The first is the growth in the concept of the brand. From its original meaning, branding has moved beyond a symbol burned in cow flesh, beyond a logo or advertising strap line to become defined as the totality of thoughts and feelings an individual has towards a company and its products. In this wider context, any material sent to a customer helps form, redress or even damage a customer's perception of that brand. Tacky direct marketing communications can destroy a carefully built brand image as quickly and as definitively as a salesmen with bad breath.

If you've ever received a letter from a company making you an offer for which you don't actually qualify or which you have already taken up, you'll appreciate the damage that can be done. This belief, that direct marketing will have an effect on the 98% who don't respond, has driven changes in some – though not all – direct marketing activity. It demands that we think deeply about non-responders, and how to leave them positively predisposed to us even if they are not currently in the market for our product or service.

We can no longer accept response rates as the only measure of success; we also have to consider the impact of our direct marketing on non-responders. It is therefore crucial that we understand how non-responders feel about our creative executions and what impact an execution may have on their attitude towards our brand. To do that we must use qualitative research.

Relationship marketing

The second key trend has been the development of relationship marketing. In the same way that a good salesman takes time and effort to cultivate his best customers, direct marketing is now frequently used to provide a relationship with customers who lack a personal sales contact. The commercial viability of this strategy rests on the fact that it is significantly more expensive to recruit a new customer than it is to develop an existing customer.

Relationship marketing is now the fastest growing sector of marketing. If the commercial argument above is the engine, it is advances in technology (the internet), society (social acceptance of receiving telephone calls from an existing supplier), and business (acceptance of the Pareto rule; i.e. 80% of your profit will come from 20% of your customers) that have provided the fuel. Today, direct marketing is neither a media selection nor a channel, but a whole new way of doing business. Ask Michael Dell if you need a reference.

Creating a 'relationship' with a customer using direct means was originally something of a challenge to our industry. We can identify what they buy, what they respond to, but what do they want from us in terms of a relationship? Christmas cards? Newsletters? Fridge magnets? To get the nature or frequency of communication wrong will be damaging and expensive, so how do we understand what type of communication (in terms of media, content, style, frequency, even production quality) is most appropriate for them? And how do we know when we have done a good job?

Again, it is qualitative research that rides to the rescue. By listening to customers, understanding who they are, what language they use, what preconceptions they have, what they want to achieve, and by gaining insight into what kind of relationship they want, we can learn how best to enhance their long-term loyalty to our brand.

Marketing databases

The third key issue is the growth of powerful marketing databases. It is old hat to go on about how a young brand manager now has sitting on his or her desk more computing power than an Apollo spacecraft, but it is a fact. Huge advances have been made in our industry by exploiting that power.

In theory, we can record as much detail about our customers as we wish and not just their purchasing behaviour. We can know what car they drive, the names and ages of their children, what sort of house they live in and where they like to go on holiday. This power gives us the opportunity to find more relevant and motivating subjects for use in creative work. It can even lead us to the selection of lists; if we know that ISA holders are also likely to be into sailing, we can purchase a list of subscribers to sailing magazines.

However, in practice, most client data is limited to purchasing behaviour. That leaves large gaps; for instance, it may not tell us much about their lifestyles. To fill this gap we can overlay 'lifestyle maps' which will tell us, for example, that if someone lives in Street Y they are more likely to take their holidays in Spain rather than, say, France. Or they are more likely to visit the cinema than eat out. However, this still tells us nothing about their attitudes. For example, are they cautious with money or impetuous? What are their priorities in life? Are they early adopters or scared rigid by new technology?

It is this attitudinal understanding that can best guide the development of creative work so that it can have the most positive impact on responders and non-responders alike. This information or 'soft data' can only come from qualitative research. When you marry it to the hard data provided by the client database you have the basis of a truly powerful marketing tool.

How qualitative research is used: case histories

In the preceding section we outlined how qualitative research can be applied to the creation of powerful direct marketing programmes. A few case histories may indicate better how precisely we have used it for a number of clients. These cases have to do with direct mail because, in order to protect our clients' current activities we have had to choose older examples. But the principles remain the same in our latest work for e-businesses using the internet, and on global CRM programmes based on telephone contact.

One of the residual mantras of direct marketing is that it is a science, and there's no doubt that many areas of direct marketing have a strong scientific bent. You won't find me hosting seminars on regression analysis or predictive modelling, but there has been a school of thought which held that the scientific certainty of a response figure could be extended to the creative idea and execution. If we could use numbers to produce the sequence of words and images that are guaranteed to work most effectively every time many of us would be redundant. 'And why not?' I hear you chorus. Because creative work is subjective, and every brief demands a different answer.

At the other extreme, many creative leaders would prefer that everything was left to gut feel and intuition. Somewhere in the middle ground is the area where creative research can help. As already discussed, it cannot give you the execution that will deliver the largest volume of response, but it can help you create work that is more in tune with your audience and therefore stands a better chance of being accepted.

How do you talk to first-class passengers?

Science met art when we worked on the relaunch of British Airways first-class. The job was to find out exactly who was travelling on first-class before we contacted them about the new improvements to the service.

A questionnaire was developed to elicit vital information. It hardly needed research to tell us that people who flew first-class had neither the time nor the inclination to complete and return 'surveys', so what type of creative treatment should be adopted to overcome their reluctance?

Direct marketing 'science' says that a prize draw is a cost-effective way of boosting response. But what do you offer some of the world's richest people who have everything? And, more importantly, is such a blatant sales technique acceptable to them?

Research to the rescue. In-depth interviews (these people don't go to groups) told us the passengers fell into two categories: patricians and strivers. The first boasted inherited wealth and were predominantly English, including minor royalty. The latter was the international business elite of the late 1980s. These two groups had different attitudes and aspirations but they had one thing in common: money.

However much they had, they wanted more, and they wanted to be associated with it (witness the throngs at Ascot, Henley and the Chelsea Flower Show). This told us that, in principle, they would not be averse to the concept of gaining something for nothing. So we could do a prize draw, but we needed to dress it up appropriately (make it fit tonally with the first-class brand). However, we still had the problem of the prize.

Again, thank you research. With the benefits of in-depth interviews the researcher was able to cover various topics including the respondent's interests. One subject that kept on coming up in conversation was art. The patricians loved art, and many had fine collections. The strivers were fascinated by the way it had become one of the sexy investments of the decade (Van Gogh's *Sunflowers* had just been sold for £26 million).

This was our clue. The next day we went out and toured the galleries of Bond Street. We found the answer: a genuine French Impressionist painting by an admittedly second division artist called Paul Vignon; but we could exploit the history and the fact that he had worked with Cezanne. In addition, it cost no more than a typical 'win a car' sweepstake, yet the perceived value was considerably higher. The result was huge levels of participation; not only did we capture something like half the total universe of first-class passengers but all the questions, including the tie-break, were answered in full.

We were then able to mail respondents – e-mail was not yet a viable communication method, and telephone contact wasn't generally accepted – with full details about the brand relaunch.

How do we build a long-term relationship?

Another client posed a very different problem. With commendable foresight it (a large building society) had realised that direct marketing was set to play a major part in the way it would communicate with customers.

The society asked two agencies to answer this brief: *Consider the next three years. We will be writing to customers about our range of products including mortgages, loans, savings and insurance. How do we talk to them?*

At face value it seems quite a simple task, but beneath the surface lay traps. For instance, in those days a building society customer's main relationship was with a branch, so where did centrally driven direct mail fit in? What would be the criteria for success? Would it be response to individual mailings or overall growth of business? Previous research had shown customers to feel very warmly about the branch staff so did they actually want a relationship with Head Office at all?

Ranges of potential direct mail executions were produced by both agencies. As it happened, the two agencies were quite distinct in their approaches. To cut a researcher's very long debrief short, the first agency produced direct mail that by and large used the tried and trusted techniques for maximising response. The executions featured flashes, special offers, long letters, PSs, etc.

The second agency produced work that was more reserved in tone. Too reserved, certainly, to generate large volumes of response from 'cold' or even mildly warm prospects. For example, the envelopes were predominantly clean and white with only the logo on the front. Any sales message was left for the back. The letters were short (less than a side) yet utilised all the data we had on our customers right down to exploiting their account information to cross-sell other products.

The client conducted qualitative research with groups held in three different locations across the country. The results were both generic and specific. We found that customers universally placed direct mail into four categories.

(1) *Personal mail*: Letters from family and friends which they read immediately and gave them much pleasure.
(2) *Personal business mail*: Letters from their bank, solicitors, estate agents, companies with which they have a strong relationship predominantly giving them information. These they deal with almost immediately.
(3) *Direct mail*: Letters from companies with which they have a relationship and who are now trying to cross-sell other products. They look at these when they can find the time, probably in the evening or at the weekend.
(4) *Junk mail*: Mailings from companies they either don't know or with whom they have no relationship with, selling stuff they are rarely interested in. Either junked or glanced at over the weekend.

Previously, our client had felt that their work had too often looked and read as though it fitted into category 4 (hence the process). At the very least, they wanted to move it into category 3.

Other findings included the fact that customers were beginning to understand the game. They knew what 'Mailsort' stamped on an envelope stood for, and from that they knew immediately it was a mass mailing unlikely to include anything of immediate personal interest. Branding on the envelope was important, too. They had a strong affinity with brand and felt reassured by its presence.

Contrary to 'pub talk', customers appreciated headlines on the envelope and at the top of the letter. It helped them decide whether the information was relevant to them or not – it would prevent them from reading about mortgages when they'd just bought a house. Not surprisingly, they wanted letters to be short and to the point, with the main benefits brought out first (English writers have an inherited tendency to beat about the bush).

They also expected us to exploit all the information we had on them. If they had £58.67 in their account they expected us to know that and to include it, even if we then used it to cross-sell something else.

If it was something they were interested in, they wanted more information, which was the role of the leaflet. Long copy here proved to be no problem. Our customers were intelligent enough to self-select the stuff they liked, and they wanted visuals to be relevant and to help their understanding. Not rocket science, admittedly, but a nail in the coffin of those who believe impact is everything.

So what did this mean for the two agencies involved? Rightly or wrongly, the agency that exploited more of the traditional techniques lost out. Customers recognised and recoiled from the clichés. 'There's no need to shout at us', they said; 'We know you, like you and trust you. Why are you talking at us as if we had never met?' The work was too close to category 4.

The second agency's work became the benchmark for future communications. It came close to acknowledging the relationship that existed between customer and brand, and understood the harm that too strident an execution might have on people who didn't respond this time but might do next.

This was the best use of creative research I have ever seen in direct marketing. It didn't try and tell us which pack would pull the most response, nor try and write the pack for us. It simply gave us a steer on the sort of things the client's customers were looking for and expecting from their relationship, and some guidelines as to what this meant in terms of creative tone of voice.

To those of you versed in CRM jargon, this last case history must seem to be prescient – a campaign designed to deliver CRM before the acronym was invented. Well, we hate to say 'We told you so' but the principles of CRM have been what direct marketeers have been saying 15 years – it's just that you needed £5000-a-day management consultants to tell you this before you would believe it. More fool you.

THE PRACTICALITIES OF QUALITATIVE RESEARCH FOR DIRECT MARKETING

Most of the qualitative techniques used for direct marketing projects are adaptations of those used in mainstream research. Few specialist tools have been developed, primarily because of a lack of researchers dedicated to serving our industry. While numerous attempts have been made to set up these dedicated research units, most have failed because the direct marketing industry has not been mature enough to generate sufficient business. Thus most direct qualitative research is handled by non-specialists, using methodologies brought in from other areas.

This is not usually a problem. Much of the work we do involves answering common marketing questions which existing methodologies can address quite well. A motivating proposition is the same whether it is communicated above or below the line.

It is only when looking at executional development that specialist knowledge is required. This expertise exists in the planning departments of large direct marketing agencies, but accessing this knowledge directly means letting planners research their own ads, and many clients reject this. Thus planners have had to brief external research agencies not only in the objectives of these projects, but also in the best way to research them.

The following thoughts are a collection of guidelines we have gathered from our experience researching direct marketing executions.

Structuring the project

The core requirements of any research programme apply as much to direct marketing research as to any other. Setting clear, viable objectives, making sure the researcher knows how the results will be used, and providing a coherent and well-reasoned research sample are all just as important here as elsewhere. As with above-the-line, researching direct marketing creative work can inform you about the clarity of communication, key messages, personal relevance, appeal and brand consonance. All this information can be delivered in a diagnostic fashion which helps the creative teams build better executions rather than simply testing them to destruction.

All this is important, but it doesn't tackle response. If the key objective of the campaign is a high response rate, qualitative research may be inappropriate in that it will guide you to develop material that will please the eye but fail to make the telephone ring. Thus you shouldn't allow a client to force in a research objective which asks for a 'winner' in terms of response.

It is also worth pointing out that while integrated campaigns are everyone's dream, integrated research programmes are often a failure. Above-the-line advertising and below-the-line direct marketing have very different roles in the marketing mix. In the debrief, researchers will pompously declare, 'the direct marketing is less emotionally rewarding than television ads'. This is generally true, usually irrelevant and always misleading. Direct marketing in integrated campaigns is typically designed to provide the rational support to the above-the-line emotional appeal. Thus it is supposed to be more rational; a fact which many researchers fail to grasp.

You should also avoid allowing the above-the-line agency to include direct marketing in any creative development research they undertake. Direct marketing will invariably be 'tacked on' to the end of the group, and will never be seen fresh.

In this case, the respondents will have already decided which TV idea they like. Direct marketing will only be approved if it executes the very same idea. There is little point in researching direct marketing material in this situation; if executional synergy is demanded, wait until the above-the-line creative vehicle is developed, and then apply appropriate direct marketing technique to the output. By the way, executional synergy, while neat and tidy, seldom leads to the most effective marketing campaigns, since it prevents full exploitation of the media; but that's another story.

Another problem with allowing the advertising agency to research direct marketing material is prejudice. I once witnessed a group where an IPA award-winning planner introduced the direct mail as follows: '*I don't suppose any of you read junk mail, do you?*'. He defended his question on the grounds that it was 'real consumer speak'. Maybe, but I was always taught that good research uses unbiased questions in order to get honest, insightful answers.

Selecting a researcher

When choosing an agency to conduct executional research, make sure you discuss the project with the researchers who will actually conduct the project before making your final choice. The first question to ask them is if they have any experience researching direct marketing in your sector. If not, let them learn on someone else's business.

Try to get a feel of how they view the industry; are they positive about it or cynical? For example, do they use the phrases 'junk mail' and 'punters' or talk about 'direct marketing' and 'customers'? The attitude they bring to the groups will affect the output enormously. Too many researchers still rubbish the sector to prove they're hip. Avoid them like the plague. In addition, avoid any researchers who claim to be able to pick which pack will get the best response. They're liars or fools.

Methodology

Groups versus depths

Focus groups have become the be-all and end-all for most consumer advertising research. They are seen as more creative and dynamic than in-depth discussions, and therefore offer more potential to develop ideas. In-depth discussions are now rejected, ostensibly because they lack this energy, though in practice because they are much more expensive, time consuming and have smaller sample sizes. As a result, both clients and agencies try to avoid them. Nevertheless, in our experience depths have generally proved a better research tool than focus groups. There are two main reasons for this.

First, some people are still embarrassed about admitting they read unsolicited mail, even if it comes from a company with whom they have a relationship, like a bank or a building society. This is particularly true if they wind up 'confessing' that they have responded to a prize draw. There will generally be someone in the group who will try and make them feel foolish. Using in-depth discussions eliminates this problem, and allows researchers to get down to work more quickly, as they don't have to spend ten minutes persuading an entire group to come clean about the fact that they've responded to direct mail.

Second, many packs attempt to use mail creatively, if not intrusively. This may mean numerous pieces in a pack, including pop-ups, fold-outs or large-format items. To better understand the problems these devices may create, we need to see how a respondent actually opens a pack and interacts with the contents. In fact we have occasionally asked respondents to stand up and open the pack in the research if this is the way they normally open their mail. We then gain a better picture of how these devices work or fail to do so. It is easier to watch how a respondent opens and handles the piece in an in-depth interview. What's more, if the interview is conducted in a person's own home it gives the researcher a chance to get a better feel for the context in which it would be read.

Diaries

One technique that often offers great value is to ask respondents to collect all unsolicited mail received between the date of recruitment and the actual discussion. If this period is a week or more, the collected material can be used as stimuli to open a discussion of what is 'good' and 'bad' direct mail.

Unfortunately, despite the fact that some people believe they receive 'hundreds' of mail shots, the fact is they don't. In order to make this methodology work, the collection of material might need to be augmented by a collection of common mail shots (ranging from local store door drops to classic mass-market mailings from organisations like Readers Digest or BT). This technique can be doubly powerful if you can send your own material to the respondents during this time, and thus gain 'real-life' response.

SUMMARY

This chapter has shown that qualitative research has a new and important role to play in direct marketing. This role has emerged because the industry has changed, and is now expanding well beyond direct sales. Understanding consumers, brands and the relationships between them is at the heart of this new world, and only qualitative research can provide the insight that leads to excellence.

What it has also endeavoured to show, however, is that while the tools of traditional qualitative research are transferable to direct mail, the interpretation is not. Failing to appreciate the difference can result in findings that are worse than useless – they can be totally misleading. Like any powerful tool, use it with caution and foresight.

KEY IDEAS

- While dismissed by some as junk mail, direct marketing in fact drives and has always driven the wheels of commerce.
- Direct marketing has always striven to become a science with rules which determined responses rates.

- Qualitative research is useless at predicting sales response and as such, was rejected by the direct marketing industry.
- Qualitative research has found a role in direct marketing due to a new interest in brands, the development of relationship marketing and the growth of powerful marketing databases which need interpretation.
- Qualitative research can also help create work that is in tune with the audience, and therefore stands a better chance of being accepted.
- The traditional rules surrounding direct response are being challenged as the role for qualitative research expands, particularly into helping agencies develop brand-enhancing work which also gets a good response.
- Unlike most areas of research, direct marketing tends to favour in-depth interviews to replicate the personal relationship between the consumer and direct marketing.

Chapter 6

The Use of Qualitative Research in Commercial Media Planning

Will Collin
Director of Strategic Services, New PHD
and

Jon Wilkins
Joint Managing Director, New PHD

Editor's introduction

There is a plethora of new media available. In print, radio, new media and even outdoors, the choice available to the consumer (and therefore to the advertiser) is vast. Added to this is the explosion in television and the resultant need to segment audiences meaningfully if advertisers are to reach their desired target audiences.

This chapter considers these changes which have taken place in the media world, but from a highly commercial perspective. It is not concerned with the development of the new media nor with the programme content, both of which are explored in depth in other chapters. Instead, Jon Wilkins and Will Collin, both renowned media strategists, have focused on the impact of these changes on advertisers and, therefore, on media planning.

Media planning has become increasingly complex as the media possibilities have grown. Understanding media audiences was once confined to quantitative methodologies which have become increasingly inadequate. This is both in terms of their scope and size given fragmentation and, crucially, their ability to really understand consumers, their relationship with the media and ultimately, their feelings about advertising and commercial messages placed in those media.

Qualitative research is a relatively new tool for the media planner, having in the past often relied on account planners to provide insights.

As the media issues have become more complex and the media function has separated from full service advertising agencies, the need for specialist media researchers has evolved.

I recommend reading this chapter after the broadcast and television chapters, as they provide additional context. However, on its own the chapter remains illuminating and clearly focused for practitioners in the field.

THE CONTEXT: THE CHANGING MEDIA LANDSCAPE

The commercial media landscape has undergone massive change in recent years, and the pace of change continues to accelerate. Put simply, there are more media, more media for me in particular, and more and more brands in the media clamouring for my attention. This chapter is concerned with the effect of these changes in the world of advertising – how to ensure that commercial messages are seen and noticed by the right target audience. We can identify three main factors at work: fragmentation, segmentation and the maturing of the advertising industry.

Fragmentation

Media as an area has never been so complex. It now stands for so many things, and has become an all-encompassing term. The main reason for this has been the growth in units of media. We have seen growth within nearly all the established media, combined with the development of new media opportunities, from ambient to interactive.

In any market with intense competition, only those brands with true competitive advantage which offer consumers real value will succeed. Those that do not will be eclipsed by the competition. In the media world, fragmentation will mean that many media will become marginalised as they fail to fulfil consumer demand. Figure 1 illustrates both the enormous growth in the number of traditional media and the arrival of entirely new media, all within a single decade.

As a brand manager in the 1980s, deciding which media to use for your brand's commercial messages was relatively straightforward. There were two national commercial TV channels, ITV and Channel Four, and a strong national press that would provide the backbone of your schedule. There were also a few women's magazines for certain 'housewife brands' and around 20 regional commercial radio stations (allowing a client with a regional brand a cost-effective upweight opportunity). By using these media you could also

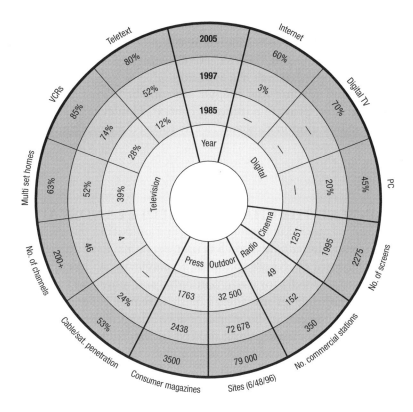

Figure 1 Growth in the number and type of media.

be guaranteed to reach large swathes of the total population rapidly and cost-effectively. However, this cosy simplicity has now all but disappeared.

Television

With the onset of Sky and multi-channel homes in the late 1980s we saw the introduction of many new commercial channels. These channels, led by BSkyB, muscled their way into the broadcasting environment and into consumers' minds, using huge amounts of marketing and by aggressively pitching for and buying previously sacred UK and US programming from under the noses of the traditional broadcasters. This included sporting rights, movies, US sitcoms and other 'must see' programming.

These twin factors have driven multi-channel penetration to where it is today (around 36% of the total population, and significantly higher among some important advertiser demographics such as the 16–34 age group, where penetration stands at 50% (BARB, November 1999)). Today, with the introduction of digital TV, the inevitability of the pay-TV future is starting to register with industry commentators and consumers alike. We are being offered up to 200 channels, countless channels offering movies on demand, and are promised the ability to select from a series of interactive opportunities. Viewers will be able to take part live in game shows, order their main grocery shop to be delivered, and move money around their accounts from the comfort of their armchairs. Services like ONdigital, the digital terrestrial provider, aim to convince the majority of the population who have so far resisted the allure of multi-channel TV that there is an offer for them that provides extra quality to their viewing agenda, cost-effectively. This is explored in depth in Alastair Burns' chapter on broadcasting.

Print

We have also witnessed enormous fragmentation within the print medium. This ranges from the huge increases in specialist supplements in the national and regional presses through to massive growth in the magazine market. Looking forward a few years one can anticipate some parallels emerging between the digital TV channels and the magazine markets: media owners will focus on more specialist interests and start to provide more segmented services for fanatics of everything, from cooking to cars, thereby fulfilling valuable niche interests.

Radio

Radio has also expanded massively. National commercial radio is now well established with four franchises covering differing formats, from talk, classical music, pop and rock through to news (Figure 2). This is supplemented by ever more local station franchises catering for more specialist and segmented needs, from dance music formats like Kiss and Galaxy through to ethnic formats like Choice. Digital radio will also offer listeners new services and, increasingly, broadcasters can reach way beyond their transmission areas using internet-based technologies to 'webcast' their programmes. Finally, one cannot ignore the illicit but burgeoning pirate radio scene.

Outdoors

The marketplace for outdoor advertising has both consolidated and fragmented simultaneously. There has been an expansion of quality poster stock, but at the same time we have seen enormous growth in so-called 'ambient' outdoor opportunities, offering new poster-type media apertures for advertisers. This encompasses everything from shopping trolleys through to hot air balloons, building-side projections and toilet door advertising! (Figure 3)

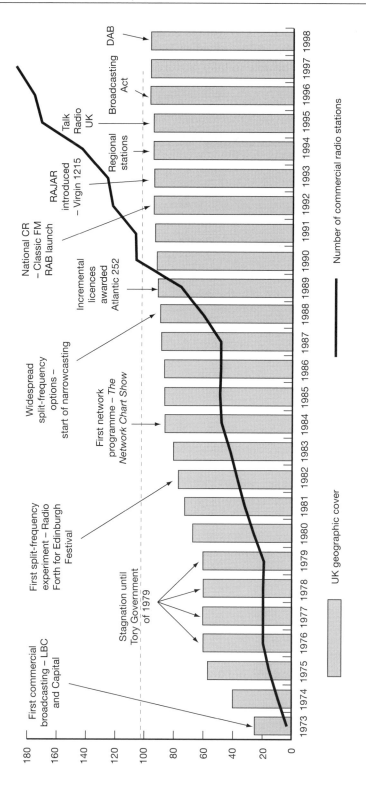

Source: RAB

Figure 2 Number of commercial radio stations.

Figure 3 Outdoor advertising.

Interactive media

Interactive media is an entirely new area that has appeared and established itself within little more than five years. The internet is the fastest growing medium ever, easily outstripping television in the pace of uptake, and this is only one of the opportunities springing up. We have also seen growth in CD-ROMs and kiosks, and we have the promise of genuine convergence between TV and the internet with the likes of Web TV and Open.

Time spent exploring interactive media is often time that was previously spent with more traditional passive media. This introduces yet another layer of experience into people's media repertoires, thus further complicating this dynamic marketplace.

New formats for commercial messages

Alongside the fragmentation of the media themselves, we have also witnessed media owners and advertisers exploring new formats for commercial messages, beyond simply the placement of advertising spots and space. This has taken the form of sponsorships, advertorials, infomercials, advertiser-funded programming, websites, databases, events and stunts, to name but a few. Traditional above-the-line communications are blurring with below-the-line, meaning that having any line at all becomes purely arbitrary, and usually just a convenient way for advertisers to develop a roster of agencies with specific skill sets. This is at a time when more and more advertisers are striving for genuinely integrated solutions.

Running in parallel with fragmentation, the media world has also witnessed increasing segmentation in the content the media owners provide. This is the second marketplace dynamic we will consider.

Segmentation

Consumers have a finite amount of time that they appear willing to spend consuming media. People are generally busier than ever before, and being time-squeezed means they become more selective in how they spend their precious 'down time'. Media consumption has to compete with other pastimes: watching TV or reading magazines is increasingly in competition with cooking from scratch or pottering in the garden. Hence (to borrow from The Henley Centre) the Niagara of increasing media supply will be met with no increase in demand.

Implications for advertisers

Clearly, in a zero-sum game such as this, something will have to give. Increasingly, people are starting to consume many of these different types of media in small, selective, focused doses. For the advertising industries this means that media planning decisions increasingly need to be made in tandem with creative decisions to ensure advertisers achieve their goal of cut through.

The impact of brand messages

In a world full of advertising, a brand's share of a consumer's mind is no longer purely determined by its share of voice. The relevance of the media environment, i.e. synergy between the creative and the media vehicle, can increase the impact of a brand message far beyond what plain audience figures might suggest. Used strategically, media can deliver brand amplification, not just brand exposure. For example, the value of the *Guardian*'s sponsorship of Channel Four's FilmFour productions lies in the challenging and independent-minded profile of the movies, not just the raw numbers of viewers they deliver. FilmFour's media brand values amplify the *Guardian*'s desired brand message, thereby delivering better quality communication.

This is an area where sensitive brand-based research has the potential to add enormous value to the media planning process, whereas traditional media industry research is often too broad or too superficial to provide useful insights.

WEIRD.
SOME PEOPLE START
THEIR NEWSPAPERS AT
THE FRONT PAGE.

NO ORDINARY LAGER   CARLING   NO ORDINARY LEAGUE

Figure 4

Me and my media

Nowadays, if consumers are particularly interested in, say, sport, they can immerse themselves in media specifically focused on that interest, avoiding other subjects with little difficulty. By way of an (extreme) example, a fanatical sports devotee can now watch any of the three Sky Sports channels, Eurosport, either ITV, BBC or Channel Four's extensive strands of sports coverage. They can listen to Radio 5 Live, Talk Radio or Capital Gold (in London) on any Saturday afternoon, and read specific newspaper sections focused on their passions. And all this is without browsing specific team websites or specialist magazines to quench their thirst for information. Figure 4 shows how some people can take this passion to extremes.

If people were genuinely to adopt such a totally obsessive focus in their media consumption, then targeting and developing content for them would be relatively straightforward. If only it were that simple! The reality is that with media, as with all brands, people exhibit a confusing and sometimes conflicting set of preferences which can be unravelled only with sensitive consumer research.

The maturing of the advertising industry

In a typical week, the average consumer is exposed to more than 1000 separate commercial messages of varying relevance and quality. In the face of this advertising onslaught, people are starting to edit out the irrelevant or crass. They are becoming ever more advertising and marketing literate, and ever more selective in what they will pay attention to.

The cynical consumer

Advertising as an industry is still only just reaching maturity. As in many maturing markets, the consumer is becoming hardened and even cynical. It has been proved that heavier viewers of TV, and thus heavier viewers of TV advertising, are much less likely to change their purchasing behaviour as a result of seeing advertising than are lighter viewers.

We are also learning that some very lucrative advertising markets of upmarket, older consumers are actively avoiding advertising, which is a real concern for all those involved in commercial media. In multi-channel homes, viewers are more likely than their terrestrial counterparts to vote with their remote controls during the commercial breaks, with men especially favouring channel grazing over actively watching the commercial breaks.

These types of behaviour mean that understanding the quality of the media environment within which a brand appears becomes crucial. If the issue of increasing ad avoidance is not addressed, then ultimately the entire current advertising model starts to break down. We can see some evidence for this in the US, where multi-channel households have been the norm for some time and zapping and zipping (fast-forwarding video ads) are well and truly ingrained in media usage patterns. The net effect on ad awareness has been one of steady decline (*circa* 20% over the past five years).

Advertising avoidance

There have been a number of studies into the phenomena of ad avoidance and aversion, using a mixture of qualitative and quantitative research. Both BMRB and Lowe Howard-Spink have shown that certain types of consumers are inherently more cynical about advertising, and thus more likely to avoid commercial messages *per se*. Furthermore, Carat Insight has shown that since people increasingly edit out the irrelevant, it's more important than ever to target your advertising at precisely the right kind of people, at the right time, when they are in a predisposed mindset to consider your product. Failing to meet these criteria may mean your advertising will fall on deaf ears, ultimately becoming nothing more than brand wallpaper.

The problem of ad avoidance is compounded by the looming spectre of ad-free environments, whether this be on niche channels (e.g. the Disney Channel) or on specific pay-TV events. Taken together, these factors clearly demonstrate the importance for brand owners, media owners and agencies to gain a deeper understanding and insight into the changing relationship between consumers, advertising and media – before it is too late.

THE ROLE FOR QUALITATIVE RESEARCH

Rapid change

The sheer scale and pace of change has meant that media practitioners – from media companies, advertising agencies or marketing organisations – have found it very difficult to analyse and understand what this has meant for consumers. Long-held assumptions and rules of thumb about the ways people consume media are becoming less and less useful or sometimes even positively misleading. Meanwhile, new opportunities thrown up by the changing media landscape may have been missed through not fitting into the traditional worldview.

Ultimately, this has meant that many media practitioners have systematically failed to capitalise on this dynamic market, while those who have been more proactive in harnessing change have benefited hugely, gaining special insights into behaviour that their competitors have overlooked or been slow to recognise.

In a fast-moving and constantly changing environment, it is important to be able to recognise when an emerging trend becomes a genuine phenomenon with real commercial implications and a real impact on business. The risk of missing a sea change in the consumer mindset is doubled by the parallel risk of mistaking a minor blip for a major trend. Companies with an ambitious approach to embracing change may make the mistake of throwing themselves headlong into an apparent opportunity which consumers are neither remotely interested in nor ready for. For every Sky there is a BSB; for every Metro, a London Daily News.

Data, data, all around

With such a great pace of change, it might be expected that the world of media would be one of the most heavily researched markets of all. Indeed, in some ways this is true, but often the research exists more to support the media-buying market than to illuminate the changing consumer mindset.

Inspect the profit and loss account of any client involved in advertising and it is likely that the amount spent on media will stand out as a considerable figure in proportion to other expenditure. They rightly demand accountability for this investment, and hence this has always been a huge issue for advertisers and media owners alike. This need for accountability has led to the establishment of industry-wide, usually quantitative, research studies that provide the statistical framework underpinning decisions regarding investment in media activity.

Typical accountability measures would be audience size and the frequency with which that media opportunity is likely to be consumed. Less common is a measure of quality or the nature of the relationship the consumer has with the specific medium. Each of the main media has its own survey, a 'gold standard' which creates a currency on which media buyers and sellers can base judgments and trade.

However, in a dynamically changing, fragmented and segmented market, the pressure on this research to deliver is immense. It has to fuel an industry that is constantly looking to develop new approaches, practices and strategies to create effective communication, and ultimately share of mind. At the heart of this process has to lie insightful, sensitive and flexible research, yet the standard industry research is constrained by its responsibility to maintain unchanging and unimpeachable standards to underpin the multi-billion pound trading market.

Therefore, while there is indeed a wealth of media research, we still too often lack the sensitive tools needed to understand the subtle yet continuous shifts in the media landscape, which would guide us to new opportunities or steer us away from false dawns.

Missing the whole picture

Inevitably, each medium's industry-wide research survey has developed in isolation, at different times and with differing methodologies, leading to an alphabet soup of joint industry committees.

One fundamental weakness of this approach is that by dividing up the industry research contracts 'vertically', we don't really get a true picture of the way people create their own 'horizontal' media priorities. Do they watch cricket on television with the sound down and the radio commentary on? Do they watch the 'soaps' as background while they are eating their dinner? Given that most advertisers use a mix of media to deliver their brand communication, this represents an 'information deficit' in industry research.

It also falls short of giving us a feel for the role each medium plays in their lives. Do they read *The Sun* for the sport? Do they have some sacred programming they will never miss, and hate being interrupted? Do they have one really trusted source of business information? These essentially qualitative criteria will clearly have a fundamental influence on how consumers interpret advertising messages carried within each medium.

A final weakness of the industry research is that its standardised structure makes it difficult to replicate consumer segmentations based on attitudinal dimensions, which are used increasingly by marketers as brands seek to position themselves to groups defined by mindset rather than by demographics.

There is an opportunity here for developing research which reflects this segmentation, by dividing consumers into smaller and tighter groups, defined perhaps by shared interests, shared career paths, race, etc. Developing a quantitative sample to analyse these markets is neither practical nor cost-effective; hence there is another information deficit in the current industry research.

Media brand relationships

Media are brands just as much as detergents or car marques. Like all brands, they exist purely to fulfil a human need. This is often to provide entertainment or information, but increasingly it can mean more, such as being the focus for communities of interest or providing opportunities for interaction such as a retail or transactional capability.

What this means is that whether one is an owner of media or a user, such as an advertiser, it is crucial for your brand development to be aware of the changing consumer needs with regard to media. It is essential to recognise that media are not simply empty vehicles in which brand messages are delivered to consumers' eyeballs. They are often living, vibrant brands with which the consumer has a strong relationship and whose values influence the take-out of advertisers' messages. Advertisers have always benefited from this strong relationship between their potential customers and the media, yet its significance has too often been overlooked in traditional media research. This issue is explored in some depth in Alastair Burn's chapter on broadcasting.

The need for change

This increased complexity, combined with the sheer pace of change of the environment, means that the industry research is in a state of flux. It can no longer answer the plethora of questions that need answering, nor provide the depth that individual media owners, agencies or advertisers require. More and more, the industry data act as a currency for trading and little else.

In a fiercely competitive market where brand differentiation is critical for advertisers, precisely the same thing is happening to media and advertising agencies. We are all looking to create an edge over our competitors. Strategies and solutions generated through analysis of syndicated research available to anyone will struggle to be unique. As a result we have seen a huge growth in proprietary research, both quantitative and qualitative. All this research is focused on a better understanding of consumers' attitudes, behaviour, and their relationships with media in order to build communication that will stand out. The holy grail is a media solution which so perfectly fits the brand that 'the medium is the message'.

It is important that the right issues are explored using the correct methodology. For some topics a quantitative approach is more relevant, for others less so. There is often a need to combine quantitative and qualitative methodologies to gain the most appropriate insights. Quantitative approaches tend to be more useful in tracking media trends, pre- and post-testing use of media, or in trying to quantify effective weights or frequency of media.

Other issues, such as consumers' media lifestyle, the fit between creative content and media vehicle, or relationships with media brands, are more suitable for qualitative approaches. We outline a number of different applications for qualitative research in the following case studies. We will also explore the variety of different methodological approaches that can be used, beyond traditional 'focus group' structures.

When it comes to commissioning research in this field, there are now several research companies with qualitative experience in media research. There is also a range of hybrid research/strategy companies which combine research services with strategic recommendations. Some clients and agencies prefer to out-source this type of research, while others put this type of interpretive research at the heart of their offering, and package these insights as central planks of their media thinking.

PRACTICALITIES – BASED ON CASE STUDIES

Fast forward – a qualitative study of media and the World Cup 1998

Enormous amounts are now spent on sports-related sponsorship, advertising and promotion, yet the benefits are often suspected to be hit-and-miss, with Nike's 'ambushing' of the Olympics seen by some to overshadow the impact of the official sponsors. Yet sport, and particularly football, has almost reached the status of a medium in its own right, evoking passions and loyalty that other media could only dream of. Against the background of the World Cup 1998, New PHD and Giant Research Consultancy conducted a qualitative study into how brands can best exploit the media opportunities offered by sport, and how to avoid the twin threats of competitive clutter and cynical fans.

This case study is an example of how qualitative methodologies can be deployed to unravel complex issues within a media event.

A mixed methodology

Conventional discussion groups were used, but the methodology also included in-depth interviews with football pundits, brand managers involved in football-related marketing, and media owners. Additionally there was 'live' research where people were interviewed and filmed while watching the event in France. This mixed methodology enabled the considered reactions of group respondents to be put in the context of manic fans in the heat of the action. It also ensured a refreshingly vibrant debrief presentation.

The conclusion was that a brand's involvement in the World Cup should be part of a long-term football or event strategy, not just as a platform in itself, as this risks the messages becoming lost in the clutter. This involvement can be termed 'turfing' (staking a claim in the event through sponsorship, e.g. Adidas) or 'surfing' (using promotions or advertising during the event, e.g. Nike). Furthermore, the 'event' starts long before the competition itself, and the timing of brand activity must take account of this.

The role of sponsorship

A universal event such as the World Cup brings otherwise disparate audiences together in a mass media experience. Communication strategies which treated the World Cup audience as if it were the same as that of the regular Premier League missed out on this unique, inclusive character. In addition, unlike the Premier League, consumers do not see a direct benefit from sponsors to the game. There is no perceived connection between a sponsor's contributions and paying for better players, unlike in the domestic league. Hence a brand needs to communicate the value of its involvement by demonstrating how it improves the event (e.g. funding the England team).

Consumers' expectations are raised across the board – not just for the event and their team, but also for brands and advertising. It is as much a competition for advertisers as it is for the teams. Everyone has to raise their game – creative, media and promotions are expected to pull out all the stops.

Magic AM – researching media lifestyles

EMAP own a number of AM radio stations in Yorkshire, which until recently used a range of different brand names, although they shared a similar 'gold' format. Following its success in developing the Kiss brand for FM stations, EMAP decided to reinvent all its Yorkshire AM stations under the Magic brand, repositioning them towards a younger and more aspirational audience.

This case study is an example of how qualitative research can be used to explore consumers' media behaviour, at a level of detail unachievable with syndicated industry studies.

Conventional plus innovative approach

The media solution for this campaign comprised two elements: the first fairly conventional, the second more innovative. The conventional element was to create brand awareness and establish a Magic personality using three commercials on ITV. This part of the strategy was creatively led. The innovative element was to leverage this personality to generate trial of the station, using media which had been identified through research to be specifically relevant to the target audience's lifestyle. This part of the strategy was media led.

Media agency Rocket sought to understand the target 30 to 50-year-olds' routines in order to drive trial of the stations at key times (breakfast and drive time). The intention was to integrate the brand into the life of potential listeners, peppering their daily routines with 'ambient media'. These would offer calls to action, each tied into a promotional mechanic to generate maximum response.

Inspiration

Qualitative discussion groups revealed a number of nuances that provided inspiration for the media solution. First, it was found that nights out at the pub really were an event, often with the whole extended family going together. This meant the pub itself was effectively a media opportunity, which was then exploited by placing free postcards (an ambient medium) which featured the 'finger game', enabling them to re-create the spirit of the TV ads (Figure 5).

Being right at the heart of the family life stage, it was perhaps not surprising that the target consumers tended to go for one major shopping trip per week by car. This led to a campaign using a promotion on till receipts, shopping trolleys and supermarket floors, as well as more conventional six-sheet posters on the supermarket walls.

Finally, given the close connection between radio listening and long car journeys (which we found were common in this part of the world), a final opportunity was in petrol stations. The media used here were ads on petrol pump nozzles and on the reverse of till receipts, backed up with on-the-ground SWAT teams offering to retune car radios.

The resulting campaign was unprecedentedly effective, achieving both a successful rebranding of the stations with increases in listening share and improvements in the audience profile. The precise lifestyle-based targeting

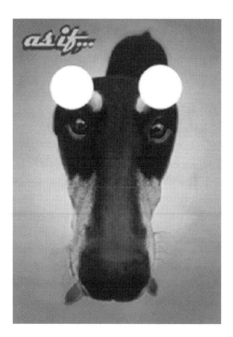

Figure 5 Postcards placed in pubs.

resulted in an extremely cost-effective campaign, with cost per response for the promotions being far lower than industry norms.

Understanding price ads in the press

Running tactical price ads in the national and local press is something of a tradition, perhaps most notably for DIY and white goods retailers where the 'Comet Price Index' and the like have become a familiar presence at the latter end of the week. However, in the telecoms market where the product is intangible and the purchase process less clear-cut, it was less certain that the press was the right medium. This was the background for a qualitative study into the way people read newspapers and the price ads within them.

This case study is an example of how qualitative research can be used to provide an in-depth diagnosis of how media are consumed in real life, as opposed to the necessarily limited measures provided by industry surveys such as NRS or BARB.

Given the personal, private nature of newspaper reading, the methodology was to conduct individual in-depth interviews. We spoke to regular readers of all three sectors (popular, mid-market and quality). The respondents were given a current newspaper to flick through and were then asked to talk through things that had caught their attention, whether editorial or advertising.

The research validated many commonly held rules of thumb, such as the greater impact of right-hand pages or colour ads, and the fact that many men read papers from back to front. However, recall of price advertising was very low as a whole, excepting the phenomenon of self-selection where respondents home in on ads for products they are actively considering. Consequently the golden rule for an intangible product like telecoms, where there is usually no purchase deadline to raise interest levels, is to be as simple and bold as possible. Complex offers and fancy ads are likely to be ignored. On weekdays, newspapers are read during limited periods of 'down time' (on the train to work or at the desk at lunchtime) and people's attention filter is therefore ruthless.

One opportunity we revealed was the area of 'functional' editorial. These are pages such as TV listings or share prices which maintain a constant level of interest and will be consulted regularly. As such they slip through the attention filter more easily than the mixed bag of regular editorial. This led to the recommendation to use small space ads on the TV listings page to highlight price offers linked to specific times of day, and to use 'share square' ads to communicate special deals to business customers.

MEDIA 2000 – researching people in the know

This case study is an example of how qualitative methodologies can be used to predict and plan media for the future. It recognises the limitations of conventional research in the area of predicting future behaviour: consumers are better at commenting upon ideas than generating them, leading to the (unfair but commonplace) allegation that planning by using qualitative research is like driving by looking in the rear-view mirror.

The idea was to assemble a number of experts in a particular field, add a couple of clever people from different but related areas, sit them down in a room with snacks and alcohol, supply moderation to set the parameters and lead the discussion, and then let the juices flow. The panels focused on certain topics or areas but were deliberately more freeform than usual research in that they aimed to free participants from the necessary shackles of their day jobs and allow them to project their knowledge, experience and creativity into the future – always with interesting results.

This project consisted of five panels, each containing representatives from one media group or one media area, from a national newspaper to a major magazines-to-radio media group, a pay-TV company and various new media organisations. The research was conducted by Giant Research Consultancy.

The opening question was as simple (and as difficult) as this: How will the world of media look in five years' time? This was placed in the context of the advent of digital TV and radio, the huge growth of the internet and a possible threat to print media. The discussion was then brought round to implications for advertisers, brands, media owners and media agencies.

Interesting themes recurred throughout the project. Opinion was that there would be a lot more media in the future but that this might well be concentrated in fewer hands. There was a fear that the huge multinational media cartels were carving up the world between them and could one day own both production and distribution. No one else would get a look in, certainly on a global perspective.

The implications

The implication for advertisers could be immense. Only large and established brands would be able to buy into mass media environments. Although there would be more outlets, there could be less room for smaller brands. But this could also have a positive impact. Participants thought that in the future creativity would be all-important. Brands would have to be creative and do creative things – in media, advertising, brand extension and NPD – to cut through the clutter. An exciting time to be alive!

For media brands it was thought that content and editorial would become ever more important in a future marketplace. Media brands will become filters of opinion and have to develop strong relationships with their consumers if they are to thrive. Thus the media brand becomes more important than the medium through which it communicates, leading to cross-media brand extensions.

The above only really scratches the surface of this project. The point being made here is that in the future all brands will have to have a dialogue with their consumers. This research methodology raises issues and platforms which can initiate that dialogue.

SUMMARY

The media world has changed dramatically over the past ten years. While the established media have expanded massively, we have also seen the development of significant new media formats, from ambient to interactive. The word 'media' has never meant so much. It has moved beyond being merely being a receptacle for advertising (i.e. spots and space). It now embraces sponsorship, advertorials, infomercials, advertiser-funded programming, websites, events and stunts, to name but a few.

Against a backdrop of huge media fragmentation, people have no more time or money to spend on media. They are responding to these changes by consuming many different types of media in small, selective, focused doses. Now, more than ever before, advertisers must make decisions on media, planning and creative at the same time if a campaign is to have a chance of standing out amid the media blizzard.

All this has complicated the profession of media planning and buying, requiring the industry to adopt new practices and strategies to create effective communication. The key to this approach is a better understanding of consumers, derived from the insightful use of research.

Media is a business driven by research. Each separate medium has its own quantitative industry survey: a gold standard, and a currency upon which media is bought and sold. However, the sheer pace of change has meant that this traditional media research is in a state of flux. It can no longer answer the multiplicity of questions facing clients and agencies involved in the media decision-making process. The data sources act as a trading currency, but little else.

The problem is that these surveys can lack depth and focus on measuring rather than evaluating quality. There is little appreciation of the fact that two TV programmes, for example, *Coronation Street* and the news, will have a very different relationship with the viewer, and be watched in a very different way. Consequently, any commercial message placed within them will be interpreted differently. Such differences in the quality of media consumption exist throughout all media; some are actively consumed, some passively, some passionately, others out of duty, etc. Yet so often we tend to reduce them all to merely 'opportunities to see'. There is a shortfall of insight in media research, which is where qualitative approaches can help.

It is these fundamental changes which have led to the introduction and massive growth of qualitative research within the media field.

KEY IDEAS

- There are more media, more 'for me' media and more brands clamouring for my attention.
- This change covers not just more media using existing routes but also more routes, such as multi-channel TV, interactive TV, specialist press and magazines, local and new digital radio and outdoors which now encompasses 'ambient' media.
- Messages are no longer simply advertisements; they include advertorial, infomercials, websites, databases, etc.
- Increasing media supply will be met with no increase in demand, so advertisers need to plan media in tandem with creative considerations to ensure cut through.

- The consumer is cynical and advertising avoidance is another pressure on advertisers.
- The existing structures for measuring consumption of media are inadequate given fragmentation of media.
- There is a need for more in-depth understanding of how people actually consume and feel about their media usage than traditional measures provide.
- Qualitative research can help unravel these issues and is being used, often in highly unconventional ways, to help clients achieve their commercial objectives.

FURTHER READING

For a good example of qualitative research used to explore media habits, see Capital Radio's *Youth Research*, July 1997: a qualitative/quantitative study into youth media habits, focusing on the role of radio. Received the IPA Seal of Approval.

For an overview of a number of qualitative studies which have explored readers' relationships with magazine brands and the role of magazines within media repertoires, see the Periodical Publishers' Association report *How Magazine Advertising Works – A Review of the Research Evidence* by Guy Consterdine, second edn 1998, available online at www.ppa.co.uk/howads/index.htm

A study of media as brands, mapped using qualitative research, can be found in Sue Gray (1999) *Harnessing Media Brands*, Admap, September.

Chapter 7
Design Research in Action

Jean Carr
Director, SRU Ltd

with

Peter Wallis
Chairman, SRU Ltd

Editor's introduction

Coming from an advertising background, I have always found research into design particularly interesting. Advertising may have copy, movement, photography and sound to communicate its message, and the task remains difficult. Design is an equally powerful tool in the positioning of a brand, but as it is integral to that brand or product it must work harder. The design of a pack, a product or a retail environment tells us so much about the product or contents themselves, the user, the usage and the brand imagery and, on the whole, we are relatively unaware that this is the case. The power of design is immense and getting it right a feat that, for me, is incredible.

This chapter explains the role of design in our lives with regard to product, packaging and retail design. Jean Carr then goes on to explore, in detail, how qualitative research can play a vital role in the development of design ideas from the starting point of developing the brand strategy right through six stages to evaluating final executions. Jean shares some of her ideas about the practicalities of conducting research in this field at the end.

Jean has extensive experience in this field and the detail and clarity of her thinking on the subject reflect that expertise. Peter Wallis contributes to the thinking and brings his own unique views on design, for which he is so famous, to the party.

THE CONTEXT: UNDERSTANDING DESIGN

What design is and does

Everything with a physical form has to be designed: cars, FMCG, shop furniture, annual reports, magazines or point-of-sale material. Nothing emerges 'organically', and very few designs are completely dictated by their technology. Whether created by a design professional with a knowledge of the sector or by a technologist, all physical forms present a series of options and design choices as they evolve.

Understanding the impact of these choices in the marketplace is commercially important; design can work for or against the acceptance of a product, retailer or medium at many levels. Ergonomics – how people sit in chairs or navigate stores with baby buggies – is only one dimension. Design also operates at an *emotional*, non-verbal level, communicating in codes that we learn unconsciously. For example (and this is by no means a definitive list) the codes could include:

- Some that are universal versus some that are culturally specific (in the Western world funeral livery is black, in India it is white).
- Symbols (in an experiment with two shapes and two words it emerged that all around the world people associated rounded shapes with soft sounds and spiky shapes with hard sounds).
- Colours (black and yellow mean warning, red means exciting and blue suggests soothing or calm).
- Textures (furry suggests warm and cuddly, metallic means hard or cold).

The moral is that design creates responses which we don't recognise consciously and thereby provoke associations. The more design appeals to these unconscious positive triggers, the greater the penetration of the message.

Precisely because design is non-verbal/non-intellectual we often don't suspect that we are being influenced by it. Therefore its messages are harder to resist than rational verbal messages. Although consumers' design vocabulary may be unconscious, it is highly susceptible to 'social currency', factoring in new iconography and aspirations derived from a variety of fields. Therefore a product/brand/store/fashion item may begin to look or feel wrong long before it becomes irrelevant in more pertinent ways.

Design mirrors the evolution of society, customs and ideas, so it needs to be constantly updated to reflect these changes (for example, the HP sauce bottle or the Marlboro pack – both apparently unchanged but in practice constantly updated over the brands' lifetime).

Market and consumer changes impacting on design

The market and consumer changes that have led manufacturers, retailers and, increasingly, designers to recognise the value of consumer input into the design development process are all ultimately driven by the emergence of more competitive, fast-moving focused offers of goods and services, targeted at more demanding, educated, fickle and fragmented consumers. They include the following.

The emergence of design as a key element in positioning

What something actually *looks* like tells you what group of people it caters for; for example, is it for young people, for someone conventional, for yuppies, for people in the know, for 'caring mums' or for 'studs'?

The level and type of design employed sends out unspoken messages to consumers about how the manufacturer or retailer sees them and what kind of relationship they seek with them. Design, for instance, can say 'you need to be clever/an insider to recognise what we're saying', or 'we understand you and share your values', or 'we know how important it is for this product to make you look modern', etc.

Design can show what emotional needs the product meets beyond its overt function. Is it fun, a duty, a pleasure, or all about self-identity? Design can tell you whether it is for public occasions, for keeping secret, for nostalgia. It can tell you what makes the product distinctive; is it cosmopolitan, gentle, modern, natural or amusing? It can be the solid state of the positioning argument. Some examples of the vital positioning role of design would include:

- The Phillipe Starck lemon squeezer – a banal kitchen object rethought as 'art' and sophistication
- The Dyson vacuum cleaner – manifest innovation and individuality
- The Ford Ka – female, young, lively
- Penhaligon – nostalgia, romantic and classy

Design, like these messages, needs to be current and relevant to make sure the positioning and identity are coherent and operate to plan.

Design differentiates and adds value in markets where products have reached technical parity

New packs – and especially new delivery systems – can give the edge to products where there is very little discernible difference. Once again there are many examples:

- Round tea-bags to fit the cup (Tetley).
- Pyramid tea-bags act like a tea pot and allow water to circulate in the bag (PG Tips).
- Toilet Duck – a lavatory cleaner designed to get under the rim of the bowl; the design also 'anthropomorphises' the pack, making it friendly and fun.
- Yoghurt for children in collectable building brick containers like Lego in different colours, provoking 'pester power'.
- Cheese strings – processed cheese in the form of 'liquorice straps' where a single string of cheese can be peeled off and eaten, adding interest to a commodity product.
- Dairylea snack packs – lunch box packs with biscuits/cheese/slices of 'ham' which can be assembled by children at school (fun for kids/saves effort for mum).
- Pringle crisps – mouth-shaped/fit for the tongue. Can be played with by adults and children (the permission is granted by advertising); they now have a new small Pringle-shaped box to carry a few of them to school.
- New air fresheners – disguised as plugs or prettified as pots, boats, etc. so they can be left on show.
- Persil tablets which give dosage control (it is clear how many washes you get in the box).

If design can differentiate and add such dramatic value to otherwise homogeneous basic product types, it is clearly vital to know where and in what ways it operates.

The increasing requirement for consumer information

Consumers, retailers and legislators all demand more information about the contents of products and how and where they have been produced.

There is now the issue of how and where the design can incorporate the statutory requirements, such as salt content, E numbers, animal testing, without overwhelming the commercial messages. Additional related design issues include Braille on dangerous products, for example, bleach, child-proof closures, instructions in bigger typefaces for older people. Increasingly, packaging itself has to be eco-friendly, re-usable or recyclable.

At the same time, packs (and products) have to carry the right messages as well as the right information, particularly about claims which cannot be made explicitly, such as nutritious, slimming or improves one's sex life. Design has to convey all the market-driven values while conforming to regulations.

There is now also a need for a design language that will translate across a number of markets (not too advanced for the least developed while not too far behind for the leaders). The need is often to retain the *look* of the brand while the name changes between regions:

- Opal Fruits – Starburst
- Marathon – Snickers
- Oil of Ulay – Oil of Olay

Global and international design have to create the right mix of symbolism/ iconography for different cultures.

All this means that 'getting it right' in design terms is ever more important, while 'getting it wrong' can be disastrous at scale.

The growth of design consciousness among consumers

Consumers are becoming increasingly educated in design. Everything is designed (almost nothing is bought as a loose commodity), meaning consumers are exposed to more and more design. Consumers have an increasingly wide range of cultural references (films, TV, music, foreign travel, dedicated media, new media, etc.) and design is itself a media subject. Consumers are becoming increasingly articulate about design, more aware and knowledgeable about how it works. In research we constantly hear such remarks as:

- 'They're trying to do a Hovis'
- 'They want you to believe it never saw the inside of a factory'
- 'That's meant to say Hollywood glamour'

Consumers are increasingly aware of what design says about them to other people, both as a positive means of self-expression – 'this makes me look modern' or 'see how ecologically correct I am' – and also as a default verdict – 'this product doesn't really say the right things about me any more'.

Design and caring about what things look like is no longer 'sissy' for men or the province of the 'design classes', women or marginal groups. It is now legitimate dialogue for everyone. Men have now been given permission to look nice and talk about 'soft factors' in relation to themselves and their clothes.

Younger groups are most acutely aware of design and what it says about them. Indeed, this is a market area where design has triumphed over content:

- The look is everything
- Nuances are vitally important
- Iconography/symbolism semiotics are all very precisely defined
- Design is central to self-definition (trainers, sunglasses, etc.)

Therefore, design needs to reflect these new more demanding sensitivities in this market.

The exponential increase in the order of design investment

The increasing demand for sophisticated professional design input, applied more frequently with higher associated costs, and the increasing dependence on design to underwrite the brand or product proposition, mean that it is correspondingly important to understand where design fits into the hierarchy of concerns. We need to know what matters to consumers about design in that particular sector, and their priorities and how they react to specific designs in the market.

The constant need to assess the effectiveness of design

As with advertising, does design do what it is meant to in specific instances and does it fit with the overall strategy for the brand? Does it say the right things and has it a clear message? We need to consider if the design conforms with all the other things that are being said about the brand, the price positioning, the advertising and other promotions.

Marketeers need to know where design matters and whether the design in question is doing its job against the set priorities.

The need to identify the overall role and importance of design to consumers in making brand choices

We need to know where design stands in relation to all the other elements in the product/marketing mix. Is it *front of mind*, as in fashion/furnishing, or is it *lower order*, whereby as long as it looks OK it will not conflict with or distract from the real reasons for buying that brand? How much investment, care or attention does design warrant for a given brand?

Understanding the design priorities of different consumer segments

Increasingly sophisticated products, services and communications are much more closely targeted today. We need to consider who likes what and the differences between various groups of people. This includes demographics but also backgrounds, ethnicities and psychographics. We need to consider what visual 'codes' people recognise and their cultural references.

Developing an appropriate design vocabulary for the sector

Research can develop an understanding of the language of the consumer or sector and identify the most important design language to use. It might need to convey 'nourishing' for babies, or for adults or cats. It might want to say 'modern' for computers, cornflakes, cosmetics or convenience stores. It might consider how to say 'trustworthy' for vitamins, sanpro products or cars.

The need to educate designers and design buyers

For design buyers

Buyers need to understand the potential for design to add value by defining positioning and identity. They must appreciate what the design has to do, convey or fulfil, and understand the importance of design for the overall brand, for example the need for various members of the brand 'family' to share the same characteristics.

Buyers should consider 'the interconnectedness of all things', how the look should fit with all the other marketing messages from advertising and promotion, and recognise the importance of thinking about design early in the process and not as an afterthought; for example, the pack as integral to the product and brand, not just a means for the consumer to carry it home.

For the designer

Designers and creatives, of all kinds, need to understand the market and the role of research as a positive input, not a constraint on creativity. Research is needed to help bridge the gap between consumers and designers (who are often very different from the target audiences they are designing for and do not necessarily understand their lives, preoccupations and value structures) and to understand specific consumer sensibilities and prioritise appropriate design vocabularies in a focused brief.

We need to involve designers in the research process, making sure the stimuli used are a fair representation of their creative ideas and giving them the best chance of obtaining a proper consumer response. Finally, we need to interpret and communicate findings in compelling design-relevant ways that enable designers to 'own' them and recognise the actionable value of research.

The whole point of research is to be of real practical use to the design development process. Being a demonstrable contributor to the process can ensure that research gets the recognition it deserves, helping buyers and designers to understand what matters about design in that commercial context and how to get it right.

THE ROLE OF QUALITATIVE RESEARCH

In this section we take three of the main design fields in turn: product, packaging and retail, and explore the role of qualitative research in illuminating these functional, emotional and symbolic aspects of design that are important to consumers, and therefore to designers and to buyers of design.

Product design

For new product development

Research can identify where design can make a difference by understanding the gaps in the market and where there are unfulfilled needs. It can develop an understanding of *how consumers make choices* between products/brands/ fashion items and the factors/dimensions that define their mental maps of the sector. Research can describe the kinds of problems and difficulties consumers encounter, such as products which are hard to use:

- Getting the last bit of toothpaste out of the tube
- Fashionable clothes that aren't comfortable
- Irons which don't turn themselves off after a certain time if left unattended

It can also identify the *gaps* in the market that could be met by designers, such as a washing-up liquid that looks good in a 'designer' kitchen, a dandruff shampoo that looks as though it will make your hair beautiful or an outsize fashion store that looks as though it's for young people.

For existing products

Research can establish how well existing products match up to consumers' functional, emotional and aesthetic needs and where they need to be updated, modified, repackaged, re-sized, etc.

At both the NPD and the 'old product development' level, research has the role of exploring:

- Ergonomics
  How well does the product function in use?
  How does it feel to hold?
  Is it easy to press the button?
  Is the kettle easy to fill/does it pour well?
  Is the hairdryer easy to hold when drying hair at the back?
  Is the bottled water container easy to pour from?

- Aesthetics
  How does the product look:
  - modern/up to date
  - traditional/classic
  - right in my home/in the place it will be seen

- attractive in its own right?
Does it say the things about me I'd want it to say?
What sort of form should it take:
  - rounded/sharp-edged
  - organic/engineered
  - anthropomorphic/neutral?

- Badging
Does it stand out from the competition?
Does it belong to the rest of the product family?

- Cultural references
Does it signal its origins appropriately?
Does it convey the 'right' messages about the consumer?

- Defining priorities
Materials:
What could/should it be made from (e.g. plastic kettles)?
Levels of finish:
  - matt versus shiny
  - smooth versus textured
  - sharp-edged versus organic?
Colours:
  - Can white goods/brown goods be coloured (e.g. Apple computers, Smeg fridges)?
  - What colours are fashionable and how 'dateable' are they?

Research can help at every stage, from concept development to fine-tuning the materials and textures.

Packaging design

The role of research in pack design is to ensure that packaging contributes as much as possible to the overall mix/adds maximum value. There are a few key issues.

Brand convergence

It is essential to check that the packaging fits with all the other messages about the brand, such as the product formulation, and the user group identifiers:

- For caring mums
- For 'Jack the lads'
- For the health conscious

Solving the added value versus cost issues

Research can identify where packaging might command a premium; for example, the resealable pack; the product in its own reusable storage jar; the air freshener that looks nice enough to leave on display; and the bottled water that looks good at a dinner party. Conversely, research can identify where improved packaging cannot justify its additional cost; for example, where the product is used in one go or decanted into another container or where packaging is already considered too elaborate for its purpose.

Point of purchase

Research can consider whether a pack stands out on the shelf:

- As an individual pack
- Collectively as a facing of products
- In different positions in the store – top shelf/bottom shelf
- In relation to different competitors

It can ask what the appropriate balance might be between packaging as signalling a brand's membership of its category and operating within the category conventions – for example, all-white toothpaste with red/blue/green (never purple) – and the need to differentiate itself clearly as an added-value brand.

Functionality in use

Research can explore how the packaging is being carried home – for instance, where is the product/pack stored? Is it in a cupboard, on the dressing-table or in the sitting-room? Research might query whether it fulfils its role appropriately, such as by looking good in its setting. It can also consider how easy it is to dispose of the pack, whether it is considered wasteful to throw away the pack or whether it could be reused for something else.

Research can identify opportunities to differentiate or add value through packaging.

Trade requirements and constraints

Packaging increasingly needs to conform to trade requirements and constraints. Supermarkets and other retailers are demanding about the size and shape of packaging in terms of its handling, its storage and how it fits on the shelf. It may be important to evaluate consumer and retailer reactions to pack sizes and configurations in parallel.

Research can help to optimise a pack at any stage in its life – by making it choosable and by reinforcing brand values, by making it easy to use or by reinforcing loyalty and adding value.

Retail design

Research can inform retail design in all its aspects – whether by the creation of a new retail proposition or the fine-tuning/refurbishment of an existing one. Retail design research operates at many levels.

Exterior design

The exterior of a store sends out powerful messages to passers-by about who and what the store is for and about what they can expect to find in it, who they can expect to find there, and so on. It can also signal the nature of the experience in that store.

Functionality of overall design and layout of the store

However attractive the exterior, consumers go into shops in the hope of finding something they want to buy. The interior of the store has to be appropriate to the *type of shopping mission*, such as planned, browsing or impulse.

It must also be appropriate for the *nature of the goods* sold; for example, what should a café in a chemist's shop be like? The overall design and layout needs to make it easy for consumers to find their way around the store and locate appropriate departments, have private conversations and so on.

Signage, labelling and merchandising

These are often a separate subject of research. Signage must be readable in the right place, have the right information and right aesthetics, and fit with brand values.

Merchandising creates the opportunity to show goods to their best advantage and to add value. Research can explore what kind of display is most appropriate for what and when. Design can create zones and concentration areas which reflect and enhance the nature of the goods; for example, bakery in-store, kids' department.

Atmosphere and ambience

Design now provides the 'theatre' in-store and creates the right mood for the purchase. The bridal shop, the high tech computer store, the toy shop, the sex shop; what should these forms of shopping look and feel like to maximise propensity to buy?

Brand image

What does the store say about the retailer and the psychological contract with the customer? What qualities and characteristics are appropriate for the definitive flagship store, which elements of that store need to be present in all the subsidiary branches, and how can they best be adapted to a local scale without losing their essence?

Qualitative research can illuminate all aspects of retail design, from the creation of a new retail concept to the design of an interview booth or a swing ticket, and thereby create much more cost-effective design outputs in the form of sector-appropriate design solutions, These can deliver greater lifetime value from customer relationships.

One reason why qualitative design research can make such a major contribution is that consumers enjoy it and therefore like getting involved in the process, because it obviously translates directly into things they can touch or feel.

THE PRACTICALITIES OF QUALITATIVE RESEARCH

The uses of qualitative research

This section describes and reviews a range of qualitative research techniques which are effective in capturing meaningful consumer input at different stages in the design process. From our experience across the field of design research it has become clear that, irrespective of the specific sector being analysed, the design development process follows the same overall pattern – and qualitative research plays an important role at each of the six stages.

- Understanding/segmenting the market in broad terms using mapping.
- Providing a context for design and the role it plays in the sector.
- Testing broad design directions and concepts.
- Fine-tuning front-runner design options.
- Evaluating consumer responses to the finished/final design.
- Monitoring the performance of the design in the reality of the competitive marketplace.

The six stages

Understanding the market

Here, the aim is to understand the overall lie of the land from the consumer point of view; to understand how close or far apart the brands in the sector are and why, and in particular to learn what dimensions are used to judge and group brands.

This consumer map doesn't necessarily fit the 'objective' supply-side view of how the market segments, but it is the map that matters in defining *overall strategy* for the brand. On the basis of those dimensions which really emerge as separating the key brands, the desirable and undesirable characteristics for the sector and those which are most closely associated with the brand concerned, clients can decide whether to reinforce their key defining characteristics, whether to bring them closer to the ideal or move them further away from the undesirable end of the market. Research can also indicate how to achieve this profile – through advertising, product reformulation, packaging, position, etc.

The attributes which consumers use to distinguish between brands may be directly related to the 'look', as these may say the most important things about the brand – e.g. the Dyson cleaner or Clinique's packaging – or may be qualities less directly related but which still have important design implications – e.g. organic; scientific; state-of-the art; feminine.

Mapping helps clients understand what the most important/desirable/ motivating attributes are in their sector and where their brand stands in relation to them. From this they can develop a strategy to position the brand to best advantage and identify which qualities the design most needs to demonstrate to consumers.

The other part of the initial mapping process is to look at how consumers segment in terms of their attitudes, tastes and priorities in relation to the brand, and particularly the design dimensions of it. Research of this kind will be particularly important when clients have an existing customer base that they do not want to alienate while they are attracting new targeted customers.

It is vital to present the brand in as visual a form as possible in order to understand those aspects of visual design which are most salient. Thus familiar, old-fashioned packaging may be comforting to existing customers but a turn-off for the new target group. Research needs to explore which parts of the design must be retained and which parts could be renewed.

A retail banking client wanted to redesign its branches to appeal to a wider audience and to identify a new way of dealing with customers. Existing and new target customers were asked to visit the existing brand outlets and key competitors' branches before attending group discussions, where they talked about their experiences, and grouped the banks, using photographs of the interiors. The dimensions that emerged included:

- Welcoming / intimidating
- Bank's territory / customer's territory
- Private / public

We identified those elements which existing customers valued and felt epitomised the brand, and which were negative or unimportant. We then overlaid on them the priorities and concerns of new target customers. We used this to produce a design strategy which optimised existing strengths in a more inclusive and appealing way and added complementary design factors – practical and symbolic – which had value for new customers.

Providing a design context

Once the design strategy has been agreed – i.e. what the design has to achieve – qualitative research can help designers gain a better understanding of the detailed context in which they will be working.

It is important to stress here that this kind of analysis does not mean research is asking consumers to do the designers' work for them, but rather to help designers get under the skin of the groups of people they are designing for and therefore to understand their perspective on design.

One key technique employed here is observation, looking at how people use products, packs, stores, etc. This involves exposing respondents to different kinds of stimuli to understand the ways in which they 'read' them. Thus we might show them different:

- Packs / labels
- Shapes
- Finishes
- Colours
- Typefaces / fonts
- Symbols

First, we ask for spontaneous associations and then go on to ask for associations with particular attributes that we know design will need to convey as part of the strategy, for example:

- Which colours say 'clean'?
- Which shape is most 'feminine' / least 'feminine'?
- Which packs are 'modern'?

We always ask respondents to explain why they make these judgments.

An example

A packaging client wanted to improve sales of toothbrushes. When a camera was set up overlooking a supermarket facing to observe how customers selected toothbrushes it revealed confusion at point of sale and very little automatic behaviour – i.e. simply reaching for a familiar pack – suggesting there was little recall of what brand of toothbrush had been bought before (used out of pack). Importantly it also revealed that consumers studied packs intently and compared them, usually looking at the back of packs for information (qualitative research supported the view that consumers were looking for reasons to buy a particular brush).

Our client's packs had nothing on the back. Designers were briefed to produce some clear graphics demonstrating the benefits of the brush. Sales of the enhanced 'reason why' packs improved significantly.

Exploring design directions and concepts

Once designers have begin to develop their ideas about potential design options, qualitative research can help to identify the concepts and design direction which are most promising, i.e. those which best reflect the design brief and provoke the desired response. These concepts can be expressed in various degrees of completeness from very rough ideas to something almost finished:

- Concept boards
- 2D illustrations
- Prototype products
- Environmental models

They can be branded or unbranded.

Ideally, research shouldn't use more than five developed design ideas to evaluate at any one time, otherwise confusion and 'snow-blindness' sets in. It's very important that all the stimulus material is finished to the same standard. It is very hard for respondents to look at a mixture of finished and rough versions and not be distracted by the different degrees of finish. It is also useful to include the existing design and key competitors to see how new design relates to these critical benchmarks.

When respondents are shown the designs, they are asked to systematically explore what the design says:

- What the products might be like
- Who would use them
- Which words/attributes apply to each

All the time, the researcher is looking for a design which says the right things about the brand and which attracts the desired target customers.

Our client was an opticians' chain with an old-fashioned image keen to update without losing authority. We developed different design directions at various degrees of development from the existing design – evolutionary to revolutionary. We then explored the reactions of existing and potential customers:

- Which were most appealing
- Which conveyed desired messages best
- Which were credible, non-credible and a step too far for the brand concerned

Fine-tuning design

Having narrowed down the design directions to the most promising candidate option, we can use qualitative research to fine-tune the details of the design.

Essentially, we use the same approach as for exploring design directions to research variants of a single design:

- Different colourways
- Different fonts
- Which cat to use on a new range of cat foods

In the case of pack design we might disaggregate the design elements so that respondents can assemble them in different ways (for example, 'that blue for the pack, with that typeface in green, and that picture of the cat').

An example

A fully finished prototype for self-catering accommodation for short break holidays was built in a warehouse. Respondent families were invited to 'come for a two-hour holiday' with their luggage. Their visits were then videoed from the initial opening of the front door to the respondents eating and relaxing and then 'going to bed'. The families were asked to comment and explain their spontaneous reaction.

The research identified the features which added value, i.e. those which were noticed and appreciated – a real fire, a balcony, a large fridge –and those which were not – a breakfast bar, a large store cupboard.

It also identified the ideal layout for kitchens. Less space was needed for food storage, but more surface area was requested for stacking and washing up out of sight of the living area. Potential 'damage' spots (where large suitcase were likely to knock walls, places to leave wet shoes/clothes to avoid stains on carpets) resulted in major savings in construction fixtures and fittings and maintenance in the 600 'lodges' then in development.

Evaluating response to final design

The last stage in the design development process is evaluating consumers' response to the final design before rolling it out. Again, the overall questions are whether the design achieves what it is intended to and whether consumers like it.

At this stage the research *should replicate real life as far as possible* – with the use of prototypes or controlled in-situ trials. Techniques move to observation and comment after trial, i.e. how do consumers respond and, if anything doesn't seem quite right, eliciting the reason why.

An example

A household cleanser combining existing formula with a different dispenser was used in homes for a week before respondents attended group discussions.

A mock-up display of new hard wax packs was produced and respondents were asked to find a pack appropriate for their last DIY task. We probed for comments on ease of locating the right product type and, within that grouping, the right specification for the task.

SUMMARY

SRU's experience of design research has developed over the past 20 years or more.

Since we saw design as an increasingly central strategic issue from the late 1970s on, we were concerned to both help our clients think clearly about its role and value and develop relevant research approaches capable of factoring in all the complex cultural issues that design development and evaluation present.

As brand strategists, we were also concerned that design should be related to the wider context of the long-term brand strategy and its other expressions in advertising, PR, public affairs, point of sale and service.

Only qualitative research can address issues of this kind. Only qualitative research can elicit the cultural and psychological factors that explain completely different reactions to ostensibly similar designs. And only qualitative research can enable you to brief a designer in detail on a new market and its deepest needs and wants.

In the early 1980s design started to be acknowledged as central in SRU key business sectors of retailing and property. 3D design became the business weapon for a new generation of retailers and developers. SRU became partners – with a major design group and a logistics specialist – in a joint venture to help shopping centre owners achieve their potential and keep ahead of new competition, and developers asked us how to add value to their office blocks or residential developments. The result was that we custom-built research approaches that allowed design decision-takers to see for themselves and 'own' the understandings afforded by qualitative research.

'Sponsored shopping' (accompanied shopping), 'dolls house' (model-building) and a range of other research applications all developed out of the intensive experience of those years when clients would demand a new design solution for a 500-branch chain that could be rolled out in months not years, and when developers wanted to break the mould of domestic residential design with houses and flats that looked like AD 1750 or 2010 rather than the 1970s.

These clients were often driven entrepreneurs with little knowledge of research, simply the absolute requirement that it would yield understandable, actionable results and thereby more than pay its way. It is testimony to the real value of custom-built qualitative research that these clients became repeat purchasers!

It is the ability to identify which details really matter to key audiences without ever losing sight of the big-picture priorities that makes qualitative design research so immensely powerful as a creator of competitive advantage. The consistent use of intelligent qualitative research in design development enhances the client's and the designer's creativity through a dialogue with the marketplace which provides a profound understanding of consumers' real priorities and sensibilities.

KEY IDEAS

- Design is becoming more crucial to a whole range of business initiatives. It can add value, create new markets for existing products and underwrite the acceptance of new products.
- Changes in the business environment are compounding the importance of design such as globalism, competition and new technologies.

- Design investment is therefore becoming more widespread, more strategic, more professional and higher cost, involving higher risks at every level.
- It behoves organisations investing in design to do so in a more informed way, by identifying and understanding target markets, informing the design development, and evaluating design options against their intended marketplaces.
- Qualitative research can contribute powerfully to informing, developing and evaluating design, and it is best conducted within a sound philosophical framework and using practical approaches based on it.
- Whatever type of design, product, packaging or retail, similar issues emerge:
  - identifying salient market criteria for the design task;
  - relating this to the overall brand strategy and its communication;
  - informing the client's thinking and the designer's understanding;
  - informing the development of design options;
  - evaluating candidate designs;
  - evaluating acceptance in the real market.
- The consistent use of intelligent qualitative research in design development enhances the client's and designer's creativity through a dialogue with the marketplace which provides a profound understanding of consumers' real priorities and sensibilities.

Chapter 8
Qualitative Research in the Development of Higher Education

Sue Robson
Managing Director, The Qualitative Consultancy
with

Angie Ballard
Market Research Manager, Open University

Editor's introduction

Until recently it seemed unthinkable that the austere, academic world of higher education would be involved in marketing methods. Indeed, marketing courses themselves are a relatively recent phenomenon in the world of universities.

Sue Robson, one of the UK's leading researchers, and Angie Ballard set the context for exploring this area by considering the massive social, economic and political, as well as the educational changes that have occurred in recent years. Their impact on the universities has been that these institutions now need to actively market themselves to their students to ensure they fill their places and meet their financial targets.

The change is not only about money; it also affects how and why students study. Universities need to be relevant to the modern student, who differs quite radically from the student of the past.

Conducting qualitative research in this field is new and far from straightforward. Clients are often ill at ease with the approach and thus require special attention and support. Small budgets and wide briefs mean that researchers need to develop innovative ways of approaching research to provide maximum value.

The Open University is a fascinating example of what can be achieved when research is used sensitively and objectives are clear. Angie has generously allowed us a glimpse into a university which has really embraced its 'customer' and used qualitative research to best advantage.

THE CONTEXT: THE MARKETPLACE FOR HIGHER EDUCATION

At one time, certainly in the 1960s and 1970s and even in the early 1980s, universities were clear about their offer and their market. They provided the traditional three or sometimes four-year degree to the small proportion of school leavers who aspired to higher education, often without any clear career goal in mind. Alongside this were vocational qualifications for those seeking entry into specific careers, including the professions. This was a neatly and simply defined educational world and the focus of university effort was then centred on the academic product. Concepts of target market, understanding the consumer, brand image, customer service and attracting new students in a competitive marketplace simply did not apply.

All this has now changed. Over the past decade we have experienced many social, political and cultural changes in the UK and overseas, which have impacted on the market for higher education – and which have significantly increased the universities' need for a greater understanding of their 'consumer', the prospective student.

The changes we have noticed are diverse: social, political and cultural changes; education changes; changes as a result of increasing use of technology/IT; and changes as a result of the increasing interest in part-time and distance learning. It is useful at this point to list some of the major considerations we, as market researchers, have had to take into account.

In terms of social, political and cultural context

- Changes in government education policy.
- The pressure on young people to gain qualifications and market themselves to employers.
- Women entering the workforce and senior management in greater numbers.
- 'Portfolio' careers and additional qualifications as a means to effect this.
- The emphasis on lifelong learning.
- A time-obsessed society, but with conventional social, work and personal time slots breaking down and with increasing service availability 'round the clock'.

In the area of education

- The large numbers of school leavers entering higher education.
- The proliferation of tertiary qualifications, beyond just university degrees.
- The conversion of technical colleges and polytechnics to university status – creating the 'new' or '1992' universities.

- The decreasing value of the student grant and, most recently, the introduction of fee contributions from students in higher education.

In the area of technology and IT

- The high penetration of television, video and audio systems in the home.
- Satellite, cable and digital TV, bringing a proliferation of channels and programme choice, including many of an informative and educational nature.
- Computer use in the workplace and at home becoming commonplace – including use of e-mail and the internet.
- CD-Roms delivering information to the home, via the PC.

The increasing interest in part-time and distance learning

- The increasing need for those in employment to gain further/higher qualifications in their chosen field.
- The target market for adult education changing from mature adults seeking a 'second chance' to those '30-somethings' seeking a second degree or professional qualification.
- The close link people make between career development and personal fulfilment when considering higher education needs.
- The increasing numbers of universities and other higher education providers offering the part-time route to degrees and professional qualifications.
- The increasing numbers of providers offering distance learning.

With all these changes, universities can no longer focus on planning degree courses on the basis of what they believe students should study. They also have to focus on:

- Who their students will be
- Where they are
- How they want to study
- What they want to study
- Why they want to study
- How they make their choices
- What will motivate them to choose one provider over another

Qualitative research has a significant role to play in answering some of these questions and we have found that it is forming an increasing part of the overall spend on research.

Some universities have risen to the challenge of a changing marketplace and are commissioning research to inform their decisions. Others are becoming aware of the need to market themselves more effectively and thus of the need for research. Probably yet others will do so in the future. In 1995 some 15 universities had staff who were listed as members of the MRS, which includes staff teaching market research in the business departments. In the 1998/99 year-book the number had risen to over 50.

For their turnover, market research budgets are still modest in the university sector and the proportion of qualitative research can vary from none to about two thirds by value. We estimate that this currently gives a gross spend of over £1 million a year and possibly a lot more than this.

THE ROLE OF MARKET RESEARCH IN HIGHER EDUCATION

Introduction to the Open University

The Open University was established in 1969 by Royal Charter. Its function is to provide university education for adults delivered to their own homes. The courses use a mix of printed texts, audio-visual materials and information technology as means of instruction and the majority of students have a tutor. The course materials are designed by course teams made up of academics from the nine faculties, schools or centres working with advisers from the Institute of Educational Technology and the BBC as well as other outside experts. At present, the university has 13 regional centres within the UK, as well as a European office in Brussels. Today there are about 113 000 students studying over 173 undergraduate courses and some 30 000 postgraduate students. Some 20 000 students were from outside the UK and 40 000 students were working online in some form in 1998 – communicating with other students or their tutor using e-mail, reviewing course material or information sources via the internet or taking part in one of the electronic conferences. Over 30 000 companies directly sponsored student study in 1998 and the postgraduate professional updating market is increasingly important. The Vice-Chancellor, Sir John Daniel, describes the OU as one of the ten mega universities in the world.

The appeal of the Open University

A number of both qualitative and quantitative studies with a wider audience than the active student body showed the university that, while its name is well known, there are many misunderstandings about the nature of its offering and methods of teaching. In university terms the OU is a young institution, and 1999 marked its 30th year of operation. However, for the younger generations it has less appeal and relevance, especially given the much wider range of competitors.

The OU has recognised that it needs a strong brand to face the future with confidence. It has acknowledged that as the environment in which the brand exists changes, so the brand must change appropriately in order to maintain its premier position as the part-time distance learning provider *par excellence*.

The need to change

The OU has also recognised that because of its distinctive offer it can capitalise on some of the changes listed above (for example, many of the IT developments, the move towards lifelong learning, 'portfolio' careers, the computer skills base among the young), while others are potential threats to its pre-eminent position. To give just two illustrations of the latter: first, with the significant increase in the numbers of school leavers going into higher education, the traditional OU market of 'second chance' mature adults will shrink in size; second, the creation of the '1992 universities' has increased the number of institutions taking an active interest in offering degrees to the mature and part-time student target market.

Qualitative research at the Open University

Thus one would think that qualitative research would be integral to its marketing thinking. However, like all universities the OU concentrates on the rational and reasonably argued case. Qualitative work that explores the emotional and non-rational can be seen as especially challenging to the supposed rational decision-maker.

Again, like many other clients, both in the higher education and the commercial, profit-making business sectors, the OU has many different 'user groups' of market research information. These can include those involved in:

- Direct marketing
- Advertising
- Brand and corporate identity development
- Promotions using publications and leaflets and literature aimed at prospective enquirers
- Publications aimed at prospective students
- Literature aimed at students, such as administrative information, course guides
- Student support services
- Different faculties
- The business school, OUBS
- Development of new courses

- Attracting corporate sponsors
- Fund-raising
- Alumni interest in affinity offerings

Thus we find that the primary role of qualitative research in the higher education sector is no different from that found in any other market sector – namely closing the gap between the marketer and the consumer and, through this, providing the marketer with an intimate knowledge and understanding of the consumer. The best qualitative research allows the client to 'experience the consumer's experience'.

Academics can live in a world far removed from their students, despite teaching them most days of the week. Marketing teams in academic institutions can be cut off from their marketplace. This is even more so with a distance learning provider, the OU, whose potential market is, in theory, for the majority of its courses, every adult in the country.

With universities, therefore, there is a particular need for qualitative research that can provide clear insight and understanding of their complex and diverse target market, their hopes, their aspirations, their motivations, their behaviour and their needs, in order to maintain a competitive edge in an increasingly complex marketplace.

Challenges to conducting qualitative research in this sector

Clients with little knowledge about qualitative research

One of the challenges of conducting qualitative research for the higher education sector is that of dealing with intelligent and well-informed people, who have great abilities in their own area of responsibility but who often have only a sketchy understanding of the strengths of qualitative research. Clearly one of the functions of the internal market research team is to provide this expertise and 'translate' where necessary, but the qualitative research supplier is also often dealing direct with the internal client, such as at briefing discussions and debriefs. A well-developed ability to 'take the position of the other' and understand the client's perspective and experience is of considerable value.

The traditional interpersonal and group facilitative skills can therefore be important in the client context as well as in the research process. Some internal users will have a clear understanding of the role and value of qualitative research and be very experienced at dealing with its 'soft' values; others may feel very uncomfortable at listening to a presentation based on the findings of a small number of group discussions or individual interviews. Some will only be comfortable with numbers and percentages; others will draw inappropriate conclusions from, say, one group held with a particular target sector.

For some studies the converse is the case and one is challenged as presenting too superficial a view. How can the one-and-a-half-hour group discussion reflect five to ten years' study experience and the evolving relationship with the institution? Breadth of sample across these different time perspectives is one solution. However, accepted qualitative market research will have limited appeal to the ethnographic and conversational analysis specialists.

All this can mean that much importance is placed on the debrief. As is often the case, this meeting can be the first opportunity many of those attending will have to hear about the research, but it can also be the forum for some attendees to air their own preferred perspective on the role and value of qualitative research! The ability to argue one's case calmly, with clarity and conviction, is paramount.

Charts and diagrams are powerful explanatory devices that can aid understanding of the conceptual nature of qualitative research findings. Later, we note the impact of the 100 figures ('little men') from the competitor preference study. Other examples are the brand onion to capture the essence and various layers of corporate brand imagery, and a pyramid symbol we used to act as a metaphor for the 'climb to the top' of the decision process and achievement of a degree.

However, it is important that such figures are self-contained and self-explanatory – they will be copied and passed around, often in quite alien contexts, and it is useful for there to be a reference to the source study as well as having details of date, sample size and authorship.

Multi-clients

Another challenge that is commonly set by many service providers' use of research is that of multi-clients. There is often considerable overlap in the needs of internal departments. Some examples are:

- Those responsible for direct marketing need to know the key messages to attract new students just as much as those responsible for the prospectuses.
- Those responsible for creating the academic content of a new course need to understand prospective students' expectations and needs, while those responsible for marketing and advertising the new course need to understand how to present the course content in a clear, motivating and relevant way.
- Those responsible for handling enquiries from prospective and current students need to understand the emotional needs of students, as well as their academic motivations and ability, as much as do those offering students' pastoral and counselling support.

- The very different perspectives that can be taken to changes in service provision between centrally based staff and regionally based staff.

The qualitative researcher needs to be aware of the different agendas and priorities in a mixed client group and take any disagreements over scale or timing back to what is in the best interest of the institution as a whole. One of the key responsibilities of any market research function is to keep the pan-institution perspective in mind.

The need to allow time within the institution

Although those employed within an academic institution to provide marketing and research expertise will have no trouble, others may not be so sophisticated in their understanding of concepts such as:

- The power and importance of the brand
- The target market – how to define, how to identify who/where they are
- Communication is a two-way process
- The customer perspective

They may also be very sceptical of the value of qualitative research.

There is, therefore, the need to allow more time for assimilation and 'ownership' of the issues. This requires researchers who are sympathetic rather than assumptive and arrogant, researchers who are willing to attend more than one meeting when planning a project, or have further debriefs, or meetings after the debrief, to discuss how to present the research in a way that will make it comprehensible – or indeed institutionally acceptable – to a wider audience.

Wide target market but tight budgets

Many projects for a university need to take into account that the potential marketplace is very wide, and can be geographically spread, fragmented and individualistic. People's educational background, life stage and personal circumstances, work experience, current job/career, study motivations, local provider options, family/friends'/work colleagues' experience of higher education – to name but a few – can all be a powerful influence on their awareness of the marketplace, image of providers, study plans, decision process and satisfaction with their educational experience. This can bring a whole new set of challenges to qualitative research design and sample recruitment.

In qualitative research, when one wants to understand the influence of these factors on a specific issue, it is often best to define the groups in a clear, separate way, creating distinctively different and homogeneous groups. In this way one can relate the views expressed to the circumstances of that group, but in a complex and fragmented market this can often lead to a very large sample design, involving lengthy time scales and the need for generous budget provision.

In higher education, funds for qualitative research are often tight, and when working in this sector one therefore develops a high level of skill in defining the optimum trade-off between depth and breadth of sample coverage and in deciding on the most cost-effective methodologies to meet the client brief. We have found that one can often gain sufficient information from 'picking off' key sub-groups in the target market as a whole, and convening a few groups just with them. Alternatively, one may sometimes opt for a mix of groups and brief, semi-structured interviews, either face to face or over the telephone (depending on sample and objectives). Groups can provide rich insights and develop hypotheses. One-to-ones provide the detail needed to come back with a robust dataset.

Thus we have very rarely found ourselves involved in the 'standard' four or six-group project, split into younger/older or north/south or user/non-user segments when doing research for a university. More often, we recommend conducting a combination of two or more of the following:

- Group discussions when it is feasible to recruit people from a local area to one venue, sometimes standard length but often extended, as the issues facing prospective students are potentially life-changing and thus need time to explore in depth.
- Mini-sized groups when the dynamic and creative interchange of opinions is crucial to achieving the objectives but we know that recruitment will be a challenge.
- Individual face-to-face interviews when we want to explore issues in the brief at the level of the individual experience and decision-taking.
- Individual interviews when lists of specific targets are being provided, but we know from experience that these lists will be small and the addresses scattered geographically, and thus it is unrealistic to even aim to conduct a group.
- Telephone interviews, again to cope with a scattered population, but only relevant if the brief is focused, tactical and the sample is list based (and thus has some 'relationship', however brief and minimal, with the provider). We do not usually find telephone in-depths a helpful methodology when recruitment is cold.
- Semi-structured interviews, which retain a qualitative identity but have an internal consistency and focus that mean we also gain comparative data across a scattered range of individuals. Again, these can be done face to face or over the telephone.

- A mix of qualitative and quantitative studies, usually undertaken sequentially, when there is a need for that powerful mix of qualitative insight and hard data to inform decision-making.

With budgets often being a considerable constraint on the ideal solution, yet with the need for the qualitative project to be robust and not just a skimming of the surface, one has to think quite laterally at times. It is quite usual in proposals for work to give two or three costed options so the clients can see what they are losing by opting for the lowest budget. It has often been our experience that with a carefully argued case small budgets can be supplemented to allow for a more meaningful project.

In a budgetary context, it is also worth noting the increasing trend towards syndicated studies in the higher education sector. Non-market research companies predominate here, such as HEIST and the recent study commissioned by CVCP and UCAS and including 15 universities undertaken by the Institute of Employment Studies, Sussex.

Defining the potential user

With the conventional school leaver aiming for higher education, there is little problem in either defining or identifying/recruiting to qualitative research.

With mature students, however, the problem can be an immense challenge. Even with the growth in interest in lifelong learning, one is still often looking for needles in haystacks. And then, when you find someone who is apparently eligible in terms of current academic qualifications and expresses interest in further study, you recruit them, begin to interview them – and then you find their interest is vague, non-specific, unfocused and of little value to you when trying to research reactions to a prospectus or direct response ad.

Over the years we have therefore had to considerably refine our definition of 'potential users'– much to the anguish of our recruiter team at times! But it is of no value to interview a group of people who think they might like to study for a degree one day, but who are so vague in their intent that they cannot contribute effectively to any debate about the key messages or executional details of press advertising that is intended to recruit new students.

List recruitment

This was briefly touched on above. Recruiting from client databases is becoming a more and more relevant method for qualitative projects across a wide range of markets and industry sectors; but universities have needed to research particular sectors of their enquiry and student base from when they first began to use qualitative research. List recruitment has therefore been a constant challenge.

It is important, therefore, to keep abreast of changes to the data protection legislation; also changes to the MRS Code of Conduct, ESOMAR Code, Database and Qualitative Guidelines. All the codes are available from the Market Research Society and the DPA is available from the Registrar. Careful study is necessary to avoid falling foul of the law and of best practice guidelines.

As in other markets clients need to be reminded of the essential differences between anonymised survey and market research and exercises in list cleaning or list building.

List recruitment is sometimes seen as the panacea for a difficult recruitment challenge. However, our experience is that one only resorts to it when cold recruitment is not a feasible option. Even with a sample as motivated as current students are likely to be, it brings with it many problems that can lead to the recruitment task as a whole being far more of a challenge.

One needs to consider how and whether to inform those on the list in advance of recruitment, to think about the different training the field force/recruiters will need, to think about the location of the interviewing, the venue, the incentives, the pre-checking, the post-checking, and so on.

Importantly, also, one needs to check with the client, perhaps via a count of the relevant sections of the database, how many eligible names will be on the list, whether telephone numbers are provided, whether these include ex-directory, and so on. It is worth noting the increasing difficulty of accessing telephone numbers, if not recorded on client databases, with the trend to ex-directory.

Client lists can take more time to access than using directories or own databases. We have found the timescale can vary from three days to four weeks depending on the sector under investigation.

Our experience is that lists are rarely as relevant, accurate or extensive as one hopes. The experienced internal client will also recognise this, and one can therefore work as a team to overcome problems and manage everyone's expectations.

The constraints of the academic year

Working with a university client, one becomes used to activity peaking at certain times of the year. There is a definite cycle to recruitment campaigns, and supporting continuing students in their further study choices.

More important than the academic year can be the budget year. The annual bulge of research projects as the year end approaches is less of a feature now that institutions are able to carry some funds forward to the next year.

Another important feature is that the enquiry process and decision to apply can take less than a month but, in the mature student market, particularly part-time distance learning, it can also stretch over five years or more. The most extreme case found for the OU has been 21 years. The outside agency can usefully remind the institution that real-life timetables do not neatly mesh with their administrative timetables.

Overview of changing use of research

Centralised marketing

The centralised marketing department gives a focus to the institution's marketing activity and provides a critical mass of staff not only to undertake the many activities but to plan for the future – building on the successes and learning from the failures. However, the amount of centralisation is an ongoing debate and, as the faculties become more conscious of the need to attract and keep students, so the debates increase. Periodic value-for-money reviews are a useful opportunity to change the internal organisation to meet changing institutional priorities. Within the OU the marketing of postgraduate degrees is a good example of an activity that has largely been faculty based and is now moving to shared ownership as the increasing importance of this market is recognised.

Those universities that have a marketing department of some sort, with a specific brief to act as a bridge between the institution and its prospective students, to generate new students and to maintain communication throughout the student experience, not only make much more use of qualitative research – they also make *better* use of qualitative research.

The request from the end user of the research will come to the agency via the marketing and research team: the request 'can we have some of those focus groups to find out X' becomes a well-written brief, with clear background on why there is a need to find out certain information, who are the relevant sectors to interview and what will be decided on the basis of the findings.

For example, the Open University has always had a commitment to institutional research, usually undertaken by the Institute of Educational Technology. In 1988, with an increasing demand for work among wider audiences than the student body, the market research post was established, attached to the business development and marketing function as a temporary one-year experiment. At that time no dedicated budget was spent on 'market research', although there were a number of studies which fulfilled that role. The spend in 1989 was £30 000. In 1999 there were two full-time staff with part-time secretarial support, and a third post soon to be appointed specifically for the Open University Business School. The total funds allocated to market research in 1998–99 were over £0.5 million: a welcome increase, although still a modest sum for an institution with a turnover of £230 million.

The growth of strategic research

Looking at the way the market research spend has developed within the OU we found that the focus of qualitative research was originally tactical as the institution tentatively engaged with the world of commercial research and allocated a small budget to commission external agencies. Over time, its use of research has become more extensive, much more sophisticated and, in consequence, now includes major strategic studies as well as continuing with the tactical work.

To give a flavour of this change: initial projects were centred around 'small' issues; for example, the design and content of a brochure aimed at a specific target, such as corporate sponsors of OUBS students or the pre-testing of three executions of a TV commercial targeted at potential OU students. As the value of qualitative research to improve and refine such executions was recognised, so the projects moved back a step in terms of planning and development. Thus, a few years later, we found we were being asked to work on early design developments for a range of brochures targeted across the potential OU student spectrum and to define and model the whole decision process from first thinking about higher education to actually registering as a student.

Explorations of the marketplace for higher education, part-time or otherwise, enabled The Qualitative Consultancy to build a body of knowledge about potential students' perceptions and image of the wide range of providers – FE colleges, polytechnics (as they then were), the 'new' universities (as they later became with the change in status and role), the traditional redbrick and 1960s universities, Oxbridge, the business schools, and providers which have always offered courses to the part-time, mature student market, such as the OU.

The role of branding

An important, more recent recognition is the power of the brand image to influence choice. This has led to universities commissioning research of a classic, qualitative kind, exploring brand image, defining brand essence and assisting in the strategic development of marketing and advertising campaigns to shift the image in the desired direction for the future.

PRACTICALITIES – BASED ON CASE STUDIES

'Observation' as an alternative to qualitative interviews

Exploring responses to a new helpline set up for current students, which required qualitative insight plus quantitative indications of take-up, reasons for use and satisfactions, might have suggested a combination of individual interviews, followed up by a CATI quantitative survey. We kept the CATI element, but the individual interviews (groups were out of the question as the sample was too scattered) were too expensive. So how were we to define the questions for the quantitative stage? We could make some assumptions, of course, but these could be missing some important details.

The solution was to sit in on the helpline desk, listening to calls and talking to the staff who had been trained to answer the calls. Two evenings of researcher time doing this, followed by some telephone calls to a few more helpline staff, led to a clear and detailed questionnaire at much less cost than interviewing the students in depth.

'Scattered' group definitions across the target market

One institution, launching a corporate image campaign on TV for the first time, wished to use qualitative research in the creative development process. The target market could include:

- Potential students – of various qualifications, academic levels
- Previous enquirers
- Students
- Staff who act as ambassadors of the institution in their role as tutors, counsellors or administrative student contact staff

Thus the number of groups could have become quite astronomic. A careful interlocking quota design enabled this project to be completed for a cost-effective budget and to a tight timetable. The central focus of the sample design was the key stages in the, often lengthy, decision process the student goes through between first thinking about the possibility of going to university, enquiring, applying, gaining entry and beginning his or her studies. We refined this into three key stages, which we could then subdivide in terms of key demographics and behavioural measures, in order to conduct a series of groups which, between them, provided a good overall coverage of the diverse student market.

Telephone interviews as an alternative to face-to-face interviews

As part of a development project on direct response press advertising, there was a specific objective of looking at the responses to two new ads, one placed in the usual type of publication, one placed in a new choice of publication. The university had the response data to the range of ads and thus knew whether they were working well against the 'benchmark' ad, which always performed well. But why were the response patterns different; what could they learn from an understanding of perceptions and reactions to headline, copy, layout, etc.?

Responses to the new ads were of course quite scattered, and an appraisal of the list of enquirers made it clear that groups were not an option. A one-to-one approach would also be more appropriate, given that responding to a direct response ad is an individual matter. However, conducting a series of individual interviews, face to face, would be expensive and time consuming. Could we gain sufficient information over the telephone, without the ads there as a prompt to respondents?

We decided that, given that the main need was to explore the reason why this sub-sample responded to this particular ad in this particular publication, we could opt for the cheaper alternative of telephone interviews. We would not be able to explore the creative and emotive dimensions of the advertising – but we would be able to answer the questions: Why this ad? Why this publication? The rest of the sample (with groups of non-responders) was to be used to explore the ad in more depth.

Qualitative in team with quantitative

One of the most extensive projects undertaken by the OU was to provide an estimate of overall market share. Here we worked with a well-known quantitative agency to give both the numbers and population estimates through 10 000 omnibus interviews undertaken in five waves. Both group discussions and individual interviews were conducted to provide the illumination and understanding of the different target market sectors.

This project was particularly noteworthy. The complexity of the quantitative analysis, with its shifting bases for the percentages, derived from the different stages and sample sources for the research, meant that the conclusions on market share and potential target market were hard to grasp by those without a strongly numerate or marketing background. As this research was frequently quoted as the foundation for marketing thinking and future research plans, it became clear that a more graphic illustration of the data implications was required. The marketing department of the OU converted the shifting bases to a visual representation of the total adult population, using clip art of figures ('little men') to demonstrate, in a powerful, graphic and easily comprehensible way, the OU share of the market, its current and future target markets.

When a heterogeneous group definition works well

When one is asked to look at the target market for 13 brochures targeted at the postgraduate market, the first suggestion for sample definitions is to take the target for each brochure and interview them in a separate group, but this alone would make an unwieldy sample size. When one also considers that there is a need to explore reactions to the brochures with people at different points along the decision process – potentials, enquirers and students – the problem of sample size begins to loom even larger. Moreover, there is the underlying issue that we are dealing with a minority sample, even among students. Since the project brief is a creative development one, there is the preference for conducting group discussions – but how can we recruit enough people from a minority and scattered population to a group?

The solution in this case was to think about what could unite respondents in a different way. The answer was faculty: a linking of subjects that have something in common. Prospective and current students all interested in/studying sciences or interested in/studying humanities would surely be able to discuss their needs from brochures in a group.

With this solution, we were able to reduce the number of groups to a manageable and economic number, and we did indeed find that respondents felt they had enough in common with other group members to discuss their reactions to brochures in a useful and detailed way. We were also able to use the differences between the decision stage which different respondents had reached to work on contrasting views to form a resolution in terms of brochure design and content.

CONCLUSIONS

Qualitative research provides illumination and understanding. For our university clients it has helped them understand the different motivations and attitudes among their heterogeneous clientele and the need for different levels of explanation and support. It has also helped them understand the complex and seemingly chaotic processes someone goes through in deciding to become a student. Several of the research studies have provided new terms and definitions that have become common currency – a notable example in the OU is focused and unfocused enquirers. The work has helped define the overall promotional strategy and is presently contributing to the development of a coherent brand strategy. As the work has circulated, so requests from new client departments have arisen. It is crucial here to keep some distance and not go native – to still be seen as an impartial outsider rather than stooges of the marketing department. One moves from market research to the consultancy role – and here each researcher has to decide where their boundaries are.

Providing an explanation of the motivations to study, especially among adults choosing to study part-time, is an area where qualitative research is pre-eminent – indeed essential – in providing an understanding of complex and seemingly chaotic behaviours. It gives marketing an understanding of their promotional work as well as reminding administrative and academic systems of the real-life users' experiences.

One of the challenges this sets the qualitative agency is to balance the need and desire to work as a team with the client while staying 'in role' as an objective outsider. Being the impartial outsider can involve having to communicate bad news. A good working relationship means this is listened to rather than dismissed as 'just a few groups'. Another sign of a good working relationship is early warning by the research function of future projects, accepting that one is often in a competitive tendering situation and will not get all jobs, being able to say no to further work on occasion, but also being offered some interesting and trail-blazing projects when the need arises.

The role of qualitative research in higher education is here to stay, and its use will increase, both of the conventional kind and working with new and innovative approaches such as 'virtual' groups and interviews online.

KEY IDEAS

- Social, political and cultural change including pressure on youth to market themselves has irrevocably altered the world of higher education.
- Education changes as a result of IT and of increases in part-time and distance learning have impacted on the market for higher education.
- Universities can no longer plan degree courses on the basis of what they think students should study.
- The OU has recognised that these changes provide opportunities, but also many threats such as a reduction in numbers of potential undergraduates due to the increase in degree courses taken immediately after school.
- The world of universities leans towards a belief in rational argument and is reluctant to adopt qualitative methodology.

- Conducting qualitative research is particularly hindered by inexperienced and dubious clients; multi-clients; the slow pace of decision-making; and wide target markets but tiny budgets.
- Marketing departments are starting to emerge with the specific brief of acting as a bridge between the institution and its prospective students and qualitative research is a key tool in this process.
- Ultimately, the universities are recognising their role as brands and using qualitative research to define and refine the brand image to maximise their commercial potential.

FURTHER READING

Alexander, M., Burt, M. & Collinson, A. (1995) Big talk, small talk: BT's strategic use of semiotics in planning its current advertising campaign. *Journal of the Market Research Society*, 17(2).

Blyth, W. & Robson, S. (1981) Resolving the hard/soft dilemma. MRS Conference.

Connor, H. et al. (1999) *Making the Right Choice – How Students Choose Universities and Colleges*. Report by Institute for Employment Studies to CVCP, HEFCE and UCAS CVCP, London.

Daniel, Sir J. (1996) *Mega-universities and Knowledge Media Technology Strategies for Higher Education*. Kogan Page, London (Open and Distance Series).

Robson, S. (1991) Ethics; informed consent or misinformed compliance. Proceedings of MRDF Seminar – What matters in qualitative research. *Journal of the Market Research Society*, 33(1).

Chapter 9

Museums, Galleries and the Arts World

Susie Fisher
Director, The Susie Fisher Group

Editor's introduction

The arts have traditionally enjoyed a privileged position. Consumed by a minority and not needing to consider the majority, they have survived on grants and taxpayers' money.

In the new accountable society, the arts institutions have been forced to change and to justify their income. Susie Fisher explains how funding has suddenly become dependent on access for the majority, and arts institutions now need to fight for their audiences, not only among themselves but among the huge range of leisure activities available.

In order to attract new audiences and visitors, arts institutions have started to take on the marketing approach normally associated with commerce. In many cases, this has been a very painful process as the marketers of the future have challenged the way in which traditional curators, directors and other purist members of the arts conduct themselves.

One of the methods adopted has been qualitative research. It is being used to help understand the potential visitors or audiences and so assist the arts institutions with their task. In this environment, research has not always been met with open arms and Susie has made her mark at the forefront of this fascinating conflict.

The reasons for change and the implications for qualitative research are explored in this chapter. Susie goes on to look at the way in which museums and galleries, forced to reappraise their approach, have started to use qualitative research. The performing arts lag far behind in this area and, while similar issues would apply, the chapter necessarily excludes them from the sections on the use of qualitative research.

THE CONTEXT: THE CHANGING WORLD OF THE ARTS

A wind of change

The arts agenda has changed. Museums and galleries have moved from being the preservers of the nation's collections to being educators and interpreters of those collections. The performing arts have to prove their relevance to a broader public or dwindle as archaic forms. Access is the battle-cry. Access for young people and for old people; access upmarket and down, physical access for the disabled and, above all, intellectual access for everyone.

How has this change come about? It may be largely a question of money. If the public doesn't get the benefit then the arts don't get the funding. A long-time tradition of elitism is under attack.

It would be misleading to think that the scales have fallen instantly from the eyes of the arts establishment. Its leaders are not, by and large, calling for intimate public consultation, and indeed often mistrust it. But there is now a new generation of professionals drawn from education and interpretation, marketing and design, who are committed to working with their audiences rather than in divine isolation.

Drawing for spiritual support on the US experience, they have named this new discipline Visitor Studies. Visitor Studies ensure that the visitors' perspective is represented in decision-making, and it exactly mirrors the role of the planning department in the early days of advertising planning.

This is partly fuelled by the universities, in particular the University of Leicester, which teaches a visitor-centred approach to museums and galleries. There is much idealism, a desire to build a knowledge base about consumers and a desire to share that knowledge. The UK Visitor Studies Group was inaugurated in autumn 1998. This thinking should also drive thinking in the performing arts which currently lag behind.

Commercial unease

But the arts world has been brought up short by lack of money. In the rarefied air surrounding performance, painting and historical artefact, commercial profit has previously been irrelevant. Perhaps art which made money didn't really count as art at all. At any rate, it was to nourish the soul of the nation rather than to stoke its coffers for which the arts expected government subsidy. The prevailing thinking was more about finding an audience (however small) to appreciate the artistic integrity of the work than about interpreting the work to be capable of touching a wider public.

The Thatcher years took a more robust view, in which ideas about commercial sponsorship went hand in hand with a reduction in state funding. By the 1990s, an arts establishment, traditionally ill at ease with commercial matters, was facing the following indigestible menu:

- Commercial sponsorship as a necessity
- Lottery funding requiring accountability
- A fiercely competitive leisure environment

Let us examine how these factors have worked together.

Commercial sponsorship

Patronage is an old idea. Shakespeare himself wrote for the Earl of Southampton, and these days the baton has passed on to the large corporations. The question has always been whether the agenda of the commissioning body compromises the integrity of the work, and today is no exception. Did the Design Museum on the Thames, for example, compromise its goals by persuading Coca-Cola to fund a large gallery on the evolution of the Coke bottle and logo? Probably not, but large corporations will want their payback in other ways.

The sponsor wants to be sure that association with the arts body enhances its image with its own customers. It also wants to be sure that enough of its customers will see the contribution it has helped to make. The arts endeavour must be demonstrably successful in terms of achieving visitor coverage and communicating something relevant and, if it can put the sponsor's product in a good light, so much the better.

Lottery funding

It is the Heritage Lottery Fund, however, which has wrought the biggest change in attitudes and energy. Between 1993 and 1999, the Fund has distributed £1285 million to heritage projects. This has had the effect of putting different arts organisations on their mettle. Projects which had lived for years in private dream cupboards began to see the light of day, and arts people painfully began to acquire the skills to pitch for them.

The Lottery required, as a bare minimum:

- A coherent vision of the project
- A named target audience
- Fit within the aims of the organisation
- Sound project management within a budget

The very act of mastering these business-inspired disciplines proved to be empowering. Even if they weren't awarded Lottery funds, organisations were understandably reluctant to renounce their worked-up ideas, and sometimes the money was mysteriously found from elsewhere.

Readers of this chapter will not have been slow to work out that an organisation needing to spell out a coherent vision and define its target audience will very soon need to consult these audiences. For example, the Natural History Museum, now justly celebrated for being accessible, went into research asking a dry question about people's relationship with arthropods, but it emerged at the end of the process with a crowd-pulling gallery entitled 'Creepy Crawlies'.

The Commission was soon overwhelmed with applications, and consequently articulated tighter requirements as it evolved.

- A preference for projects with wider demographic access (this was where the political will lay).
- A stipulation that the public was to be consulted.
- Provision for evaluation at the end of a project to assess what had worked and what hadn't.

Relevance and intelligibility to the intended audiences became important issues, requiring a listening ear and willingness to debate. The process of thinking through the interpretation in line with the visitor can help to clarify the funding process.

A competitive leisure environment

The arts are good for you, therefore people should visit. This may be so, but would you put your trust in the moral high ground to make sure you got your audiences? The arts establishment would certainly have done so once, but cannot afford to now.

In the mind of the consumer, a decision for the arts is one of a range of options available to be enjoyed as a leisure activity. It is on the criteria of enjoyment and entertainment that leisure activities are assessed. The temptation is to opt for the easier, glitzier world of entertainment; pubbing and clubbing, cinema and shopping rather than to slope off to a boring gallery or heavy Shakespeare play in your spare time.

Today's audiences are steeped in a highly stimulating soup of interactive media: computers, screen games, television, video. This means they won't settle for simple objects, facts or lofty performances which make no attempt to engage them or respond to them. The traditional opera and the 'dry as dust' museum are non-starters.

However, families with children often rediscover their desire for the culture from which they sprang. The well-meaning parent has found a more sympathetic environment than the pure arts in the commercial world of heritage and theme parks, where there has been spectacular growth in recent years. Recreated environments such as Beamish village in the northeast or the Epcot Centre at Disney World have brought their subjects to life in a more palatable way. They offer both entertainment and wonder. On the London stage, musicals rule the roost.

These alternative attractions aren't going to go away, and they have siphoned off an audience which the arts covet for themselves. The more successful arts ventures have taken on board people's love of big production values and hands-on involvement.

The skill lies in achieving the aims of the institutions through the new media of entertainment and display, but this has plunged the arts organisations into conflict. They need to acquire these modern world skills in order to attract their audiences and justify public money, but at the same time there is a deep-rooted fear that the very nature of the arts will be subverted. How commercial do they need to be?

Conflicts of interest

This mistrust of popularisation is at the heart of the arts establishment's ambivalence about market research. In making a subject popular to suit public taste, will they betray the integrity (both aesthetic and intellectual) which gave it worth in the first place? By using the techniques of Disney, do you become Mickey Mouse?

Museums and galleries can feel they are the final and proper guardians of scholarship and aesthetic appreciation. Museum professionals can be as worried about maintaining status among their peers as about bringing in the public. Theatre directors notoriously believe that if they make any concession to popular taste they are betraying their art.

THE ROLE FOR QUALITATIVE RESEARCH SPECIFICALLY IN MUSEUMS AND GALLERIES

The exchange of old versus new views

The need for mutual understanding has been amply demonstrated, but is this the same thing as saying there is a need for qualitative research?

In reality, yes. The organisational culture within arts institutions is typically strong, sometimes ingrown. There is little existing opportunity for a frank exchange of views between the arts providers and their audiences, unless it is through some external agency.

Qualitative research contributes uniquely by:

- Providing an external discipline to help organisations articulate their plans from the audience perspective.
- Letting professionals hear the frank experiences and feelings of both their visitors and their non-visitors.
- Creating a common forum in which interpreters, curators, designers and directors can integrate the visitor into the planning process.

Although laudable, this basket of delights is not always welcome within the institution it seeks to serve. Let us explore this through the experience of the museums and start by considering a typical structure (Figure 1). Each of the stakeholders has an identifiably different stake in, say, setting up a new gallery, and each will argue for his or her own interest. Visitors of course occupy an anomalous position. First, they lie outside the organisation, and second, they are the *recipients* of the museum's services, arguably, the people for whose benefit the museum exists at all. If you consult your visitors in the first place, it is difficult to justify not taking their view into consideration, and they could be a bit of a loose cannon in the hallowed halls.

Traditionally, the direction and content of a gallery has been the responsibility of the old school: directors and curators of high scholarship who have been educated to believe in their duty as specialist decision-makers on the public's behalf. Many are distrustful of the public's patchy grasp of their mission and values, and are therefore reluctant to have their ideas undermined by the public's easy criticism.

Ranged on the other side is the new school: the educators, interpreters and marketers who have been tutored in dialogue and communication. They are more aligned with the advertising and marketing world, and see the input from the consumer as a way to develop more effective messages. The new school has a ready use for qualitative research, whereas the old school does not.

Because qualitative research with consumers is relatively new in museums, there is hesitancy about how to interpret the visitors' pronouncements or, indeed, whether to listen to them at all. Do you have to slavishly follow everything they say? Could you just do the research and safely ignore it?

Research can therefore be an unwanted intrusion for the old school, and threatening to boot. There is a terrible fear of adverse criticism of displays even among curators who want change, variety and input from the public.

Some of the problems occur because the museums don't think through their ideas from the public's perspective at the outset. Slowly but surely, qualitative research pressures museums to express their ideas in a form which visitors can grasp. If they don't, they can't get feedback on them at all.

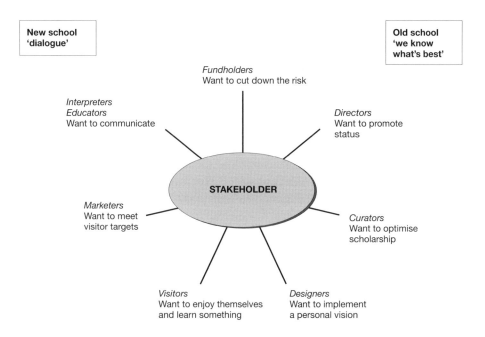

New school
'dialogue'

Old school
'we know
what's best'

Fundholders
Want to cut down the risk

Interpreters
Educators
Want to communicate

Directors
Want to promote
status

STAKEHOLDER

Marketers
Want to meet
visitor targets

Curators
Want to optimise
scholarship

Visitors
Want to enjoy themselves
and learn something

Designers
Want to implement
a personal vision

Figure 1

Innovators in qualitative research

Some museums have embraced qualitative research with vigour and have innovated and benefited from it, while others have been more reluctant. A shining star in this particular firmament has been the Science Museum in London. Under the patient vision of Dr Ben Gammon and his team, working on the new Wellcome Wing, the museum has developed an effective internal system of audience advocates.

These advocates reject confrontation as a way of operating with curators and design teams, and are resolved instead to identify the ways in which they can best support their teams. The role they have drawn up for themselves is an amalgam of:

- Adviser
- Educator
- Communicator
- Strategist
- Trainer

They then put themselves through an assault course designed to help them feel closer to their visitors:

- Accompanied visits
- Observation in gallery
- Attending group discussions

They finally visit an outside exhibition on a subject which bores them rigid. This has proved wonderfully liberating for gallery development, with the advocates humbled and full of feeling and able to see the visitor's perspective from the inside.

Part of the advocate's responsibilities is to identify where there is a knowledge gap and to commission research, usually qualitative, to fill it. There is logic, confidence and completeness in this approach, and the Science Museum has some of the highest visitor numbers in the UK.

The critics

Organisations such as the V&A and the National Gallery would argue that the Science Museum has an easy time of it. Asked merely to dramatise and communicate scientific concepts, with a little help from the objects in its collection, it can interpret visitor interests with relative freedom.

The arts galleries are essentially collection based. The objects are primary and must sometimes speak their story without any interpretative support at all. In fact, in many art galleries, the visitors dive past the exhibits because they have so little context and learning to help them. Because visitors often don't know how to look at the objects, they take them at face value – 'Yes, that's a cup and saucer' – and move on.

It is the fine arts end of the spectrum which has been slow to find a role for visitor research; similarly with theatre, architecture and the other creative arts. Is this to do with aesthetics? Is it that the creators feel their subject should be understood in its own terms as the fruit of a compelling creative vision? Are they expecting the *observer* to do the work and make the leap, rather than meeting them halfway. If so, bending to public taste would be anathema and visitor research likewise.

Nevertheless, opinions are on the cusp of change. Once organisations realise that research insight can *feed* rather than *dictate*, there is a gradual opening of the doors. Many arts organisations just don't have much experience of qualitative research. It can come as a surprise to them. They still have to make judgments, but these will now be informed rather than purely subjective.

What is becoming more apparent is that the central role of qualitative research is to find the bridges between visitors and visited, between consumer and product. This is the same exercise whether the product is genetic engineering or the Victorian Gothic. Once you know the visitor's natural take on the subject, you can guide them across this bridge and through to a treasure house of which they were previously unaware.

The functions of qualitative research

The arts world acts through the medium of projects; these may be performances, events, seasons, galleries. These are its products and, like any other product, they can derive strength from the corporate brand. I should be more likely to find you looking at an exhibition of twentieth-century painting in the Tate Gallery than at Devizes Road, Swindon, even though the paintings are of comparable quality.

Research in the arts is categorised according to product and brand development, but the jargon is different for each. Research for *product development* is known as evaluation, and is usually divided between formative evaluation (creative development at the front end) and summative evaluation (post-testing). Both are research whose purpose is to help with interpretation.

Brand research comes under the heading of marketing and is thought of in a very different light. Its purpose is to get visitors through the door. Like any marketing department, it poses questions concerning brand image, pricing policy, positioning, catchment areas, key targets, purchase decisions, frequency of visits, competitors and so forth.

While this is essential information for the commercial side of the operation, brand research has done qualitative research no favours. Designers looking to understand the subtlety of the *gallery* product experience can find themselves facing what they regard as crass segmentations and naive pronouncements from the marketing side. They may well assume that all research is as bad. There is scepticism about people who focus on marketing.

It has been my experience on the other hand that *formative evaluation* can actually be very useful to the marketing department. Once you've discovered the spark which lights people's interest, it is very often the same spark which will tempt them to visit. This transfers directly into advertising and promotion. Hence, when the Museum of Science and Industry in Manchester discovered that the excitement behind their new Textiles Gallery lay in the world of fashion and the feel of material, they gave it the title 'Fibre, Fabrics and Fashion', and featured brilliant silk banners and fashion shots in their advertising.

Corporate branding still has a long way to go in the arts. The arts are full of strong brands, which have not yet accessed their marketing potential. This will surely come, and with the help of qualitative research. Only think what you could do with, say, the RSC or the Tate Gallery as brands.

Formative evaluation

It is formative evaluation, then, where qualitative research is making its biggest contribution. The main themes are characterised and discussed here.

- *How does the target audience relate to the subject area?*
  How much do people know? What is familiar? Where are their misconceptions and where do their emotions lie? On the basis of this insight, the subject can be explored using touchstones which already mean something to the visitor.

  Thus the Museum of Liverpool Life wanted to know how ordinary people related to the Army, and Swindon Borough Council posed the huge question, 'How do people relate to art in the public arena?'.

  In a ground-breaking project first begun in 1990, the London Borough of Croydon asked both visitors and non-visitors how they felt about museums and arts. They then scooped up the resulting mix of inspiration and despair and fashioned a new museum which dominated the specialist literature for a decade. It loaded a treasury of local anecdotes, photos and newsreel on to computer and challenged visitors to an onscreen quiz. It organised its objects pell-mell, and without a single boring label.

- *Will the visitor understand this gallery approach and feel motivated?*
  This second strand involves offering the visitor a proposed gallery structure, with main headings and supporting content. This is more difficult territory, because the gallery is often trying to educate the visitor just so he or she can take a view on whether the new approach sounds interesting. The visitor has a lot to take on board; first, to learn the subject, then to assess if it will be interesting as an exhibition, and then to criticise it. What's more, the visitor is unlikely to be offered alternatives to choose from, if he or she doesn't like it.

  Fortunately, in practice it is possible to *feel* the areas of enthusiasm; for example, the Willis Museum in Basingstoke wanted to update its Social History Gallery, using discrete chronological periods, from the Victorian Age through to the 1960s. It discovered that people dismissed the Victorians as a grey, grim, distant era, but they did get very emotional when Old Basingstoke was demolished during modernisation in the 1960s. The curators made the decision to tell the story of the 1960s modernisation at the beginning of the gallery, rather than at the end. This riveted their visitors at the outset and then allowed the museum to lead them back in time to the Victorians. And it worked like a charm.

  The Walker Art Gallery in Liverpool had the chance to open a new Decorative Arts Gallery, and boldly decided to link the collections back to methods of making, shaping and patterning the objects. It turned out that only if the gallery involved people in the *user*'s story would they then extend their interest to methods of making and patterning, which they otherwise found rather dull.

● *Is my content working successfully in executional terms?*
The analytical work done, the gallery designer swoops in on the strategy and content documents and brings it all to life... or not. All galleries have a need to test their prototype exhibits to see if they work and communicate, but by this stage the money has often run out. In principle, research can test out the prototypes and examine the effectiveness of their communication. In practice, this may well not happen until the summative evaluation, by which time it is all done and dusted, and the mistakes either avoided or built in.

Summative evaluation

With Lottery money and accountability in the ascendant, it will be increasingly difficult to avoid a post-mortem by research. But this can be a low point. At its most helpful, the evaluation follows visitors through the exhibition, event or show, working out pathways, points of absorption, communication, barriers and successes. What worked and what didn't? If a brave venture hasn't quite come off, what went wrong? In theory, the climate is one of learning for next time. In practice, it is full of anxiety about criticism. After all, what can they do now?

The Museum of London ran a summative evaluation on its new Prehistoric Gallery, to find that its low-tech dioramas worked brilliantly. Unfortunately, at the same time, visitors completely missed a signalled transition from the Stone Age into the Iron Age, and consequently failed to spot the significance of the sudden rash of swords and jewellery. Summative evaluation usually gives with one hand and takes with the other.

Architecture Week '98 was surprised to learn that almost nobody had spotted that it was on, even though the same people had visited some of its events. It discovered the need for a long publicity run-up, and also that its participating architects needed more support. Importantly, it identified an unsatisfied hunger for public dialogue with architects, which will guide the next Architecture Week.

Arguably, it is repeated events and performances which can best benefit from constructive feedback because they have the opportunity to evolve.

Qualitative research skills

In this climate, the qualitative researcher has to acquire new skills.

A client may have only a hazy idea of what he or she wants from research, and it is not unusual to be asked for some research in general. This leaves the researcher to put the structure on the project and divine the objectives by talking to as many of the stakeholders as possible.

Clearly, respondents can be most helpful when they are responding to specific stimuli, communication and plans. These are often not forthcoming, because the development team itself may not have articulated them. The researcher must be able to formulate working propositions, in the right spirit, and be adept at interpreting the nuances he or she hears in return. Tight budgets can mean overcrowded research, with parts of all three formative stages crowded into one. You are looking to use every fragment of information, and nothing is redundant.

At the debrief stage it will be important to:

- Bring the visitors to life
- Be clear about what need not be taken seriously and what must be

and most urgently to:

- Spell out the implications for action

The more upfront effort goes into specifying objectives, plans and communication goals, the more actionable the research will be. But the client may not like doing it. After all, he comes from a different world where he can wing it on expertise.

Integrating research into action

Thrilled though many arts organisations undoubtedly are to get real information from their visitors, there is a hiatus once the results are in. It is quite difficult to convert research into action, and this often leads to a type of inertia. This particularly applies in big institutions, where lots of petty problems can build up into major obstacles.

Not only are the galleries tripped up by events and logistics, there is often a more fundamental problem. We now understand our visitors' point of view, but this doesn't tell us directly what we have to do. We still have to make that decision. If they were developing advertising, galleries would work to achieve one focused, perfect message. As it is, they are trying to create an orchestra of messages, which must work as a whole.

The researcher can help by staying alongside the development team in the manner of the audience advocates at the Science Museum, acting as surrogate visitor and distilling the wisdom of other studies. The research report will often be passed on to the designer and brief chunks summarised for political purposes, but ultimately it appears that much of the insight cannot be mobilised.

Some effects of audience feedback

A body of knowledge has gradually accumulated about visitor preferences as a result of increasing research. This has contributed dramatically to the evolution of museums and galleries over the past decade. If you haven't been, say, to the Natural History Museum for ten years, you will be shocked and delighted by the change in atmosphere and the riot of things to do. This is starting to become the norm for all museums.

People now acknowledge visitors' needs for creature comforts:

- Good lavatories
- A pleasant place to eat
- A place to sit
- Fresh air
- Clear signs and orientation

Also, willy-nilly, displays have become more entertaining. Learning is fun. This means lots of hands-on and interactives, with buttons to press and screens to play with. Knowing that if they fail to engage the children they will lose the parents as well, museums have created child-friendly environments, and discovered coincidentally that this is how adults like to learn too.

The ordinary visitor is people-centred and this has often been the key to interpretation, expressing objects through the people who use them. Nothing goes down better than seeing a whole environment recreated before you and recreations of rooms, shops, even whole streets are to be found in the most respectable museums these days.

Nowadays, it is the executional tone of the organisation which accounts for brand identity at least as much as content. But the search for the perfect communication vehicle for the task arises afresh with every new idea to be expressed. This will surely lead to an increased need for visitor input, but whether this role is taken up by qualitative research or by in-house advocates remains to be seen.

PRACTICALITIES

All right, so qualitative research is to provide the bridges between the audience, the subject matter and the collections. And it is going to prove itself as an agent of enrichment and enlightenment to an arts establishment which is leery of public taste. How exactly does it go about it?

The techniques are the same as qualitative research anywhere: a mix of group discussions and in-depth interviews plus a good number of accompanied visits and audience observation sessions. There are, however, issues concerning recruitment and stimulus material which are specific to the arts, and to museums and galleries in particular.

Arts services are not commodities in the way that Mars Bars or even television programmes are. They have a unique relationship with the local community they serve. Museums, galleries and theatres are local landmarks. Everyone in the land who visits the National Gallery will have to come to Trafalgar Square. Everyone in the land who wants to see the Willis Museum at Basingstoke will have to come to Basingstoke town centre.

This raises a problem for targeting and recruitment. Should each establishment address itself to a *local* or a *national* audience?

Defining the target audience for research

The Willis Museum in Basingstoke may confine itself to serving the local community, but the National Gallery enjoys a remit of national UK significance, even though the bulk of its visitors are drawn from Greater London and from overseas tourists. This is a dilemma both for marketing and research. Who is the target audience?

It is more practical to go for the Greater London audience, as they offer the most immediate prospect of increasing visitor numbers, but a national resource must mould itself to the needs of its national catchment area. The Gallery and its researchers have to make hard choices about where the most effective research will be done – in the regions? In Greater London? In the museum itself?

In reality, the recruitment and running of group discussions often takes place in the museum itself, because of the practical difficulty in finding clusters of respondents from outside.

Sample structure

Clearly, the sample structure needs to be designed to further the goals of the project under discussion, but this is easier said than done. We have seen how potential visitors in the regions can be sacrificed in order to take advantage of visitors on the spot.

Sample design too is under great pressure. The Lottery considers £5000 to be an appropriate sum for an individual research project, and this is the industry norm for all but the very largest projects.

Picture a sizeable museum and gallery, say in Birmingham or Liverpool. They would like to segment their audiences as would an fmcg product, identifying the optimal consumer and speaking to them. But this is a luxury. Remember, the arts are now mandated to become accessible across the board. They must address the broadest audience possible. The result is that they elect to address very broad audiences indeed, perhaps with no more than a split by life stage or perhaps by visitor/non-visitor status. The information obtained is, of course, useful and valid, but perhaps less easy to work with than if they had been able to identify precise segments of opinion.

Segmentation

A simple segmentation, currently much invoked, is between independent visitors, and parents visiting with children. This is a dramatic split, as parents will put up with almost anything to engage their children and get some learning into them. Independent visitors, on the other hand, are typically more childlike in their own right, demanding personal gratification and entertainment and impatient of poor production values.

Visitors are necessary, of course, to test how galleries and events are experienced and to help with the development of new projects, but the arts will not achieve growth unless they address non-visitors too. Visitor numbers are the magic statistic being bandied around at the moment. Arts organisations are at the beginning of the process of segmenting their non-visitors in order to help with successful targeting.

The museums often want to leap in and carry the word to every non-user in the land, but in practice the most helpful non-users will be those who are in a competitive marketplace. By consulting people who visit Disney, Tussauds, Heritage sites, pop concerts, the Trocadero and so forth, ideas from popular culture can invigorate the methods of traditional culture.

Interview methods

Group discussions are widely used and, where the subject is generic, for example, 'the future of family theatre' or 'people's relationship with GM foods', groups can be held in homes in the usual way. Very often, however, the ambience and layout of a particular venue are important to the task. Interviews then take place in the galleries or at the event itself. Holding group discussions over a sandwich lunch in the museum can turn out to be a successful tactic for inducing visitors to break off their visit and talk.

Observation and accompanied visits are extremely useful, often with time to consolidate the discussion by sitting down and talking at the end of the interview. The technique is not unlike accompanied shopping and aims to shadow consumers, noting their interests and encouraging them to clarify their reactions and decisions as they go.

All these methods require skilful recruitment on the day, and a heart-stopping business it is too. It is sometimes necessary to hold evening groups within the museum itself, and this can involve laborious planning and security.

Stimulus material

Clearly, where the performance, event, gallery or publicity is to be evaluated, the best stimulus material is the product itself. Similarly, if a new concept such as a museum and country park is to be developed, it is not too difficult to present the elements of the planned venue using trigger boards, for example, exhibition hall, seafront café, auditorium, etc., together with some visualisation.

On the other hand, the closer a gallery comes to researching its aesthetic subject matter, the more towering the problem of stimulus material becomes. This is a riddle which is only partially solved to date. Borrowing from the world of concept research, a gallery can craft together key images and propositions which give the shape of the planned development, but it is rarely adequate.

One reason is that pictures and key phrases too nearly resemble the old, dry display methods which have now become discredited. Another is that the potential visitor is being given a short cut to the bottom line. He or she gets the communication and thematic take-out without any of the evocative objects and displays which give the subject its resonance.

Oh dear, it becomes chicken-and-egg.

- You can't design a range of gallery displays and interactives until you are sure the themes are on the right track and you know what you are meant to be communicating.
- You can't evoke an aesthetic and intellectual engagement with these themes until you give people an evocative means of access using objects and displays.

Problem: How are you going to gauge the appeal of the themes?

The answer seems to lie closer to launching the visitor on an imaginative journey through the actual gallery experience. Storyboards, video collages, narrative tapes, all describing what the visitor will do and will discover as a result. But it's not ideal. Which ever way you look at it, there is a lot of duplicated work involved, and the gallery planners still have to sort out the effects of the gallery interactives from the content themes they are trying to assess.

Not everything can be checked out in advance, and at some point the planners must make their own leap of faith. Perhaps it will become more practical to research only the contentious issues in detail and to rely on the exploratory work upfront to guide the general thinking.

Doing it yourself

The draconian background of resources allocation is forcing both researchers and arts personnel to invent new ways to get the most out of their budgets. Some organisations, full of missionary zeal to get to grips with their visitors, resolve to conduct the research themselves. Involving a professional researcher to coach on method is not uncommon these days. The results are not entirely happy but, as a researcher, I would say that, wouldn't I?

Certainly there have been as many panics about recruitment, chagrin at no-shows and thin levels of data collection as there have been triumphant successes. Clearly, if the choice lies between running research yourself or having no research at all, the client is better off having a go. However, I am still haunted by the natural historian from Norfolk who went out to do qualitative research on the social history of the herring industry, and came back recommending a policy change towards the ecology of the marshland. Objective? I don't think so.

CONCLUSIONS

Qualitative research looks set to grow in the arts, not least because it is a useful tool for reassuring funders and sponsors. As the arts battle to define their place alongside the world of entertainment and leisure, they will need, increasingly, to harness the communication and media skills of the commercial world. Visitors will vote with their feet if content and production values are not up to standard, so the arts organisations will have to continue to consult people.

It will be interesting to see how the integrity of object and message will be preserved under these circumstances, and how the visual and creative arts in particular respond to input from the marketplace. The urgent question of how people learn from objects is still waiting to be answered. Before audience feedback can really take off, however, qualitative researchers have to develop more creative and effective ways of designing stimulus material.

This will be part of a growing desire on the part of arts interpreters as a whole to build a body of knowledge about visitors which will unify, guide and stimulate further work. Currently, each institution is reinventing the wheel. It is likely that qualitative researchers will contribute to this body, even though, poised as we are between the commercial world and academia, we do carry a health warning.

The gap which exists between research insight and action in the fields of interpretation and design will, over time, demand to be filled. Will these arts planners spring from qualitative research? I wonder. In the meantime, the arts world is experimenting, taking risks, asking big questions. In my role as researcher in the past few months, I have been asked to ponder:

- the meaning of art in the public arena.
- the public understanding of energy, and
- what gives Ancient Egypt its mystery?

What philosopher could ask for better?

KEY IDEAS

- Shifts in funding have fundamentally changed the agenda in the arts – the funding has now become conditional upon public benefit.
- The arts have resorted to seeking commercial sponsorship.
- Lottery funding is dependent upon clearly defined areas and objectives, including an understanding of the intended target audience, and this has forced arts organisations into the commercial world, starting with museums and galleries.
- Museums and galleries have moved from being the preservers of the nations' collections to being educators and interpreters of those collections, with access as a key issue.
- The competitive marketplace includes a huge range of options, and museums and galleries have identified families with children, and adults without children, as the two groups most easily targeted.
- Internally, museums and galleries have had to face a conflict between traditional curators with the increasing numbers of educators and interpreters who are opening up their world to critical visitors.
- Qualitative research is starting to act as a forum for the exchange of views of all parties.
- Research exerts pressure on museums and galleries to express their ideas in a form which visitors can grasp.
- Qualitative research is particularly useful and accepted for product development and formative evaluation, effectively creative development. Research at the front end is particularly fruitful. It explores how the target audience feels about the subject areas and how to help them feel motivated by the gallery idea.
- Audience feedback from existing or new exhibits and galleries has been invaluable in making displays more entertaining, and learning more fun.
- The performing arts face many of the same issues but, as yet, are still highly resistant to qualitative research methodology.

FURTHER READING

Durbin, G. (1996) *Developing Museum Exhibitions for Lifelong Learning*. The Stationery Office Group for Education in Museums, London.

Gammon, J. & Graham, B. (1997) 'Putting the value back into evaluation', in D. Thompson, A. Benefield, S. Bitgood, H. Shettel and R. Williams (eds) *Visitor Research: Theory, Research and Practice, Proceedings of the First Annual Conference*. The Visitor Studies Association, London.

Gardner, H. (1993) *Frames of Mind: The Theory of Multiple Intelligences* (2nd edn). Fontana Press, London.

Graham, J. & Gammon, B. A case study of how the Science Museum, London, is seeking to make learning central to the development of exhibitions.

Hooper-Greenhill, E. (1994) *Museums and Their Visitors*. Routledge, London.

Susie Fisher Group (1990) *Bringing History and the Arts to a New Audience*. Qualitative Research for the London Borough of Croydon, Croydon Clocktower, Katharine Street, Croydon CR9 1ET.

Chapter 10

Politics and Qualitative Research

Deborah Mattinson
Founding Director, Opinion Leader Research

with

Tim Bell
Chairman, Chime Communications Group

Editor's introduction

Political parties have recognised the need to better understand the electorate for many years. The Labour Party, stung by the electoral disaster in 1983, were relatively late in fully recognising its importance and in utilising qualitative research for this purpose.

This chapter outlines the issues facing party politics with regard to listening to the electorate and accepting research as legitimate. It explains how the careful use of research has enabled the Labour Party to tap into the beliefs and views of a highly apathetic and disillusioned electorate. It explores the controversy surrounding the use of research in the sphere of policy development – whether this is legitimate or a replacement for conviction and belief among politicians.

Deborah Mattinson and Tim Bell explore the issues from a highly personal perspective, having been deeply involved in this field for many years. They give us an invaluable and highly illuminating insight into an area which has become the focus of media attention and much public debate.

THE CONTEXT: THE POLITICAL FRAMEWORK

A brief history of the political focus group in the UK

All the main political parties have been conducting quantitative opinion polling since the 1960s. Typically, this was used to map voter behaviour and to monitor the ups and downs of campaign success and failure. Giving comfort to those who take solace in numbers and despite its lack of diagnostic, in-depth information, this sufficed until the late 1970s. In 1978, it fell to adman Tim Bell at Saatchi and Saatchi to introduce qualitative techniques to British politics via the Conservative Party. Bell says he recommended using focus groups as he would have done to any client: to help develop the advertising which the agency was working on – the highly successful 'Labour isn't working' campaign.

Tim Bell, now a Conservative working peer, was to remain critically involved in Conservative Party campaigning over the next decade.

> 'We did not set out to do anything radical. We simply used the tools that we would have used for any client to help us to refine the message we were sending to our key target audience – disaffected Labour voters. It worked because it spoke an obvious truth.'

The 1983 election

It did work, and a slightly baffled Labour Party was ushered into the obscurity and internecine warfare that left it with little stomach for the punter's point of view. Labour's lamentable performance in 1983 demonstrated how far out of touch it had become during that period, while the Conservatives seemed to hit the button every time. Says Bell, 'It was the politician's (Mrs Thatcher's) instinct that was right, and that was why it worked. She understood the voter's dreams and aspirations. Her vision was their vision. Qualitative research could never have invented her conviction. It had credibility because it was real. Where the research came in was to help refine our advertising messages.'

Neil Kinnock

Meanwhile the election of Neil Kinnock as party leader and his appointment of an impressive new team, including the young and talented TV producer Peter Mandelson as Director of Communications, heralded change. Mandelson hired Philip Gould, another prominent adman, to conduct a review of the party's communications. Gould recommended, as part of a far-reaching and radical programme, the use of qualitative research 'to help to understand how the Party is seen by its natural constituency'.

The first Labour group discussions

The Labour Party's first group discussions took place in October 1985 during the Party Conference among Labour voters who had 'switched' to the Conservatives. A researcher and a planner, Roddy Glen and Leslie

Butterfield, took the pulse of that eventful two or three days, during which Neil Kinnock made his powerful 'expulsion of the militants' speech. The vivid nature of the feedback had never been experienced before. The Labour Party did not like everything it heard, but it rang true. The party was hooked.

With Gould, around that time, I set up and co-ordinated the Labour Party's Shadow Communications Agency – a group of communications experts who were to advise and implement campaign recommendations on a freelance or voluntary basis. Unlike the Conservatives, who were still riding high in the opinion polls, Labour was felt to be incapable of attracting a decent advertising agency. The semi-covert operation added glamour, while enabling the party to cherry-pick sympathetic talent, who often offered their services for free.

Within this framework, I organised a group of some 20 qualitative researchers and agency planners who were eager to help, and we applied ourselves to the task of helping the party to understand how the electorate felt about it.

The 1987 election

So the 1987 General Election was the first in which all main political parties were using qualitative as well as quantitative research, and the game was raised across the board. Why had this move happened at this point and what were the consequences? Had the voter changed, had the politician, or both? To fully understand the changes that led to this, the beginning of an ongoing trend that is continually reinforced by all parties, it is necessary to go back a step and examine the nature of the relationship between voter and politician.

The legacy of a dysfunctional democracy

More than a quarter of the population never vote in general elections, and this figure masks a greater deficit among certain groups: for example, young people, working-class people and people living in inner cities. Worse still, twice as many people vote in general elections as vote in local and European elections.

Yet voting represents the zenith of most individuals' political activity, not the nadir. Only 28% have ever attended a public meeting of any kind, just 12% have ever contacted their local MP, a mere 5% take part in local or political campaigning, and fewer than 1% have ever stood for public office. Again these figures are still bleaker among certain key groups, often the same people – the young, the working class, and women.

Disillusionment with politics and politicians

Over recent years government, politics and politicians have been held in lower regard than ever before. Perceptions of incompetence and sleazy behaviour have combined to give a sense that politicians were in it for themselves and out of touch with the way ordinary people live their lives. The distortions of the tabloid media can take some share of the blame for this, sensationalising the private lives of individuals in the public eye in a less than edifying way.

But most politicians would accept that the rarefied hothouse atmosphere of Westminster has not always been helpful in connecting them with the electorate. The above statistics suggest that people who join political parties, who get involved in political (or other) campaigning, who even go to see their MPs are in the kind of minority to strongly imply that they may not be typical. Yet for many MPs these were their main point of reference; the closest they would come to dialogue with the ordinary electorate. Thus, a further distortion is added to the mix by politicians' own misperception of how people live and what they care about.

Combined with the resulting poor communications, it is small wonder that the electorate has often seemed apathetic and cynical. What is surprising is not that so many choose not to vote, but rather that anyone voted at all:

'They're just in it for themselves, they couldn't give a damn about the likes of us!'

'They're all the same and they're all a load of bloody rubbish!'

'Useless – bloody useless – just out for themselves!'

A vicious circle

So, dysfunctional democracy had become a vicious circle, fired at best by mutual misunderstanding between the public and the people who represent them, and, at worst, by mutual contempt. Its legacy had been an electorate so disenchanted by its politicians that it had become almost entirely detached from the political process: passive citizens de-skilled in democratic practice and locked in a moribund and unrewarding relationship with those in power.

THE ROLE FOR QUALITATIVE RESEARCH

Reviewing policy

The debate

Tim Bell remains adamant that qualitative research in politics should be confined to message refinement, and not used in a more general marketing sense for 'product development'; in this area, policy development. 'The politician's instinct should prevail. Politics designed to have popular appeal will smack of artifice. The voters admire political conviction not expediency…that is not to say that qualitative research does not have a vital role to play in presentation.'

Labour shared some of the same reservations. Yet the post-1987 Policy Review, brainchild of NUPE leader Tom Sawyer, member of Labour's National Executive who was later to become Labour's General Secretary, was designed to be a response to electoral failure. The general view was that the campaign and presentation had worked but that the product itself, the policies, had been unpopular.

Labour's policy review

Labour set about a systematic review of all the main policy areas. The starting point for this was a programme known as 'Labour Listens', in which a series of 'listening exercises' among party members as well as experts in specific areas and the wider public were consulted on key issues.

This was in part a device to bring party members and policy experts along with the new thinking by involving them from the beginning. It was also a genuine and radical consultation exercise: the first of its kind, and one that has recently been imitated by the defeated Conservative Party – even using the same name, 'the Conservatives Listen'. Damning qualitative research evidence during and after the 1987 campaign had convinced Labour Party leaders of the communications breakdown between party and politician. Part of the programme even involved a party political broadcast in which voters talked about the issues dear to their hearts, before the camera pulled back to reveal that they had been talking to a brick wall.

Presentations of voters' views were a vital part of the process, but the overall programme was carefully planned to ensure that these acted as an aide to decision-making and not a substitute for it. Six core review groups were established, covering the economy, industry and the workplace, social affairs, democracy, the environment, and foreign affairs and defence.

The research

These review groups were managed overall by a mix of party officers and politicians and chaired by Kinnock himself. Each review group included politicians, policy experts and party officers. Sawyer remained closely involved with the process, and reinforced the role of the qualitative research programme in meeting the review's objectives. Speaking in June 1988 he said a vital component would be to 'ascertain people's hopes and fears' and pointed out that 'people often had only a "distorted caricature" of Labour's policies…the party might not like that fact, but it had to start from there'.

The findings

He was right. The qualitative research I briefed into each of the review groups on a regular basis was unequivocal. Voters' two strongest perceptions of Labour were, first, that it remained dominated by 'extremist' activists whose presence initially provoked ridicule, but ultimately was a source of fear, especially among women.

Second, and linked to this, their view was that Labour's overarching objective was 'anti-success' in favour of a levelling down towards the most needy members of society. It was felt to be opposed to personal prosperity. It was seen as drab and out of date in some areas of policy and worryingly 'loony' in others, notably defence (with its long-standing commitment to unilateral disarmament). Areas governed by local authorities, often voters' only experience of Labour in power, also came in for much criticism. Supposedly 'politically correct' measures on race and gender were much derided by the tabloid media, and often cited anecdotally by respondents. They provided vivid images of how a likely Labour government would look, and fed into the hands of the Conservative Party.

These were big problems to tackle. During this period, other members of the Shadow Communications Agency and I reported back on the detailed findings from dozens of group discussions on a range of issues covered by the review. These attempted to define the status quo, generally in terms of each party's strengths and weaknesses. They looked at specific views in each policy area, then went on to pre-test possible ideas developed by the working group, and finally to explore communications strategies for certain policy initiatives.

That the Policy Review was successful cannot be in doubt, but it took longer to achieve its ultimate objective of electoral victory than anyone involved might have expected, even the most pessimistic.

The electorate's anxieties

The Policy Review managed to address some of the electorate's greatest anxieties, perhaps most notably the commitment to unilateral disarmament. However, many of those closely involved, including Philip Gould, by then my business partner, would argue that the qualitative research was only used in a manner consistent with the approach developed by Tim Bell and the Conservatives. He believed that we sought to understand how to persuade voters to our view rather than to 'meekly acquiesce in the light of public opinion'.

For many aspects of the review this is probably true. It is well-illustrated by the ingenious development of 'symbolic' policies, designed to demonstrate Labour's deeper convictions. Our role model for this was Mrs

Thatcher's sale of council houses to dramatise the Conservatives' commitment to a property-owning democracy. Bell and Thatcher instinctively understood the popularity of such measures and qualitative research informed their views. Led by Patricia Hewitt, then heading Kinnock's policy team, we used research to help promote the most popular areas of the policy package, especially those that could act as shorthand to the party's values and beliefs.

Qualitative research and policy

However, I strongly believe that qualitative research at times played a more fundamental role than this: that the stark findings surrounding voters' perceptions of many aspects of Labour's policy were vital in hardening the resolve of those brave enough to seek revision. Without it the will might not have been found to make some of those fundamental policy changes; changes that would ultimately pave the way for electoral success.

Communications strategy

The gender gap

One of the best examples of the use of qualitative research in political communications was as a tool in addressing the 'gender gap' – the historical problem that women were much more drawn to the Conservatives and, conversely, much more rejecting of Labour than men. It was true to say that if female suffrage had never happened, Labour would have won every election since the war!

The gender gap was encouraged and nurtured by Mrs Thatcher. With Bell and his team advising, she understood well the strength of admiration of female voters for Conservative values as personified by her. They also knew the levels of mistrust felt towards Labour, and, unsurprisingly, sought to enhance the Conservatives' poll lead among women at every turn.

By the mid-1990s, Labour realised that neither a new package of policies nor even a new leader was shifting the deadlock of women voters' lack of engagement with the party. I was invited to join a working party established to investigate the problem under the political stewardship of Clare Short. Members included Patricia Hewitt, by now at the Institute for Public Policy Research, publisher Carmen Callil, lawyer Helena Kennedy, and other policy and communications experts.

The first task was to provide an update of women's views of the party. This time the news was more encouraging. It quickly transpired that the core problem was one of communications, not one of substance or policy. In fact many of Labour's policies were extremely appealing to women, especially its strong focus on health and education. The problem was that too many women simply did not know what Labour stood for any more – there was a vague sense of change but no sense of what the change had brought about. It appeared that there were too many barriers preventing the party's communications from reaching their target.

Further research

In a further stage of research we set about preparing a more precise diagnosis of the problem. We spent many hours showing potential female voters TV footage of key politicians in different modes of communication: speaking in the House of Commons, in a formal 'Newsnight'-type interview, in documentaries and in more relaxed chat-show formats. We also explored newspaper and magazine news coverage, interviews and features.

The findings were clear. Politicians, in their attempts to communicate with women, missed the mark again and again. They were too verbose, too jargon laden and too pompous to connect. In the case of exchanges in the House of Commons they were also too childish and ill-behaved. As one respondent put it:

'I mean if we were behaving like that you wouldn't be running this meeting would you? You just wouldn't be getting anywhere if we were all just up and down and shouting. I think it seems a waste of time and a waste of our money. That, I think, is very frustrating for the ordinary person.'

Control groups of men

Groups of men set up to provide a 'control' strongly suggested that although the problem was less pronounced – men were less intimidated by jargon, and more comfortable with the adversarial nature of much of the politics that was served up to them – it nevertheless did exist on both sides of the gender gap. This was reassuring, meaning that, at worst, attempting to solve the problem for women would not turn men off. At best, improving communications with women would also improve communications with men.

'Winning Words'

The group produced 'Winning Words' which I presented to the Shadow Cabinet in 1996. This concluded that Labour must urgently address a number of key issues relating to media strategy and targeting women voters.

Choice of media

The first key finding was that one of Labour's main problems was choice of media: that too little active involvement with women's press, daytime TV and radio meant that too few women were actually reached by Labour's messages.

This was not simply a point about ratings. The qualitative research strongly suggested that when the party did 'get it right' (in particular we looked at a highly successful women's magazine interview on crime with the then Shadow Home Secretary, Tony Blair), the effect was powerful: the media became, in part, the message, with women voters noticing the media choice and believing that a special effort had been made to reach out to them: 'You think they must really want to talk to the likes of me or they wouldn't do it would they?'.

Respondents also pointed out that politicians were forced to behave in a rather different way in this less familiar medium, and this is always to the advantage of the viewer/reader: 'They (Richard and Judy, etc.) know what we want to hear – and it's on our level.'

Getting the message right

Remaining points focused around getting the message right and speaking the right language. This included being seen to really take the issues seriously by use of appropriate behaviour, rather than behaviour which was regarded as an abuse of the time, money and responsibility vested in MPs (such as Prime Minister's Questions, now seen because of the televising of Parliament):

'It's just embarrassing – I don't watch it any more.'

'Just a load of shouting – you don't know what point is being made.'

Also vital was the use of simple language; being responsive and actually answering the question:

'You never know where you are with them, do you?'

'A politician never answers a question. They give us chit chat chit chat, but they never answer the question. They go all the way around it, but they never answer the question.'

Respondents' suspicions

Respondents revealed themselves to be suspicious that over-complication and too much reliance on jargon would often be a deliberate attempt to obfuscate: 'Sometimes you think "what on earth was all that about?" They do it just to confuse you.'

Use of statistics was one of the examples of obfuscation most often used. Statistics appear to be devalued to the point where using them at all implies attempting to support a shaky argument or to shore up a dodgy case. The perception is that they can be used to manipulate the meaning of anything and are absolutely not trusted:

'I don't trust statistics because you never know if they are true or not – I mean anyone can throw figures around can't they?'

'One side comes up with one lot of figures and the other side comes up with a different lot – you don't know where you are, so you end up not listening to any of it.'

Effective communication

By contrast, the use of real examples and anecdotal evidence always seemed to be more powerful. This proves the old adage drawn from Third World charity fund-raising that one child dying is a tragedy, while one million dying is a statistic.

'When she got specific and talked about the woman who came to her for help it all started to mean something to me.'

'That story about the security guards supporting their families on £1.19 an hour – it breaks your heart, doesn't it?'

This approach appears more effective still when politicians use examples from their own lives, creating empathy in a way that nothing else can: 'She understands the emotions behind choosing who is going to look after your child – she's been there.'

Respondents also demand that politicians respect the viewer both by giving a strong performance and looking the part – expectations are high yet easily dashed, and appearances count for a lot, especially, like it or like it not, for women politicians. Mrs Thatcher was the role model again:

'I think all politicians when they are elected should go to acting school or something like Mrs Thatcher did to learn to project themselves.'

'They are like an ambassador. They are going to be the centre of attention wherever they go. It's a question of looking the part.'

'Some of these Labour women I think are an absolute disgrace. Their hair is greasy and unwashed – they wouldn't inspire me to vote for them because you've got to have the right image.'

This presentation had a major impact. Combined with other initiatives led from Blair's office, Labour's media strategy targeted women more effectively and, by the General Election, the gender gap was closed for the first time in decades.

PRACTICALITIES

Recruitment

There are a number of practical considerations raised by the specific nature of political qualitative research. The first relates to recruitment. Highly skilled and efficient recruiters up and down the country sigh when my office calls up to arrange a political job.

The problem stems from most people's lack of connection with the subject matter. We are all aware of the problems posed by attempting to involve people in a discussion in an area in which they feel unconfident or disinterested. In this context, politics is a bigger challenge than anything else that I have ever worked on.

Many potential respondents feel they know nothing about the subject, and naturally fear 'being put on the spot'. Women in particular (often, as revealed above, our key target audience) feel disengaged. Our recruitment attempts in the early days too often resulted in half-empty rooms, with respondent drop-out rates dramatically higher than might be usually anticipated and aimed for.

Subterfuge

I am opposed to subterfuge in recruitment, believing strongly that the 'contract' between researcher and researched demands honesty and transparency as vital ingredients for creating the mutual respect that results in the best research outcomes. However, the brutal truth is that if we tell people that the topic is 'politics', they will be scared off. We usually find a formula that refers to more specific topics under discussion, for example, views of the health service or views of education. Politics then arises naturally in a context that most respondents feel more comfortable with.

The punter

A related problem is the need to avoid 'the punter'. Again, this will be a familiar problem to most practitioners, but it is magnified in political work. In many groups of 'normal' respondents, whose confidence in the area is low, and desire to discuss issues even lower, there lurks the 'expert' who has strong views, passionately held, and who will dominate the group (to the relief of everyone else involved except for the hapless moderator). This is, of course, principally an issue of group dynamics and management, but if such respondents can be screened out in the first place, our jobs are easier.

This approach calls for a fairly sophisticated recruitment questionnaire and very well briefed recruiters. Over the years we have developed a team of specially trained interviewer recruiters who really understand the very specific requirements, and, remarkably, are able to deliver again and again. This is essential.

Group dynamics

People's lack of engagement with the topic also leads to predictable problems in group dynamics and management. Respondents' confidence (and often interest) is so low that they can be very reticent. There is also a greater than average temptation to 'go with the flow' – if one person (see notes on the punter above) expresses a strongly held view – why argue? Deference is the instinctive reaction: 'he/she is bound to know more than I do!'.

> 'If I'd known we were going to be talking about politics so much I'd have brought my husband along – he knows all about this!'

> 'When they talk about it at work or in the pub I just switch off. My eyes glaze over!'

> 'I agree with her – well she sounds as if she knows what she's talking about.'

Yet, as with many other subjects, the underlying views of those who are naturally reticent are interesting and valuable. The issue is how to elicit them and prevent steering within the group.

We have practised many useful techniques over the years, with this in mind. One of the most valuable is the simple written trigger test as a preamble to debate, thus ensuring that each individual commits up front to their own view and is then obliged to defend this view. I always use this in controversial areas, and often early on in groups as a simple warm-up device. Well-prepared 'questionnaires' can overcome the literacy problems that sometimes arise.

Projective techniques

The full range of projective techniques can also be useful in unlocking underlying feelings in this very emotional area. We often use similes (the old chestnut of what kind of animal is Tony Blair can be very revealing – no, I'm not saying!). We also use picture sorts, word sorts, thought bubbles and sentence completions. Drafting obituaries, wedding announcements and other familiar constructions can work well. We often encourage respondents to work collaboratively in pairs or mini-groups, making the sessions very interactive and involving. Respondents gain confidence and surprise themselves:

> 'My husband would be amazed if he'd heard me talking tonight – he'd never have thought I'd have anything to say!'

'It's incredible what you actually do know isn't it?'

'You'll have to chuck us out now – you'll never shut us up!'

Urgency

A further practical issue is not unique to this field but is very prevalent: urgency. If you are in the middle of an election campaign you want feedback on the findings almost instantly if they are to be 'actionable'. This is the most extreme example, but in my experience politicians are an unusually impatient bunch and when they know that work is in the field they want their findings fast.

We have had to develop a number of methods of operating to deal with this. The first is about casting, and it probably goes without saying that political research is not an ideal training ground for young, inexperienced researchers. First in the Shadow Communications Agency and now at my agency Opinion Leader Research, we have built a seasoned team of very experienced pros who can handle this subject matter and, in particular, have the analytical maturity to be able to feedback topline findings accurately.

They are helped by a number of systems: a team to provide fast turnaround transcripts, and, where necessary, a stenographer to attend the groups and produce instant notes from which a topline debrief can be prepared. During the 1997 General Election we ran a qualitative monitor of key marginal seats which involved being in the field most evenings covering a very wide geographic spread. Typically, a fast feedback debrief would be with the client by 10 a.m. the following day. Results were then analysed thoroughly and fed into a twice-weekly detailed report and presented to the weekly campaign strategy committee.

Over-enthusiasm

A final point on practicalities is how to 'aim off' for the sheer enthusiasm of any politician who is converted to 'listening to the people' in this way. Many politicians, like the voters themselves, start off the process as reluctant participants, sceptical of the process and concerned about manipulation. This is particularly true since the 'focus group' rose to fame as a tool in New Labour's armoury. However, in my experience, any politician who has witnessed the work at close hand soon changes this perspective, often adopting the passion of the convert.

For many politicians, the authentic voice of the voter, especially if witnessed directly by observing groups, is compelling to the point where he or she can be tempted to act on impressionistic findings without recourse to systematic analysis and without setting those findings in the context of other work. This is where building a close client relationship based on mutual respect is even more important than in many other projects. The researcher must be able to offer his or her mature view of how to interpret the findings. This implies a long-term relationship and a deep understanding of the work in hand. It also strongly suggests the need to use qualitative research alongside other methodologies, particularly statistically reliable quantification.

THE FUTURE

Thus qualitative research has made its presence felt in the world of politics with dramatic effect, and perhaps most apparently in the immediate afterglow of the 1997 election. Perhaps the landslide victory could have spoken for itself, but qualitative research conducted in the days after the poll revealed a stunned electorate who, for the first time in many years, felt excited and enthusiastic about politics in Britain. They felt involved in the change process that the government was embarking on:

'It's a fresh start!'

'It's out with the old cynicism – it's bringing in hope!'

'A couple of us went down to Downing Street to see him in – it was fantastic to be part of it!'

'I didn't even think I'd vote until the last minute and now I feel incredibly excited to be part of it!'

Amazingly, even now, as the 'new' government approaches mid-term, voters' enthusiasm has not waned – and neither has the politicians'. As might be expected from a party that used public consultation and market research to develop its own positioning, the new era of Labour government has brought with it a very different agenda. Civil servants were astonished to find themselves working with ministers who not only briefed market research and took detailed interest in the findings, but also asked to sit in on the discussion groups themselves.

The government is run by men and women who have seen how important it is to engage citizens, and who remember what happens when politicians forget to listen. Ironically, it is now the Conservative Party, once an arch exponent of the art, which now needs to learn the same lesson.

New techniques

Since 1 May 1997 the government has set about involving people as never before. The people of Scotland and Wales have taken part in referenda to determine their own futures. Innovative new consultation methods such as citizens' panels, citizens' juries and citizens' workshops are now being built into the planning stage of many departmental programmes. All seek to actively involve the public in the decisions that affect their lives.

There is now pressure on us as market researchers to rise to this challenge, keeping pace with government initiatives with research solutions that are both sufficiently imaginative to truly engage citizens, and methodologically rigorous to withstand the kind of scrutiny that will inevitably follow.

By adapting the traditional researcher's repertoire of panels, polls and focus groups and continually refining more active and participative consultation such as citizens' juries and deliberative polling, we can ensure that public consultation and market research remain at the heart of government decision-making.

In conclusion, I believe that if we succeed, the seismic shift in terms of political will that has found its voice, at least in part, through qualitative research can now translate into open accountable government in which citizens are truly empowered.

KEY IDEAS

- The Labour Party became interested in qualitative research after the disastrous election of 1983 when they realised that the party needed to understand the electorate much better.
- Most people have very little involvement in politics and, especially among certain key groups, voting turnout is very poor.
- People are highly disillusioned with politics, and the inability of politicians to communicate effectively with the electorate has made this worse.
- The role of qualitative research remains controversial, particularly with regard to reviewing policy where some feel that this should be led solely by the politicians' instinct and conviction.
- Qualitative research can contribute to policy development by helping to harden the resolve of those with strong beliefs to initiate changes.
- Qualitative research has a clear role in the development of better communications between politicians and the electorate.
- Research has been used to help refine the media, the message, the use of language and the tone.
- Methodological problems are complex, as respondents may be apathetic, anxiously ignorant or loudly expert.
- Techniques are required to help unlock underlying feelings in a very emotional area where respondents often lack confidence or the right words to express themselves.

- Qualitative research is now established in the political arena, as the government is increasingly run by men and women who recognise the need to engage citizens.

FURTHER READING

Coote, A. & Mattinson, D. (1997) *Twelve Good Neighbours: the Citizen as Juror.* Fabian Society, London.

Gould, P. (1998) *The Unfinished Revolution.* Little, Brown, London.

Hewitt, P. & Mattinson, D. (1989) *Winning Women's Votes.* Fabian Society, London.

Mattinson, D. (1998) *People Power in Politics.* Market Research Society Conference.

Radice, G. & Pollard, S. (1992–94) *The Southern Discomfort Series.* Fabian Society, London.

Wintour, P. & Hughes, C. (1989) *Labour Rebuilt.* Fourth Estate, London.

Chapter 11

Qualitative Research in the Social Policy Field

Alan Hedges
Independent Research Consultant

with

Sue Duncan
Director of Policy Studies, Centre for Management and Policy Studies

Editor's introduction

This chapter explores the development, implementation and evaluation of social policy for public sector bodies. These range from central and local government through government agencies and quangos to housing associations, trade unions, charitable and voluntary groups and so on. Pressure on public bodies has grown through changing structures, rising public expectations and a new emphasis on consultation and partnership. Government is now pushing for policy-making to be evidence based, and 'joined up' across departmental boundaries.

However, as Alan Hedges explains in detail, understanding the public in this sphere is very different from understanding consumers in the commercial world. For a variety of reasons, policy-makers and their social researchers are not just dealing with simple customer relationships. The policy issues are often highly complex, issues like 'fairness' need to be considered, and trade-offs may need to be made between conflicting interests.

This chapter explores the importance of understanding the public in the context of developing and evaluating social policy, why this is problematic, and how qualitative research can help.

I was delighted that Alan was joined in writing the chapter by Sue Duncan, then in charge of research at the Department of Social Security. She brings a wealth of experience to the chapter and knows firsthand about the realities of implementing policy and using research in the public sector. This combination of hands-on experience with one of the most respected thinkers and writers in the field of qualitative research makes this chapter a fascinating and enlightening read.

THE CONTEXT: UNDERSTANDING THE PUBLIC SECTOR

Why public bodies need to understand the public

Pressures on public bodies have grown in various ways that increase the need to understand their public.

Questioning of top-down authority

People increasingly expect public bodies to develop policies and provide services that take account of the public's needs and wishes. The days are gone (if they ever existed) when voters were content to elect MPs or councillors every so often and leave all the decisions up to them between elections.

As a society, we are becoming dissatisfied with top-down decision-making, and less inclined to assume that those in authority know best what is good for us. As the public gets more information and governmental processes are more subject to inspection by the media, it becomes increasingly apparent that 'experts' don't have all the answers. In recent years this has been evident in public responses to the BSE crisis, and latterly to GM foods. Research shows that in some fields people are now more likely to believe pressure groups like Greenpeace than official government information. This subject is explored in Deborah Mattinson's chapter on politics.

Rising expectations

Public expectations about services rise with increasing affluence and developing technology, but the ability of public bodies to deliver those services satisfactorily has often been under pressure, particularly after a long period where cost-cutting has been a key policy driver. This has increased the need for policies to be effective and carefully targeted.

Cohesive policy

There is an increasing realisation that the activities of different departments and agencies interact, and that public needs flow across organisational boundaries. But departments and agencies are still inclined to view the world in terms of their own policies – they are having to learn that real people take a broader view, and are both motivated and constrained by a richer and more complex web of factors.

Evidence-based policy

Increasingly, we see an insistence that policy should be based where possible on evidence and not on assumption. One of the functions of social research is to challenge and explore assumptions about how people operate and what they want.

Consultation and partnership

Government is now recognising not only that people dislike being excluded from policy-making, but that things usually work better if they have been involved in its development (see also below).

Changing structures

The 1980s and 1990s have been periods of rapid change in public services, structures, regulations and technology. Many familiar services are being delivered by different bodies, in different ways, under different rules or different names. These new bodies have to learn about their public – and their public has to learn about them. The culture in which they operate has also been changing, and organisations have had to find out what is happening, and more importantly why it is happening.

There is a growing range of semi-autonomous government agencies, quangos and other bodies to which the public cannot directly elect representatives, but which people may feel are important to them – for example, NHS Trusts.

All the above developments have made it increasingly imperative that public bodies should understand what their public does, thinks, feels, knows and wants. The 1999 *Modernising Government* White Paper says, 'We must understand the needs of all people, and respond to them. This too is a crucial part of modernising government.'

Why understanding is crucial

There are three main reasons why understanding is crucial.

- It is necessary to the development of effective and appropriate policies in a complex and fast-changing society.

- Authorities increasingly realise that if you want to change behaviour you often have to change the culture that generates it – and that means understanding quite a lot about:
  - *why* people do what they do;
  - their attitudes, values, images, feelings and beliefs;
  - the broad context within which policy operates.
- Many aspects of public sector policy involve communicating and marketing – policies don't work well if the public doesn't understand what is supposed to happen, and if the culture is pulling people in the opposite direction.

How public and private sectors differ

On some levels there is a lot in common between the public and private sectors, but it is worth focusing briefly on some differences.

Limitations of the 'customer' model

It became fashionable for a while during the 1980s to see the relationship between public bodies and the public they serve as essentially the same as the relationship between a commercial supplier and its customers. Up to a point this view provided a valuable and refreshing perspective. Customer orientation helped to enliven some organisations which had become monolithic and unresponsive.

But the 'customer' model fits only part of the complex relationship between public bodies and the public, and the mood has swung to recognise people as citizens and taxpayers as well as consumers of public services.

Some important spheres of public policy have little to do with customer relationships. We might think (for example) of issues like the management of nuclear waste, food safety, air pollution, global warming, measures to reduce drink-drive accidents, the ways in which the Health Service should set priorities for using limited resources, the problems of attracting staff into important public services like nursing, and so on. In most of these cases there is no one whom you would normally describe as a 'customer'.

Moral issues

There is also a range of issues that might seem more consumer-like, but have broader implications for public bodies than for private sector organisations. Public bodies are not usually concerned only with marketability; they typically have to consider wider moral dimensions, for example, 'fairness', 'rights', 'needs' and 'the public good'.

A commercial supplier normally has no obligation to consider minority needs if these cannot be met profitably; for example, we would not normally criticise a commercial company for concentrating on the profitable parts of the market, but we expect public authorities to act 'fairly' and to take account both of the needs and rights of minorities, and also of the interests of society as a whole.

Captive markets

Commercial markets are essentially competitive, but in some public sector fields people have no alternative supplier. They cannot choose a different source of welfare if they don't get on with the Benefits Agency or a different source of planning control if they don't approve of what the local authority does. This is sometimes less true than it used to be because of privatisation and the introduction of market mechanisms, but it still applies over a wide area.

Moreover, legislation and regulation *bind* members of the public in ways that have no private sector parallel, so there is a moral duty to consider their outcomes and implications for the citizen.

Stakeholder dialogue

Policy debate has latterly begun to shift from the simple 'customer' model of the 1980s towards the concept of 'stakeholders'. In any social policy field there is a wide range of 'stakeholders' who may need to be researched or consulted:

- *Direct customers* of a service are of course important stakeholders, but the term potentially includes anybody who might be directly or indirectly affected, who helps to fund it, who is important to its delivery or who has useful views on it by virtue of their knowledge and experience. In the case of healthcare, for example, stakeholders might include not only patients, but also carers, doctors and nurses, Social Services and Social Security, voluntary care organisations, advice agencies, NHS Trusts and their managers, GP practices, drug companies and, of course, the taxpayers who ultimately foot the bill. The relative importance of these will depend on the particular policy issues under consideration.

- *Those who deliver the policy* (for example, staff and management) are also important stakeholders. Not only do they have a right to be consulted, but they have a distinctive perspective on the issues, and successful implementation may well depend on the extent to which they understand and buy into the policy. For example, it is one thing for a housing association to devise a policy for handling tenants' requests for repairs, but it won't work in practice if repairs staff or housing officers don't understand what they are supposed to do, or choose to operate in a different way, or don't have the systems or resources needed to make it happen.

Moreover, many public policies depend on multi-agency operation, sometimes involving private as well as public sector organisations. For example, the government is currently grappling with issues arising from the need to provide 4.4 million new homes in the 25 years starting in 1991. What kinds of development does the public want, and should it be located on greenfield sites or on previously used urban land? Addressing this kind of issue not only involves talking to the public, but also to a range of different types of organisation and profession – architects, engineers, planners, managers, officials and economists, working for developers, architectural and engineering practices, banks and building societies, planning authorities, environmental groups, and so on.

Comparisons with political parties

Research for public bodies has to be carefully distinguished from research for political parties, although the line between them sometimes becomes worryingly fine. Political research is discussed elsewhere in this book, but there is a key distinction between policy research and party political research. Public policies have to satisfy two main sets of requirements.

Political requirements

If a party wants to stay in power it needs to appeal to the voters. Therefore, much political research is to do with marketing existing policies, and/or finding new ones that appeal more to the electorate. In this sense a political party is like a commercial organisation trying to sell its wares – the acid test is *whether the public will buy*. A growing range of public bodies (like NHS Trusts and housing associations) have no elected members, but they are also likely to be concerned with their public image.

Operational policy requirements

A good government concerns itself not only with the *saleability* of policies, but also with their *effectiveness*. Will they deliver what people really want? Are they viable and affordable? The acid test here is *whether the policies will work in practice*.

A public authority which is only concerned with policy saleability may be successful in the short term, but it will ultimately fail because its policies will not eventually deliver. Operational delivery is ultimately much more important to the public, but much harder to research than immediate appeal.

Difficulties of understanding the public

Complex issues

The policies of government departments and other public sector bodies often hinge on complex and ramified issues. The subject matter is sometimes difficult, and can involve technical, financial or legal matters. The public often has a very incomplete understanding of what happens, and sometimes significant misconceptions – which may be important to clear up before finally sounding out opinion about future options. Consider, for example:

- A major new policy initiative like the New Deal introduced by the incoming Labour government in the late 1990s, which raises many questions both about the basis of policy itself and about how successfully such a major reform is implemented. The research programme involved looking at (for example) the attitudes, knowledge and motivations of different types of jobseekers (bearing in mind that the situation of a 24-year-old lone parent woman is very different from the situation of a 40-year-old long-term unemployed man, and so on); and the barriers and triggers which determine whether and how someone will seek work.
- Assessing public views about the disposal of radioactive wastes – which demands a better understanding than many people have of the scientific and technical issues, and the nature of the options available.

Exploring the context

Reactions to policy options may often also be affected by contextual or cost factors, which it is important to understand. For example, in a study of pensions and retirement planning it was easy to establish that most people thought the current level of the state pension inadequate and wanted to see it increased. This is an interesting finding in itself, but the acid test is whether those in work would be prepared to pay what it would cost to fund the kind of increase they would like to see. Their reactions to this would in turn depend on various factors; for example, *how* extra charges were levied (which runs up against the problem that many people do not understand how the National Insurance system works); and whether it was an isolated increase or part of a broader tax hike. It is therefore important not just to accept what might be superficial responses without exploring their context and implications more fully.

Assessing what people want

Apart from the complexity of the issues, we also have to grapple with the essential complexity of human beings, who have a great capacity for ambivalence and for holding inconsistent views. Qualitative research is good at dealing with this, because it doesn't have to seek single answers to questions.

In any case, developing public policy is not just a matter of drawing up simple wish lists of what people would like. Good government is a difficult blend of leadership on the one hand and responsiveness to public wishes on the other. Governments sometimes need to make unpopular decisions.

Transport policy is a good example of this. There is growing collective unease about the problems caused by traffic (pollution, congestion, accidents, noise nuisance, etc.), but also a great personal resistance to restrictions on the use of cars. In this case the public could be said to 'want' different things at different levels. If you ask them whether they want curbs on car use most will say 'no' – but equally there is a widespread feeling that government should 'do something' about the unrestricted growth in traffic. This is one of many cases in the public sector where the sum of individual consuming decisions results in a system which most people find unsatisfactory.

In any case people don't always *know* what they want. It will doubtless sound arrogant or elitist to say this, but it is a simple truth, and it applies to all of us. There is a vast range of public bodies that might want to consult us, and no individual can possibly have worked out views about this great mass of potential subject matter. There will be some topics on which we have strong and considered views, but many more about which we need to reflect, learn about what options there might be, consider the implications of these, and feel our way to a conclusion.

Moreover, it could often be unsatisfactory to base policy on 'knee-jerk' responses. We can express views on issues we don't know much about and haven't thought through properly, but we wouldn't necessarily be satisfied with the outcome of policies based on such shallow foundations. The public may have misconceptions, which would make a poor basis for future planning. The *Modernising Government* White Paper talks about an 'outcome-focused culture', but only considered, informed and matured opinions are likely to lead to long-term satisfaction.

Conflicts and trade-offs

There may also be conflicts between different requirements, which make it necessary to explore trade-offs and priorities. These conflicts may exist within individuals – as in the above example about curbing car use, where on one level someone wants to enjoy unfettered use of their car with plenty of roads and parking spaces to enable them to get about freely, but on another level that same person may be anxious to reduce the pollution, noise and hazards caused by traffic.

Other kinds of tension may arise between groups of people with conflicting desires or interests. For example, policy for regulating neighbourhood noise nuisance has to strike a difficult balance between two opposed kinds of freedom: on the one hand people want to be able to enjoy themselves without being tied down with oppressive rules, but on the other, one person's right to make noise can infringe another person's right to live in peace and quiet.

Even where there are no conflicts of this kind there are often resource constraints. It is often necessary to consider how limited resources should be shared between desirable alternatives – or whether the public should be asked to pay more tax in order to achieve their goals.

Research and consultation

There is a range of models which public bodies can apply to the way they use research techniques to find out about the public:

- *Market research model*: the organisation wants to find out more about the attitudes, aspirations and activities of the people it serves, but it still wants to determine the agenda and take the decisions.
- *Consultative model*: the organisation wants to know what people would like it to do, but still takes the final decisions.
- *Participative model*: the organisation wants to work with people and involve them in decision-making.
- *Delegation model*: the organisation wants to let people make their own decisions.

Staying at the top of the scale tends to imply a powerful authority providing services at its own discretion to a largely passive public. This is still probably the dominant model in the private sector, but many people no longer feel comfortable with it for the evolving public sector. It is certainly a long way from notions like 'stakeholders' and 'partnership', which seem to belong lower down the scale.

There is still scope for operating at all these levels, and the appropriate model will vary between policy fields. However, over time the focus has tended to move down the scale. The *Modernising Government* White Paper gives a further push in this direction when it says, 'Rather than imposing solutions we must consult and work with people'.

ROLE OF QUALITATIVE RESEARCH IN SOCIAL POLICY

Growth in use of qualitative research

Over the past 25 years there has been a massive growth in qualitative research for the public sector. In the 1960s and early 1970s only a few pioneers were commissioning and carrying out this kind of work. Now it has become a central strand of public sector research.

There are three main reasons for this.

(1) Public bodies were often slower than their commercial counterparts to accept that research based on small numbers could provide a valid and reliable basis for action. This reflects various factors:
   ○ the pressures of public accountability, which likes the reassurance of large samples;
   ○ the traditional conservatism of the sector, expressed in an initial reluctance to break new methodological ground;
   ○ the academic tradition – public bodies had always looked mainly to academia for research, but qualitative techniques were largely forged in the commercial world;
   ○ a culture historically dominated by statisticians and economists, and hence by numerical information. It took time to realise that the traditional reliance on statistical information alone was limiting.
(2) More qualitative researchers have been attracted to operate in this field, and the available experience and sophistication has grown accordingly.
(3) It is only in more recent years that the importance of *understanding* as opposed to simply *measuring* public attitudes and behaviour has become increasingly apparent in public life, for reasons explored above. The particular value of qualitative research is precisely that it can help public bodies to understand the public they are serving.

Public sector applications of qualitative research

Qualitative research methods may be used by public bodies in various ways:

(1) Developing policy
(2) Evaluating and implementing policy
(3) Communications.

Developing policy

Research can provide a valuable input to the development of social policy. Successful policy needs to be workable and to deliver satisfactory outcomes.

Public attitudes and values cannot be the sole determinants of policy, but they should be a significant factor. The issue of the role of research in policy-making is explored from a party political perspective in the chapter on politics.
    Qualitative research can help us to understand:

- How existing policy is understood, perceived and experienced, how successful it is seen to be, and what is thought to need improving or changing.
- The values and goals of the target public, and their needs, concerns and problems.
- How attitudes and information relate to behaviour in the field – understanding behaviour is as important as understanding attitudes, and the link between them (*why* people do what they do) is crucial.
- Which options for future policy people favour, and why.
- What are the likely barriers or constraints to successful policy implementation, and what conditions are necessary to its success.

Qualitative research can also help policy-makers to understand emergent policy issues – for example, statistical evidence may show a growth in claims for disability benefits, but it will rarely throw much light on *why* this is happening. Qualitative research can help untangle what is going on – which greatly helps in formulating effective solutions. It can also get the public to look at alternative policy options, at different ways forward.

Evaluating and implementing policy

Once policy has been determined and implemented it needs to be monitored and evaluated. Ideally this will involve both quantitative and qualitative research. The qualitative component has a particular role in evaluation, because it can increase our understanding – not only of *what* is happening, but also of *why*.
    The ultimate aim of evaluation is to assess whether a policy is achieving its objectives. Within this there are two main strands:

- *Policy implementation*: is it being implemented effectively and fairly (and if not what is going wrong)?
- *Policy content*: is the policy itself soundly based and properly formulated? Even a well-implemented policy may not deliver if the public does not respond in the expected way or if it has unintended side-effects.

A policy could fall at either of these hurdles, and it is important to know which, because in the latter case it is the policy itself which needs to change, whereas in the former case it just needs to be differently executed. The Child Support Agency (CSA) is an example of the way things can go wrong at both levels – some (although not all) of its original policy objectives seemed widely endorsed, but their implementation clearly went badly awry.

Qualitative research can have a valuable diagnostic function in evaluation. For example, evaluating the government's current New Deal programme which is designed to get people off benefit and into work would need a lot of statistical information – how many people from different target groups get involved in the programme, how many of them get into various kinds of work and training? However, qualitative research is also being used extensively to look at the factors which encourage or deter involvement, and identify triggers and barriers to successful participation.

Another role for qualitative research is providing early feedback about what is happening when a new policy is implemented. Formal evidence takes time to assemble, but policy-makers also need to keep an ear to the ground to pick up early intimations of what is going on. They can listen in through early groups or in-depth interviews while the implementation process is still cooking. This can facilitate rapid identification of delivery problems or unintended consequences.

Communications

Authorities often need to be involved in communications with the public. This can be important both for the functioning of the system and for public accountability:

- How satisfactorily a system works may sometimes partly depend on how well it is understood. If people don't understand what is provided and how they can access it the service will not perform effectively for them. For example, people who may be entitled to benefit need to know what is available and how they can claim it. Voters faced with new electoral systems need some information about how these will work – group discussion research was used recently to find out what voters want to know about new electoral systems, how and when they want information delivered, and how to design effective ballot papers.

- There has been a growing mood of accountability, and the public feels increasingly entitled to know what authorities are doing on its behalf, and whether or not there is a direct consumer relationship. As a society we are no longer content to leave food safety, the introduction of GM foods or the management of toxic wastes entirely to the authorities and their 'experts'. We want to know what is happening in areas like these, and we want to be heard if we don't like what they are doing.

- Sometimes, public services need to be promoted to increase usage and take-up, a function analogous to marketing in the commercial sphere.

Qualitative research is particularly good at dealing with communications issues – much of the original impetus to develop these methods in market research was fuelled by the needs of advertising. What do people know and understand? What do they want to know? How much information do they want, and how much can they cope with? How do they interpret what they are told? What kinds of message will influence behaviour? How can meaning be conveyed simply and effectively? What are the key points to get across? And so on.

What qualitative research contributes

Qualitative methods have various features that are especially important in the public sector context described above.

- The quality of communication with participants is potentially high.
- This communication is bi-directional and interactive: it is possible to input information as well as collect it from participants, and therefore a genuine dialogue can be established between participants and researcher.
- People are viewed holistically, in the round.

These features are particularly advantageous in the following situations.

- *Providing understanding.* A recurrent theme of this chapter is the growing need for public bodies to understand their public – not just to know what happens, but to appreciate why and how it happens. Qualitative research is especially valuable here because of the depth and richness of the information it produces, and because of its scope for dialogue with participants. It by no means replaces the vital need for good statistical information, but at the very least it helps to make sense of what the statistics tell us.

- *Two-way flow of information.* In questionnaire-based surveys the information flow is largely unidirectional, but qualitative research offers scope for giving as well as collecting information. As well as finding out what's already in people's heads we can get reactions to various kinds of stimulus – which may include information, ideas or concepts, policy options or different ways of communicating.

- *Handling complex issues.* Qualitative studies are good at handling the difficult issues often found in the public sector because they put the researcher directly in touch with participants, so that a genuine dialogue can be established. This makes them good at handling policy issues which involve:
  ○ complex and ramified subject matter;

- ○ subtle or amorphous topics, in which the players have to feel their way towards mutual understanding;
- ○ topics which people haven't previously considered in any depth;
- ○ ambivalence and ambiguity (often crucially important in human affairs, and hard to handle in questionnaires);
- ○ exploring context as well as upfront subject matter;
- ○ handling conflicts or trade-offs.

- *Looking at policy options.* Different policy options can be presented, explained and debated. These options can even be developed in discussion – for example, it may become obvious that a particular bundle of policies is favoured apart from one ingredient, and ways can then be debated of modifying or removing the feature people object to. This may or may not lead to a workable revised policy, but at the least it increases understanding of why some options are less popular than others.

- *Assisting policy development.* Qualitative research can be creative and generate new ideas and perspectives – particularly from the use of group discussion techniques, since people in groups tend to spark ideas off each other. Sometimes this may suggest other ways forward for the development of policy.

- *Avoiding knee-jerks.* Questionnaire-based opinion polls can give a useful snapshot of current public attitudes, which have some political relevance but are not likely to provide a solid basis for developing policies that would satisfy the public if they were implemented. Simple polls tell us little about the deep-seated beliefs and attitudes that underlie expressed opinions, and aren't very good at dealing with inconsistent or conflicting views. Again, scope for dialogue and information input makes it possible to allow participants to mature their opinions in response to evidence and discussion.

- *Stakeholder dialogue.* Qualitative research facilitates dialogue with a variety of possible stakeholders – it is even possible to collect different interests around the same table where relevant.

- *Cohesive policy.* Looking at people in the round is valuable for developing cohesive policy instead of being limited by organisational blinkers. Qualitative research is cohesive by nature.

- *Consultation.* Qualitative approaches have a powerful role in consultation and public involvement, not only because they create a dialogue in place of a one-way flow of information controlled from the top, but also because they are accessible in form – people who might be inhibited from taking part in a public meeting feel more confident in a small and informal setting with a group of between six and eight people. The political temperature also tends to be low, and there is scope for people to exchange views rather than engage in political harangues, even on controversial or strongly felt issues.

- *Testing assumptions.* Policies are often based on assumptions about how and why people behave – often unspoken and usually untested. The understanding it yields enables qualitative research to challenge and explore those assumptions.

PRACTICALITIES

Practicalities of qualitative research

Developing and maturing views

If we want to avoid misleading knee-jerk responses we need to give people some opportunity to reflect and mature their views. Qualitative studies are good at this, because the conversation evolves rather than being linear, and the same issues can be approached from various angles. Group-based projects are particularly useful here, because participants are exposed to other people's views, and take part in discussion.

The 'deliberative' process is helped by giving participants good access to relevant information and plenty of time to absorb it, often longer than a standard one-and-a-half hour group. Various more specialised deliberative techniques have been developed, like reconvened groups and citizens' juries (see below).

Looking at outcomes

Social research is interested in long-run policy outcomes as well as short-run popularity. This makes additional demands on both researchers and participants. Researchers need to explore people's goals and values – not merely *what* they want, but *why* they want it. Participants need to be prepared to absorb information and think things through.

Researching complex policy fields

Research needs to be able to cope with the intrinsic complexity of much public sector policy. Again qualitative research has good potential for this, but it is important to make sure that there is enough time for participants to get their minds round the subject, and enough information to help them understand the policy issues and constraints. In addition, researchers themselves need a strong intellectual grip on the material and the policy background, and a restless determination to unpack the public's responses.

Inputting information

'Stimulus material' is often used in market research to explore advertising ideas, marketing concepts or product positionings. In social research there is sometimes a lot of detailed information to convey, often in a context where people do not know much about how something as complex as (say) the pensions system actually works. Lack of awareness is interesting in itself, but in order to progress we need to tell people something about the system.

An example may be useful. Qualitative research for the Department of the Environment to explore public attitudes to the disposal of radioactive nuclear waste was confronted by the problem that many people have very limited understanding of the nature of ionising radiation and the kinds of threat these wastes pose. Before exploring reactions to disposal options it was therefore necessary to provide a simple explanation of some highly complex science (alpha, beta and gamma radiation, half lives and so on). An illustrated booklet was produced, and in the first of two reconvened research sessions this was used to explain the background. In the second session it was then possible to look in a more informed way at the management options.

The need to inform makes particular demands on stimulus material for social research:

- It is important not to overload people with a deluge of complex data which might confuse rather than enlighten, and deaden rather than stimulate conversation. However, experience shows that the public at large is surprisingly capable of getting to grips with difficult and complex matters, *providing* that the information is clearly and gently introduced and people have a chance to exchange ideas and talk themselves into the subject.

- Stimulus must be inventive, to try to engage interest and get across difficult ideas in simple terms.

- Care must be taken in selecting the material to avoid imposing a pattern on the group. The input should give a fair and unbiased account, and the nature of the stimulus used must be clearly shown in reports, and borne in mind during analysis. Ideally, participants should also be able to *ask* for information to avoid any risk that the researcher or research customer may be too selective or not give them what they feel they need.

It is important to explore what is already in participants' heads before inputting any material. This minimises the risk that the materials will dominate the opinions expressed, and provides a sense of how people's views are affected by the inputs made.

Getting responses to different policy options

Sometimes policy development can proceed from a thorough exploration of what happens at present, and what people would like to see happen in the future. In other cases it will be useful to get reactions to particular policy options. It then becomes necessary to find simple and comprehensible ways of presenting these.

Again it will be important not merely to establish preferences, but to find out why particular options do or do not appeal, and to give participants some scope for suggesting developments. It is therefore usually important not only to look at the policy options themselves, but also at the policy context – this will help us to understand why people respond as they do to the policies, and how these could be developed to improve their responses.

Exploring trade-offs

It will often be important to explore priorities and trade-offs, because of limited resources, or intrinsic conflicts between different policy goals. This can be a difficult field, but again is well-suited to qualitative methods.

Trade-offs are more than expressions of preference. They recognise that real-life choices are usually constrained and not free. I may endorse a policy goal (like reducing class sizes in schools), but baulk at the cost of providing it (like higher taxes). I may want to park right outside the shop, but object to the amount of traffic in the high street. In a simplified opinion poll I can vote both ways but in the real world some kind of balance has to be struck, and often hard choices made.

One approach is simply to talk through the issues, and try to highlight and then resolve conflicts during discussion. The more the underlying dynamics of people's preferences are understood, the better the chance of producing policies which will work to the public's ultimate satisfaction. Sometimes it can also be useful to use an allocation exercise which obliges participants to consider trade-offs directly – for example by giving them a fixed number of points symbolising available resources to be spread across the options.

Getting the most out of the information

Thorough, intelligent and objective analysis of qualitative evidence is vital in any market, but is particularly crucial in public sector work because of:

• The density and complexity of much of the material.

- The importance of some of the issues, which often involve human rights, health, safety, income, homelessness, environmental pollution, jobs, etc.
- The need for public accountability – much social policy research is now published (still comparatively unusual in commercial market research), and it needs to stand up to political or media scrutiny.

'New product' research

Researching new products is always difficult in any sphere, but social researchers do not usually have such developed toolkits for dealing with new social products as do their market research counterparts for new commercial products. Yet new social products (like NHS Direct or the New Deal) are usually much more difficult to handle. For example, a new grocery product is typically a fairly hard and small bundle of physical product, packaging and price, wrapped in a much larger and woollier bundle of concepts and images. Social products are usually much denser, more complicated and more extensive by nature, and the devil is often in the detail.

Government now uses more pilot tests of new policies, but there is still scope for more 'new product development' research, aimed at getting policy and implementation right in advance rather than just trying out what happens when you do actually implement it. This means making more use of qualitative research early in the policy development process, when ideas are still forming.

Recruiting difficult target groups

Recruitment of participants is always likely to be a difficult issue for qualitative research, but recruitment can pose special problems in the social policy field. We may be looking for target groups which are hard to identify, hard to locate or difficult to recruit, for example, people who:

- are homeless, in temporary accommodation or sleeping rough;
- are entitled to a particular benefit but not claiming it;
- drive while over the alcohol limit;
- use banned drugs;
- have a particular illness or disability;
- have experienced harassment from their landlord;
- have left a rented council or housing association property without giving proper notice.

Recruitment for social research sometimes operates from addresses rather than doorstep or street sampling, which may make it more robust in some ways – it has to reach corners of the population unvisited by other studies. Sometimes public agencies will have lists of addresses, but there may be ethical and data protection problems about releasing these even for confidential research. Addresses may be very dispersed, and some populations move around a lot, which means lists date quickly. Sometimes lists are incomplete or not available, as with rough sleepers. In these cases researchers need to be inventive in finding ways of locating relevant people and it can sometimes be helpful to use a multiplicity of approaches.

Sometimes we may want to define samples in terms of attitude or educational level. A richly informative sample can be created by taking a variety of approaches to group structure – for example, a study of public perceptions of air pollution in which some groups were defined by each of the following: car usage, education level, 'green' attitudes, state of health (asthma, lung or heart disease). Researchers need to be inventive in finding illuminating ways of slicing the population.

Some social policy issues involve recruiters working in difficult or even hazardous conditions – for example, in difficult-to-let inner-city estates or areas with high crime levels or serious racial tensions or among high-risk groups like heroin users. It may sometimes be prudent to work in pairs.

Issues of scale

Qualitative research for the public sector varies greatly in scale – ranging from the very small to the gigantic. At the upper end projects are vastly bigger than are normally found in commercial market research – 20 or 30 groups and/or over 100 depth interviews in some cases. Large size is driven partly by the need for public accountability – it is important to avoid pushing up sample numbers simply for quasi-quantitative respectability. However, the large scale is often right and necessary, driven by the sheer scale of the problem, the heterogeneity of the population, the importance and diversity of minority groups, and so on.

Qualitative research on a very large scale brings its own problems. It demands powerful frameworks for analysis and for co-ordinating what might be a large group of researchers. But this kind of research also deals essentially with *qualities*, and there is a perpetual risk that the essential vividness and empathy it generates can be lost when transmuted through successive levels of aggregation.

Problems arising from sector growth

The enormous growth of qualitative research in the public sector is welcome, but it raises various issues:

(1) *Fitting supply to demand.* Growth demands a major increase in the number of practitioners, but training and experience are not acquired

overnight. The market for qualitative social research is growing, but the pool of good qualitative social researchers is still fairly small. Demand is beginning to outstrip supply. Attention needs to be paid to recruitment and training issues if the expansion is to be handled effectively.

(2) *Lack of buyer expertise.* Some major government departments have impressive research departments, but many organisations who need to buy qualitative research have no tradition of doing so. They may have no specialist research staff of their own, or any internal experience in this field. These include housing associations, charitable and voluntary bodies, GP practices, small Health Service Trusts, some local authorities and many other smaller public sector organisations. Some of these also have very limited resources to put into research, but a growing need for information and consultation.

(3) *DIY research.* While public bodies are under growing pressure to consult their public, they are often strapped for resources to accomplish this. One of the seductive features of 'focus group' research is that it looks like something anyone can do, and there is an increase in 'do-it-yourself' research carried out by housing officers and equivalent staff. The apparent conversational simplicity of the method can be deceptive. The profession needs to ask itself why people often view qualitative research as a game anyone can play rather than as a demanding specialist skill.

(4) *'Government by focus group'.* Around the time of the 1997 General Election the media discovered 'focus groups', hyped them to the skies, and then set about demolishing their own edifice with scathing comments about 'government by focus group'. Any research method is potentially dangerous if badly executed or improperly applied, but the media representations were a travesty of good qualitative practice. The implication of many of the accusations is that focus groups are used only to maximise short-term popularity and duck responsibility for political decisions. The message of this chapter is that the method can be (and often is) used to grapple with serious and complex long-term policy issues – indeed, that it actually helps us to avoid treating policy research merely as an instant political beauty contest.

(5) *Political credibility.* Public sector clients new to qualitative research can be nervous about its political credibility. How can studies based on so few people carry conviction and weight? In practice this does not usually prove as much of a problem as it may appear. Qualitative research is now well-established in the public sector, and its findings tend to carry conviction because they usually make sense, and portray a familiar world in vivid terms. Good qualitative research does not merely

describe people's attitudes and behaviour, it gives insights into the underlying reasons and mechanisms.

Developing qualitative methods

Types of qualitative research

The two classic formats for qualitative research are group discussions and individual in-depth interviews. For most social research purposes these should remain the staple methods, either alone or in combination.

However, variations on this basic model can also help in social research. Small groups consisting of anything from two to five participants can be useful – for example:

- in staff or professional interviews;
- with participants who may be harder to interview successfully in larger groups – for example, people with learning difficulties or speech problems, some young people, rule breakers, etc;
- where numbers are too thin on the ground to make it feasible to get larger groups together.

Developing qualitative applications

The following 'new' qualitative methods are essentially variations on the basic group technique, stretched or modified in various ways to meet different needs. Researchers and social policy customers need to be inventive in trying new approaches, and diligent in collating experiences to see what works. At the same time these are not panaceas, and the value of a piece of work ultimately depends on good craft skills imaginatively and intelligently applied, combined with sheer hard work in grappling with the material.

Deliberative methods

This is a family of approaches rather than a single method. It aims to enable participants to evolve and mature their decisions.

- *Deliberative polls.* In the early 1990s samples of members of the public were given a benchmark questionnaire interview about their attitudes in a given field (like crime and punishment or the future of the NHS), and invited to attend a weekend session. Before attending, they were given briefing material expressing balanced opposing viewpoints on the issues under consideration. During the weekend they discussed the issues, and formulated questions to put to a range of 'experts' with diverse views.

There were several successive waves of discussion and expert evidence, and at the end of the weekend the original benchmark questionnaire was re-administered.

The difference between the two sets of questionnaire responses indicated how attitudes had changed as a result of hearing and discussing the evidence. The first measure tells us something about the state of public opinion, the second about the way this changes and matures when people have a chance to think and learn. Sometimes views did change substantially.

These were essentially events made for (and funded by) television broadcast. In this format they would be expensive to apply to live social research problems, and the qualitative element was perhaps not used as fully as it might have been in analysis. However, the approach illustrates an important point about deliberation. Spin-offs of this approach are now being developed for use in studying public views about gene therapy, which clearly embraces a very difficult set of issues.

- *Reconvened groups.* Since the late 1970s various people have used 'reconvened groups' – standard discussion groups recruited on the basis that they would come back for a second (or sometimes even a third or fourth) time, to continue the discussion. This provides more time for discussing complex or detailed issues without fatigue, and scope for absorbing information, deliberating about it, and hence developing matured opinions. The approach works well, but is inevitably more expensive per capita than conventional groups.

- *Workshops.* Extended workshop-type sessions lasting up to a day are another way of expanding the capacity of basic group techniques. These can be useful with professional target groups, but also sometimes with members of the public where the issues are extensive or difficult to get to grips with.

- *Citizens' juries.* In the last few years the concept of citizens' juries has attracted a lot of attention. It has been developed internationally, and was introduced to the UK by IPPR and Opinion Leader Research. It has elements in common with deliberative polls and reconvened groups, but the model is rooted in the notion of a jury as a body of lay people who hear evidence and reach conclusions. Commonly, a panel of about 16 people is invited to attend for perhaps four days, during which they hear (and can often summon) expert witnesses, and review evidence. They tend to be asked to develop conclusions and recommendations rather than simply express views – and in some applications can even be given decision-making powers. This is a very interesting approach with various possibilities. The main problems are the high cost, and the small numerical base. Actually delegating decisions to citizens' juries is perhaps pushing the jury analogy too far. There are obvious risks in handing decisions over to such a small group of people on sheer sampling grounds.

Panel-based methods

Over the past year the government has set up a people's panel, a large national sample of respondents with known characteristics who can be used by government departments as a basis for recruiting respondents for both quantitative and qualitative studies. Some researchers questioned the value of this approach, and at the time of writing it is too early to say whether or not it will prove successful, and how useful it will be for qualitative applications – but it will be interesting to see what it produces.

SUMMARY

The social field has some features in common with the private sector, but the 1980s customer-based model of service delivery is yielding to a broader 'stakeholder' concept.

Public bodies' use of qualitative research has risen rapidly with the increasing need to understand their public in the context of changing structures and cultures, growing expectations and dwindling resources. This understanding is often difficult in relation to social policy – issues can be complex, public knowledge may be limited, and people often need to work out what they really want in a context of conflicting desires and constrained resources.

The public sector mainly uses research to help develop, implement and evaluate policy, and to improve the effectiveness of communications. The value of qualitative research lies particularly in its scope for high-quality bidirectional dialogue with participants, and for giving as well as collecting information. This equips it well for exploring complex policy issues, where participants may need to learn, reflect, discuss and mature their views.

Public sector studies pose many challenges to qualitative researchers. Policy should be concerned with long-run outcomes, which are more demanding to study than short-term saleability. Imaginative ways must be found of grappling with complex issues, providing sometimes extensive and technical information in a digestible form, and presenting policy options as a basis for choice. Time and space need to be allowed for participants to learn and mature their views. Ways have to be found of coping with conflicting desires, and enabling people to prioritise and make trade-offs. Qualitative research is by nature well-suited to these needs – but it still needs to be skilfully and creatively applied.

The need for 'matured' opinion is breeding a range of new 'deliberative' variations on the traditional group discussion – such as deliberative polls, reconvened groups and citizens' juries. Initiatives like these are welcome, and the technology should continue to evolve, but that is no reason to jettison the traditional forms (group discussions and in-depth interviews), whose flexibility and versatility is one of their main assets and which should continue as the staple methodology.

Finally, the rapid growth of public sector qualitative research poses challenges:

- Demand for good researchers may exceed supply.
- Some organisations new to research lack commissioning expertise and may take a do-it-yourself research approach without having the necessary experience.
- The vogue for 'focus groups' has attracted ill-informed and potentially damaging media attention.

KEY IDEAS

- Qualitative research was adopted relatively late in this field, which traditionally relied heavily on large-scale quantitative studies. However, it is now well-established, and used in many ways.
- The main uses are helping to develop policies and to implement, evaluate, and communicate them.
- The public sector is not like the private sector. Stakeholders as well as direct customers must be consulted, and matters like fairness, public interest and the rights of minorities need to be considered.
- It is vital to understand the public when developing and evaluating policies, yet public policy issues are often highly complex and may not be well understood.
- Participants therefore often need to reflect and absorb information before making sufficiently mature responses to provide a useful basis for policy.
- Qualitative research can open a real dialogue with participants, and provide deep understanding of social issues so that policy researchers can:
  - explore issues that would be too complex for questionnaires;
  - provide as well as collect information;
  - ask the public to consider alternative policy options.

- Qualitative research in this field faces various problems; for example:
  - a limited supply of researchers with relevant experience in a growing field;
  - a lack of buyer expertise among some public bodies new to using research;
  - the need to find better ways of explaining complex policies to the public, and helping participants to deliberate about them.
- Basic qualitative research methods are being extended to meet the latter need – including reconvened groups, deliberative polls, workshops and citizens' juries.

FURTHER READING

Bryson, C., Budd, T. Lewis, J. & Elam, G. (1999) *Women's Attitudes to Combining Paid Work and Family Life.* National Centre for Social Research (formerly SCPR).

Harrop, A. (1995–96) Measuring customer satisfaction: some methodological issues. *DSS Research Yearbook.*

Hedges, A. (1996) *Confidentiality: The Public View.* DSS Research Report 56.

Hedges, A. (1998) *Pensions and Retirement Planning.* DSS Research Report 83.

Hedges, A. & White, C. with B. Seyd, P. Kahn & K. Woodfield (1999) *New Electoral Systems: What Voters Need to Know. A Qualitative Study.* National Centre for Social Research (formerly SCPR).

Lessof, C. & Squires, E. (1996–97) Quality not quantity: using qualitative research for policy analysis and evaluation. *DSS Research Yearbook.*

Modernising Government (1999) White Paper Cm 4310, March. HMSO, London.

Prescott Clarke, P. & Hedges, A. (1987) *Radioactive Waste Disposal: The Public's View.* National Centre for Social Research (formerly SCPR).

Stewart, J. (1996) Innovation in democratic practice in local government. *Policy & Politics* 24(1), January.

White, C. & Lewis, J. with G. Elam (1999) *Citizens' Juries: An Appraisal of their Role Based on the Conduct of Two Women Only Juries.* National Centre for Social Research (formerly SCPR), Cabinet Office (also 1999 Market Research Society Annual Conference paper, Appraising the Role of Citizens Juries, by C. White and J. Lewis).

Williams, T., Hill, M. & Davies, R. (1999) *Attitudes to the Welfare State and the Response to Reform.* DSS Report No 88.

The ideas contributed to this chapter by Sue Duncan express her own views and not necessarily those of the Department of Social Security, or the Centre for Management and Policy Studies.

Chapter 12

Qualitative Research and Religion

John Griffiths
Communications Planner, CDP

with

James Jones
Bishop of Liverpool

Editor's introduction

The Church of England is under pressure to change. As the world moves on, both secularisation and also radicalism and cultism have taken their toll on mainstream, established religion.

The Church of England is starting to recognise the need to formally explore and better understand the needs of the people, both in and outside the Church. This process is difficult for an establishment which, until recently, acted primarily as a doctrinaire organisation rather than one committed to listening and evolving in line with the people. This chapter shows how, using largely volunteer professionals, the Church is starting to change. The skills of researchers and other marketing and communications specialists are being harnessed to address the issues.

This chapter considers how qualitative research is helping and how it could help more. While recognising considerable reluctance from some within the Church, the new professionals are trying to help the Church become more relevant to the needs of today's community.

The experiences of the Jewish community are also briefly explored, and many parallels can be seen as both communities need to address serious attitudinal and financial constraints to progress.

John Griffiths has worked with the Church in a voluntary capacity for many years and his passion for the subject shines through. We were privileged to have James Jones, a forward-thinking bishop who has worked closely on the development of the Church, to join in and share his insights on the future of the Anglican faith.

THE CONTEXT: THE NEED TO UNDERSTAND PEOPLE

'The priority is not so much to draw people in. It is to get those who are inside the Church out into the communities to listen to the needs of the people. All evangelism is through relationships. The Church needs to establish a relationship with the world.' (James Jones)

How new people are drawn into the Church

For the Church of England, the parish structure has been the primary point of contact. The majority of non-churchgoers in the UK still perceive themselves as having a marginal connection with the Church. This used to be exercised through the rites of passage: baptism, marriage and death, and through Christian education in Sunday schools. However, for the majority, none of these rites can be taken as a given. For most people contact with the Church is now unpredictable and intermittent. Furthermore, the licensing of other places for marriage and the increasing numbers of unlicensed people conducting funerals have undermined these traditional platforms for mission.

Engagement not involvement

This makes the portrayal of the Church in the media (real and fictional) particularly instructive. For many it is their primary perception as to what religion is about and what the Church is saying. But even when the Church is satirised and the clergy caricatured, these programmes can attract major audiences, suggesting that there are still large numbers of people who, while not considering themselves churchgoers, still find the subject of religion engaging.

James Jones comments, 'Ballykissangel, Father Ted, The Vicar of Dibley, and also the soaps indicate that the so-called secular audience is not completely detached from religious ritual and outlook. The humour in these programmes is not necessarily negative and suggests an empathy with rather than any antagonism towards these religious characters and storylines.'

The Church needs to decide how long it will continue to work with the assumption that some kind of connection exists and at what point to switch to the assumption that, for the majority, there is no longer a real connection. The starting point for the second position is radically different. What should the Church be saying to people to draw them in? What is the Church for? What rites of passage are important for people and why? Who is responsible for the religious upbringing of the children: schools, churches or parents?

Intermittent contact

Paradoxically, once there is an assumption that the constituency the Church is addressing is post-Christian and with little experience of what the Church is like, the Church may actually find it easier to manage it's image rather more effectively. Where contact is intermittent and uncontrolled, communications can be used to force reappraisal (though this will only be effective if the 'product' lives up to expectations when people do return).

Reaching out to outsiders requires radical change in how the Church operates. It may mean designing activities for outsiders rather than insiders. It may mean adopting marketing practices (viewed with huge suspicion) and adopting the tone of voice of the target group instead of insiders.

The Bad Hair Day advertising campaign suffered as a result of this. It was developed by a co-operative of Christians working in advertising on behalf of the Church Advertising Network (a coalition of denominations), and was used in the run-up to Christmas 1996. Largely accepted and enjoyed outside the Church, the campaign was roundly condemned by certain groups within the Church who failed to grasp that they were not the intended targets. But how can the Church reach out to people unless it talks in a language they can understand and relate to? And how to draw people in when church services are modelled to meet the expectations of insiders?

The nature of proselytising

Proselytising particularly among Evangelicals has taken the form of communicating a series of propositional truths. Success is measured as converts assent to these truths. Surveys following crusades run by Billy Graham and Luis Palau have highlighted a high drop-out rate as converts fail to migrate successfully into churches. Strategies employing small groups have gone awry when members have failed to integrate into the larger body of the Church. In the journey of faith there is an essential socialisation process alongside the individual's personal spiritual growth. Evangelistic activity needs to understand and develop the socialisation process as well as helping the individual to understand the wider implications of personal commitment.

The socialisation process lies at the heart of the Alpha Course phenomenon.[1] It is the making of new friendships, and sharing meals that binds people together in their spiritual quest. This is particularly successful among groups of highly mobile people who need the friendship when they move, as well as the faith.

How churches structure themselves and operate

Single issues have succeeded ideologies as banners around which people gather. There is an interesting parallel with the rise of issue politics and the way it has cut across political parties. Theological groupings such as the Evangelicals and the charismatic movement have cut across denominational structures and give a much better indication of the kind of churches people join than the traditional labels.

In the non-conformist churches there can often be a drift into monocultures with dissidents pushed to the edge. Within the Anglican Church huge efforts are made to make room for everyone since the parish church is the local church. This puts an increasing strain on resources as the parish church infrastructure tries to provide for everyone.

Segmentation and the spectrum of needs

Churches need help in finding ways of drawing people together instead of servicing them in small groups. The different theological emphases and life stages mean that, in any particular service, there will be in the congregation a whole spectrum of expectations which are virtually impossible to meet. There are those for whom preaching is central, and also those for whom the liturgy and the sacraments are essential. But sitting alongside these are the people who come for 'worship', by which they mean extended periods of singing, and those who come for prayer and quiet meditation. There are also the special needs of children and young people who are often broken down into age groupings of two to three years at a time. A typical response has been to target services at different groups, but the degree of fragmentation has been such that no single service can cater for only one group. What is the optimum way to provide for people's individual needs?

James Jones comments: 'There is a spiritual instinct in everyone. It comes to the fore episodically. One such time is when you have children and you wonder about the world in which they will grow up. Moral and spiritual values begin to surface. This is one of the reasons that family services have mushroomed in spite of fierce criticism from liturgical purists. Also, over a quarter of all toddler groups in the country are held in church halls. This, combined with the awakening spiritual instincts of parents, has provided the Church, accidentally and providentially, with one of its major mission engagements with our culture.'

Good news and bad news

The secret lies in the interface between the good news and the bad news. The Church cannot effectively connect with the community until it understands the community's issues, especially the bad news. When we've audited the parish we need to expose the bad news to that facet of the good news which is relevant. Thus where loneliness is the issue we need to present belonging, where fear of death, the hope of eternal life, where youth are bored and with no faith in the future, purposeful belonging and activity, where parents are fearful, support for their parenting.'

Membership

The whole notion of membership is changing. The Church population is finely balanced as births match deaths and conversions match those who have lost their faith. However, statistics from Christian Research (Brierley 1996) highlight slippage of 74 000 people a year as members move to a new area and attend a local church without formally joining it. If the trend continues, the impact at a national level will result in the net loss of a million members between 1992 and 2005, taking total church membership down to 5.7 million. How does a church raise funds and organise itself if the notion of membership is weakening?[2]

This slippage is uneven and it arises from many causes of which local leadership may be key – where there is good visionary and collaborative leadership locally there is growth in membership.

The clergy find themselves under increasing pressure partly through having to take on larger workloads as parishes merge, but mainly because the vast majority are expected to be people managers when they have received little or no management training. The minister may be disconcerted when their authority is challenged or flatly denied. In past years ministers could rely on a traditional deference to the clergy. This is passing as the institutional structures weaken. Authority needs to be reinterpreted to take into account the expectations of a laity who are learning in other areas of their lives to see themselves as stakeholders and who expect to be involved in decision-making.

THE ROLE FOR QUALITATIVE RESEARCH

Drawing new people in

If ordinary people have less and less to do with the Church, we have to reckon with a growing gulf in understanding between the clergy and many church people and the communities in which they live. The Church very often insists on addressing outsiders as if they are already insiders who understand and agree with what is being said. Worse, the construction of the message can be given divine right as if it would be wrong or misleading to frame the message in words which the audience might use themselves. Qualitative research can be used to help the Church reframe its message in a way that can be understood by non-churchgoers. Effective communication talks the language of the target audience, not the language of the speaker.

Indeed, a characteristic of growing churches is that they often make provision for small groups where people can frame their own questions and interrogate the answerers in their own language.

Drawing people in from the parish

The Anglican Church in Sydney has carried out a sociological study into the number of contact points a church needs in order to grow. Fewer than four and the Church is likely to decline. Rapidly growing churches can have as many as 40 or more. Many of these contact points arise from community activities: fêtes, whist drives and the like, which maintain a large ragged fringe around the Church. If the amount of time which church members can give for church activities is reduced or if their perception of who is in the faith narrows, the number of these contact points is correspondingly reduced. The congregation in effect professionalises its relationship with the community. The line between the insiders and the outsiders becomes much more strongly defined.

Research can identify the number of contact points and audit their effectiveness by surveying those who have become involved in the Church. However, this will not show which channels are failing. By conducting a communications audit from an outsider's viewpoint, it is possible to discover potential contact points where new links between Church and community can be opened up.

James Jones illustrates this point well: 'When in the parish we got a huge number of non-church guests to a barn-dance, and I was asked why so many had come. "Where," I said, "can you entertain a whole family with a three course meal and an evening's entertainment – all for £10?"'

The role of the fringe

James Jones continues. 'The fringe is the key to mission. The fringe, when they become committed, are the most fertile in reaching out to others because they bring with them a new fringe of family friends and associates. Unfortunately, all too often the missionary imperative falls on long-standing church members who, because they are up to their necks in maintaining the Church, have few contacts outside it.'

The Church has for a long time taken responsibility for the spiritual development of young people through the Sunday School movement. There are new opportunities for churches to take initiatives in providing support in the community in parenting skills, and in relationship counselling. All these need to be negotiated with local communities. The expectations of the Church and those being invited to participate are usually very different. Perhaps the dramatic decline in the number of children attending Sunday School is a sign of such differences in expectations.

Community expectations

The pace of social change is now so rapid that it is likely that such 'contracts' ought to be regularly renewed and renegotiated. If the explosive growth in the service sector has introduced new kinds of service products and offerings, we cannot expect that the facilities provided by churches can continue to be effective unless they are regularly reviewed and updated. Again, research can play a valuable role in identifying the actual needs which the constituencies feel the Church can supply. What is needed is more than consultation; it is a profound understanding of the community's expectations and how they wish their needs to be met.

Case study 1: Attracting young people back into the synagogue

The Jewish community has seen synagogue membership figures plummet for a variety of reasons. A generation ago the synagogues provided a natural meeting place that helped to glue the Jewish community together. But a younger generation has had to consider the importance of Jewish identity when intermarriage and assimilation is a very real option. Twenty to 40-year-olds were no longer joining. Jewish Continuity, an organisation concerned that the Jewish community was facing extinction within 40 years through assimilation, mounted a qualitative research programme to determine how to keep Jews within the community. Group discussions were held among young Jews who were not involved with organised Judaism at the time. It was found that the vast majority of Jews *did* wish to keep their cultural identity but had limited opportunities to meet other Jews. Synagogues were the natural place to meet, but projected entirely the wrong image. The primary benefit of membership was tied in with securing a burial plot, not a primary motivator for this age group!

One of the initiatives that came from this study was the Saatchi synagogue positioned as 'a synagogue for people who don't like synagogues'. It was designed expressly around the missing 20 to 40 age group. Although in real terms the content of services and the round of events is not that different from other synagogues, it has found a ready clientele who go primarily for social reasons. From this beginning the synagogue comes into its own as marriages take place, and parents bring their children to be raised within the tradition.

Clearly, research played an integral role in determining how and why people were using synagogues and what needed to be changed to draw people back into involvement.

Effective outreach is often based on children's holiday clubs and after school clubs (ideas now being taken up by the state). Many children are no longer available on Sunday morning – they're with their parent they haven't been with during the week or playing football. They're free on Sunday afternoon, however, which is becoming a very good time for all-age worship.

Attracting new believers

Research can assist in finding out what effectively draws new members into the churches, mapping the psychological and socialising process. Conversion is more than a cognitive assent to theological certainties. It involves an entire reorientation that has emotional and behavioural dimensions as well. There is a socialising process when new believers start to derive part of their revised identity from the group of fellow believers. This may come about through small groups such as the Alpha course referred to above, and there is a universalising process when the believer discovers that the implications of the new faith are not just private religious experience, but relate to every aspect of life. Arguably, what happens to many converts is that the conversion process is protracted and incomplete: converts get stuck or lose their faith after a short time, having never been properly grounded.

Research can help illuminate the main stages that people need to go through to come to a life-changing belief. To understand the process is not to mechanise or reduce it, or to curtail the freedom of the individual, but it would illuminate the points of difficulty for many people. This is vital when those leaving the Church (while not necessarily losing their faith) match the numbers of those joining because they have found it.

The structure and operation of churches

In the area of how churches structure themselves, members may be only dimly aware of the assumptions that undergird these structures. Even self-completed surveys fail to bring these to the surface. Qualitative research with a trained moderator can explore the foundations of people's need for the structures that exist. Respondents are usually divided up along lines of commonality to enable them to work together better. However, where there are major areas of difference, research can be used to explore areas of disagreement. This serves to identify areas of common ground that can be used to build bridges between opposing points of view.

Coping with pluralism

When there are limited resources and many groups competing for these, one of the most valuable contributions which qualitative research can make is to identify the underlying needs and to explore new ways of meeting them. The usual way to meet the needs of multiple constituencies is to segment the congregation by life stage or church tradition, but this addresses symptoms rather than the root causes. Is the Anglican communion celebrant devoted to the 1662 prayerbook primarily motivated by the structure of the liturgy, its familiarity or the aesthetic dimension? By identifying the key drivers, it may be possible to find forms of service which can more easily leap generational and theological divides. Reflective services are not only the province of an older generation any more than noisy services are *de rigeur* for younger churchgoers.

To meet the needs of many constituent groups, service structures are under great pressures, which normally means that they become longer! Again there is an expectation that a church service of an hour to 90 minutes in length must contain a number of elements which, in a sitting, cover all the corporate needs of the congregation. Looking at alternative ways to meet these needs using qualitative research can help to take pressure off the service format itself. Research can explore alternative ways in which these needs can be met with resources other than services.

James Jones' view is that 'churches or deaneries need to offer a range of worship from the classical to the contemporary so as to meet the different needs of the various groups within our multicultural society. Different denominations and traditions are no longer a stumbling block but a virtue to missions in a pluralistic culture which needs many different doors into the Christian faith.'

The role of the clergy

It might seem an odd use of research. Surely this is to smuggle opinion polls in by another name? Call it congregationalism or democracy, doesn't this undermine the authority of the clergy? Not at all. The issue is not authority but how that authority is exercised and understood. Perceptions of authoritarianism can come about because of poor communication. Without feedback, the clergy often have little idea how decision-making is interpreted. Churches are, after all, voluntary organisations whose members need to be motivated through clear communication and proper consultation. Qualitative research can act as a feedback loop to clarify how misreporting has taken place.

Why use research? Because the systematic sampling of a congregation for research interviews allows a quasi-objective framework to be placed over an area before misunderstanding generates resentment that can very rapidly escalate into open conflict on grounds of personality. The clergy badly need models for making and communicating decisions, which achieve consensus without the need for extensive consultation.

Research can help to map out how power is exercised through the organisation. Internal culture research can map trails of influence rather than official power. If consultation takes place along these channels there is far more likelihood of achieving consensus. How well are these trails understood? They may not necessarily lie along the usual lines of formal administration. The Church is, after all, a voluntary organisation and needs to be understood and managed as such.

Finding new ways of belonging

Membership is a central notion in most churches and a central tool in keeping churchgoers involved and ensuring that the Church's financial and organisational needs are met. However, if there are influences which are undermining the notion of membership, it is important that the issues are exposed and alternatives found.

The first step would be to determine what membership actually means to church members and what it is about membership that alienates those who reject formalising their involvement. We need to establish whether the same

---

Case study 2:
Listening to the clergy and the laity of the Church of England

At the beginning of 1999 the Archbishops' Council agreed to initiate a research project designed to get feedback at a parish level on the concerns of laity. Twenty group discussions with the laity were carried out across England using non-professional moderators who were given limited training and a very structured discussion guide. One of the issues which came out of the project was a sense of frustration experienced by the laity where they wanted to give more time to working within the Church and the community, but felt there were few real opportunities to do this. Such opportunities as there were, were limited and structured as roles (such as lay readership) for which many of the volunteers were obviously not suited. Simultaneously as you might expect, they believed that their clergy were struggling with a workload that was higher than ever and that they desperately needed more support from church members.

Jayne Ozanne who directed the project commented that only a research exercise of this kind could have unveiled the strength of people's feelings. A paper-based survey might have provided a percentage of additional time that people were willing to give. A poll canvassing opinion might have generated a torrent of criticism with little hope of a positive outcome. What qualitative research contributed was an understanding of what people were feeling and how much they wanted to get involved. Lack of involvement was no indicator of apathy. By identifying the barriers to involvement and setting in train initiatives to overcome these, it should be possible to find ways for people to get involved that will fulfil their desire to serve and provide badly needed support to the clergy.

---

views are substantially held but are under pressure because of time constraints, or if the problem is with the way membership is defined within the Church and the expectations that accompany it. Is this weakening of membership confined to the Church alone or is it a general weakening that applies to other forms of participation elsewhere in society? Projective exercises can be used to explore the image which non-members have of members and vice versa. Again, using research, it is possible to explore new ways whereby the organisational needs of the Church can be met while taking into account the need to belong in less formalised ways.

Communicating

Qualitative research has become an essential tool in modern communications because it allows the entire message and the way it is communicated to be deconstructed and reassembled to ensure that communication is impactful, clear, persuasive, motivating and ultimately memorable. In the light of what is now known about how to construct effective communications it is extraordinary how much time is spent in church in some form of instruction and how little is understood as to whether any of this is effective. Arguably, most of what happens in church services represents socialisation rather than education, which creates many more barriers between outsiders, who have great difficulty in understanding what is taking place, and thoroughly socialised members who can't see the problem.

Books are an obvious and trivial example. Many churches have in their pews at least one liturgy book and a copy of the Bible. At the door, the hapless newcomer is given one or perhaps even two hymn-books representing traditional hymns and more modern choruses. They may even be given a printed order of service for that week as well! The facility with which the regular membership shuffles all this paperwork is a wonder to behold.

If the same techniques used to develop advertising were used to develop, first, the structure of services, and secondly, the specific content of the teaching programme, there would be dramatic increases in understanding and maintaining the attention of the congregation.

Service content

We have already touched on using research to identify the drivers which draw people to favour one kind of service over another. Research can be used to determine how effectively the elements of a service are communicating. In many traditions the layout of the building, the items used in worship and the behaviour expected of the congregation have symbolic importance, but often the congregation has never been taught the significance, so either completely or largely misunderstands it. It is also possible that the metaphors driving the original symbolism have lost their power, and would fail to connect even if the symbolism were explained.

Many of the elements may be remnants of technical solutions that are obsolete. They have no actual symbolic importance. How much chanting was originally designed to overcome acoustic problems that a modern sound system renders irrelevant? Has the liturgy been constructed on the presupposition that the congregation is predominantly illiterate or has no access to printed materials?

Research could test comprehension of the core creative ideas within a service format and could also look at where misunderstanding was occurring and why. It would also be possible to draw out what metaphors individuals were using to overlay and translate existing metaphors to make them relevant. Arguably, new metaphors could be researched in development as it were. Much experimentation with new liturgies is happening, with the testers having little understanding of how the new liturgy is supposed to be an improvement on the existing one and what constitutes success. There is a distinction here between researching and trialling. The criteria must be understood before they can be applied.

Sermons

If so much time in services is given to teaching shouldn't there be more effort put into evaluating input and take-out of religious teaching in order to improve its effectiveness? A 1998 survey by Mark Greene of the London Institute of Contemporary Christianity illustrates the dangers inherent in maintaining traditional forms of communication without checking their effectiveness. He researched a sample of 400 individuals. The conclusion was that 50% claimed that the sermons they heard lacked relevance, depth or challenge. Half the sample had never heard a sermon on work, and home and personal issues fared almost as badly. Only 1% of the sample had ever been asked by their preacher to give any feedback, and this from a communication form used in every church at least once a week lasting from between five and more than 40 minutes!

Discussion groups could also be employed to give feedback on the key communication points of the sermon. A group could even be convened a week later to determine how much had been retained. The group discussion need last no longer than 15 to 20 minutes. A small group could be convened regularly to play back the key points and to highlight areas of confusion.

THE PRACTICALITIES OF QUALITATIVE RESEARCH

Little qualitative research has been conducted within religious organisations, and no chapter on how it could be used would be complete without a discussion of why so little has been done. There are two main issues. First, there has been suspicion about the appropriateness of using research. Second, in a climate of decline there has been a problem with limited resources.

The appropriateness of using research

Is it appropriate to use a set of techniques that have been developed in a consumer framework where man rather than God is the measure? Should not policy be determined by tradition, by interpretation of the Holy Scriptures trying to find the will of God? Doesn't the use of research represent just another inroad for secular humanism?

The Jewish and Christian scriptures hold that God sees and listens and responds. Research is a method for gathering and interpreting what people think and feel. Reportage, on the other hand, uncritically relays whatever is said. Interpretation is an essential part of the research process. The researcher is trying to uncover what people mean rather than what they say. Much of the scepticism around research derives from a suspicion that it is a tool of demagoguery that undermines tradition and religious authority: what everyone thinks. Hopefully we have shown that research helps to uncover the voices of minorities as well as the big guns. It enables a religious community to remain in touch with the cultural community from which it is drawn, and separate from which religious life will become increasingly irrelevant.

Resources

Finance and people. Individual congregations do not have the resources or knowledge to buy qualitative research, and the other issue is employing sympathetic researchers to carry out the work. Many congregations would require that the researcher be a believer who understands their tradition. These two combine to make research a virtual impossibility.

Finance

There are two responses here. One is to examine how, at a regional or denominational level, research programmes could be funded which would support and develop local congregations. This is after all what a denominational structure is for. The second is to consider whether congregations might be able to conduct simple forms of qualitative research to monitor their effectiveness in communications. The principles of group moderation can be taught relatively easily and quickly. However, without a framework in which the issues and pitfalls are clearly understood, there is a great danger that such exercises may confuse. Qualitative research is dependent upon interpretation, and the ability to distinguish between outputs that are a function of the process and those that are genuinely insightful. Programmes of diagnostic research carried out at a macro level could provide the framework against which local initiatives could be measured. In the recent listening exercise carried out within the Church of England, moderators were trained by a professional researcher and the discussion guide was highly structured to ensure consistency of the material gathered. The interpretation was overseen by research professionals.

People

The faith of the researcher is an issue partly for cost reasons. However, I would argue that the involvement of the researcher in the process is such that a project would benefit as much from a researcher who, while sympathetic, did not totally identify with the beliefs of the church concerned. Qualitative research provides a quasi objectivity. By virtue of the small numbers being interviewed it cannot claim statistical objectivity, but where a sample of the target group is recruited and interviewed by an independent interviewer, a conceptual framework can be drawn out which can illuminate a situation.

Methodologies

The following are some specific methodologies that may prove useful in religious research projects.

Accompanied shopping

Borrowing methodologies from retailing research may prove fruitful. If those outside the church are interviewed immediately after 'using' a church or perhaps even accompanied and observed by the researcher, it is possible to get to the specifics that are deterring an outsider.

Conflict groups

Where there are major areas of difference it may be worth using conflict interviews. Interviewing respondents in either pairs or triads where there are strongly differing views does this. In the case of the triad, one of the respondents is undecided, and it is the task of the others to try to draw that person to their side. The technique is particularly useful when respondents are asked to construct an argument which would be persuasive to the opposite point of view. This serves to identify areas of common ground, which can be used to build bridges between opposing points of view.

SUMMARY

I have sought to argue that the Church of England needs to make use of qualitative research as an essential tool for seeing itself as others see it and being willing not only to serve the community but to obtain feedback on the effectiveness and relevance of that service. In the area of how the Church is structured there is a constant danger that symptoms and not causes are treated: in the area of church services we may be rearranging the deck-chairs rather than finding out why people came aboard in the first place. Finally, for an organisation to have any hope of sustaining itself, it has to understand what draws in newcomers.

Qualitative research is not a closed subject; it continues to evolve new methodologies. What drives qualitative research is the need to provide insight into the beliefs and attitudes of ordinary people. Crucially, it also illuminates the ways in which these are lived out. If a religious organisation only monitors itself against the formally and informally expressed beliefs of members without uncovering the changing attitudes behind these and the behaviours coming from them it will lose touch with belief itself.

KEY IDEAS

- The Church of England used to have regular contact with many people via the rites of passage and Christian education. This is no longer the case.
- Nowadays, for most people contact is now unpredictable and intermittent.
- There is little real connection for most people, and reaching out to outsiders requires radical change in thinking and practice.
- Drawing people in can only be successful if it includes a socialisation process alongside the individual's personal growth.
- The Church of England suffers from having to meet the needs of a huge spectrum of people and circumstances.
- In addition, the role of the clergy has changed, and untrained ministers may find the new demands of management and of dealing with people with choices very difficult.
- Qualitative research can be used to help identify the role of the Church (or synagogue) and so draw people in. This may be different from that previously thought.
- Research can be used to help restructure the Church to cope with segmentation, the role of membership, the need for better communication and ways to evolve the services.
- The process is new and difficult, given some existing views about change and the role of the clergy and also the financial and practical hurdles associated with research.

NOTES

1 Course providing an introduction to the Christian faith which originated from Holy Trinity Brompton in the early 1990s and has since been used around the world.
2 In *Gone but not Forgotten* (1998–99) Philip Richter and Leslie Francis use a combined quantitative and qualitative methodology to analyse reasons why people leave the Church in the UK.

REFERENCES

Brierley, P. (1996) *Changing Churches Briefing No 3*. Christian Research Association.
Religious Trends No 1. Christian Research. www.christian-research.org.uk
Richter, P. & Francis, L. (1998–99) *Gone but not Forgotten.*
UK Christian Handbook. Christian Research Association.

Chapter 13

Qualitative Research and Innovation

David Spenser
Director, Direct Dialogue

with

Stephen Wells
Principal, Wells & Company

Editor's introduction

Innovation is not an industry like the arts or politics. However, each and every industry covered in this book is constantly changing and innovating, and the ability to innovate successfully will be a key determinant of future success. In addition, innovation requires a deep understanding of the consumer, and in many cases it relies on the philosophy and methodologies of qualitative research. This chapter therefore fits very neatly into this book and much of the thinking is relevant to almost all the other chapters.

I was particularly privileged to have two practitioner authors contribute to this chapter. David Spenser is one of the most respected researchers working the field, and Stephen Wells has spent many years considering how to use the skills of qualitative research to encourage innovation in organisations.

David's basic premise is that consumers and organisations are increasingly distant from one another, with the consumers often leading the way in fashion, ways of behaviour and attitude change. The chapter discusses why this is the case, and how organisations can not only try to keep up but actually move one step ahead of consumers, so developing truly innovative brands, services or products.

Many different methodologies are used nowadays to assist clients with innovation including scenario planning (building 'memories' of the future) and ethnography (experiencing the lives of relevant consumers). David explains in detail how he approaches the process of introducing innovation to products and services based on his intelligent and unique interpretation of the problem.

Stephen's section is at the end of the chapter and he brings examples of this process to illustrate the theoretical framework. The context is the rapidly changing consumer, and the qualitative approach is shown operating within it.

THE CONTEXT: THE CONSUMER–COMPANY GAP

Divergence

'The greatest social change is the
accelerating rate of social change.' (Alvin Tofler 1973)

We are experiencing increasing rates of change in our lives; it seems that the only thing we can rely on is the unpredictability of the future. Tofler's comment (from back in 1974) seems more prescient than ever as we move into the new millennium.

While they have shared accelerating rates of change, the world of consumers and the corporate world have changed in different *directions*: the realities of consumer and corporate life are diverging. This has profound implications for how the processes of sparking and progressing innovation can be managed through qualitative research. Before we explore these implications, let us pause and consider some of the key trends in the corporate and consumer worlds. So, with apologies for the inevitable generalisations and simplifications, I want to hold up a mirror to each of these worlds.

Consumers

- Increasing fragmentation in consumer markets has been well-documented. We can no longer explain or predict markets using the old demographic models of age, sex, class, region. Consumers are aggregating in new kinds of allegiances resulting in the emergence of different kinds of target groups; for example, the rise of greys and gays as primary consumer segments.

- These are not just macro market trends, however – even on an individual level we are seeing greater diversity and variation. 'Portfolio careers' are now becoming the norm as people do not expect to remain in the same occupation, on a predictable track throughout their working lives, or even from one decade to the next. Consumers are having to become accustomed to much greater levels of uncertainty and unpredictability than they have faced in the past. While for older consumers, used to greater levels of security and predictability, this is unsettling, younger consumers are increasingly seeing it as a source of interest, opportunity and personal growth. For younger people, it makes life more interesting and exciting.

● Consumers' use of brands is reflecting these trends. We are seeing the rise of 'portfolio consumers' who use brands in different ways over time and indeed use them in different ways according to different aspects of their identities: 'which part of me are we talking about?'. The old, unidimensional definitions of brand usage seem inadequate now to explain the complexity of brand repertoires. Savvy marketers realise that 'mindsets', 'need states' and 'viewpoints' are a better way to understand and explain their consumers than demographics; they target their brands/communications at these 'ways of being'. (By illustration, someone's brand usage might change according to whether they are in the mode of 'me at work', 'me with my family', 'me with my friends' or 'me as a father'. These repertoires might be quite different.)

● We are seeing consumers evolving different relationships with brands. They have become much more marketing-literate, confident and self-assured in their use of brands. They are no longer happy merely to take what's given, but are demanding a say in creating the brand's agenda, either with or without the involvement of brand management. This has resulted in consumers becoming dramatically more demanding of brands: even over 'how they behave' (the organised resistance to the threatened sinking of Shell's Brent Spar platform is a particularly dramatic example of this). Paradoxically, they are also becoming more playful and creative in the use of brands for their own ends.

Fashion provides some of the more obvious examples of consumers adopting and using brands according to their own agendas. I understand that the Tommy Hilfiger brand was originally intended as a preppy, upscale fashion brand (similar to Ralph Lauren's Polo range). It was discovered and adopted by urban black youths, who bestowed upon it an immediate street cachet. Fortuitously, this represented a marvellous platform from which to imbue an international brand with mass appeal, and the label has been skilfully marketed to exploit this (unintended) early lucky break. Similarly, brands such as Timberland and Caterpillar have been quick to exploit the use of industrial and combat apparel by modern-day 'urban warriors'.

There has been something of a sea change in the relationship between brands and consumers. Technology means that consumers now have all the information; they are not the ones trying to 'work it all out'. Increasingly, that is becoming the manufacturers' job. And this is before the impact of online communities has fully hit us, with their potential to fundamentally change marketing and retailing dynamics.

The marketing game

The picture I am painting is one of consumers *enjoying* the 'marketing game' and participating in it as *equal partners*. 'Clever marketing' is now one of the highest compliments to be paid to a brand by the public (superseding plaudits for 'believability', 'realism' or even 'truthfulness'). UK consumers now enjoy and applaud subtle, clever tactics as never before. They greatly value imagination and wit from companies. They are predisposed to respond positively to innovation. As I write, the current UK advertising campaign for VW Polo engages consumers in an entertaining 'game' around a central but often elusive price/affordability message. The success of the campaign is testament to the enjoyment consumers derive from rising to the challenge of decoding the advertising. The message is straightforward, but the wit and style with which it is conveyed are applauded.

Again, with apologies for over-simplification, when we look at the corporate world, we see a very different set of trends.

Corporate

If consumers are characterised by increasing diversity and playfulness, the corporate management of brands is characterised by more uniformity across markets and greater singularity of purpose. The cost-stripping culture of the late 1980s and early 1990s has resulted in leaner, more centralised management structures, to the point where strategic management of a brand may even be in a different global region to its markets, as a result of the drive for economies of scale. The holy grail today is a communications campaign that is entirely consistent across all global markets – neat, clean, decisive and efficient. For all the talk of 'think globally and act locally', the appeal of a singular campaign is so alluring for international brand management that it can prove hard to resist.

These trends can result in brands – and those managing them – becoming progressively more divorced from the 'buzzing, blooming confusion' of consumer life. Marketing management attempts to capture a brand's essence in a single pithy phrase which is then applied across all markets. This practice is unkindly called 'megaphone marketing' in some circles as it rides roughshod over the differences between markets, never mind the difference between consumers! This, sadly, is unlikely to result in the cleverness, imagination and creativity increasingly appreciated by the consumer. One is left with the image of 'battleship brands' steaming ahead on their predetermined courses. They certainly offer impressive money-return, efficiency and clarity, but lack real dynamism, internal variety, playfulness or flexibility. While these battleships are forging ahead, consumers are busy having fun in speedboats – buzzing around between the brands, and jumping on and off them for a laugh.

What this means for 'innovation'

In a nutshell, all this means that innovation is getting harder for larger companies to achieve, particularly multinationals.

A widening gap

The divergence between corporate and consumer realities is resulting in a widening gap between those on the 'client-side' and those on the 'market-side'. On the one hand, we see consumer fragmentation, media proliferation and playful, even anarchic consumption / use of brands; on the other we have corporate procedures and structures that could have been designed to thwart imagination. Risk-taking with big brands is, well, risky. The sheer volume of information generated by modern brands can slow decision-making to a crawl – and anyway, the decision-makers are so remote from the market that they might be in another country.

It is easy to intuit how wide 'the gap' feels between oneself and different companies. There is nothing particularly scientific about this, just a sense that some brands are more 'in touch' with their consumers than others. For example, I bank with both Barclays and first direct, but 'my gap' feels smaller with first direct. It feels smaller with Virgin than British Airways. Larger with Sainsbury than Tesco. Quite why is difficult to say; it might be their communications, the experience of brand contact, the nature of service I receive or even their design aesthetics, but it is easy for me to judge which of these brands feels more 'on my wavelength'.

Some companies do work hard to keep the gap as narrow as possible. As consumers are taking a more active, equal role in establishing the meanings and values of brands, smart companies have endeavoured to enlist their co-operation. In effect, they aim to 'share' the brand, and achieve agreement with their consumers over the way forward. Some companies create specific procedures to achieve this – for example, most US grocery brands display toll-free numbers to gain customer feedback, suggestions and comments. Increasingly, websites are becoming truly interactive – allowing a direct dialogue between the brand and those comprising the brand community. The web is a great means to create a forum in which all those who are interested or associated with a brand or a company can have a voice. This interaction can help to guard against brands which are literally 'losing touch' with their communities. The brands with the highest quality dialogue are in the strongest positions to innovate. We see this trend particularly in the 'younger' industries and markets such as IT/computing, where there is an obvious fit with interactivity and technology. Organic food, cosmetics, clothing (especially street/athletic wear) are also arenas in which new brands are notably moving forward in league with their consumers.

The street as the hunting ground

It is the consumers now who have greater reserves of dynamism, imagination and creativity; they are now the ones with fleetness of foot. The street is a better hunting ground for new ideas than head office, or even the research and development department. Companies will find it ever more difficult to seize the initiative from consumers. Ultimately, consumers will assume an even greater upper hand when online communities reach their full momentum, as Hagel and Armstrong have noted:

> '[Online communities] turns the traditional market model, in which vendors seek out customers, on its head. Virtual communities put customers in this more powerful position by providing them with a rich source of vendor information, forums in which to interact with other customers, and the capability of interacting with specific vendors to negotiate the most advantageous terms of sale.... Increasingly, customers will pit one vendor against another to secure the best deal for themselves.' (Hagel and Armstrong, 1997)

Consumers have control over their communications and sources of information. They have the savvy, and are more in touch with subtleties. In short, they are becoming smarter and more powerful than the companies providing them with products and services. Many brands' innovative heartbeat is shifting to those consumers on the edge of their community network, and they are making up their own minds over what they want.

Catching up with consumers

Companies that lose touch with the brand communities are doomed to play a game of 'catch-up', or simply to attempt to spot trends among opinion-leader groups (the youth, gay culture, clubbers, etc.). This latter strategy will ultimately fail, as its relative success depends on how close to these leading-edge groups you can get (are you *really* on the pulse, or lagging a little way behind?). The diversity and fluidity of the new consumer reality means that it is not always easy to spot (or even choose) which leading-edge audience you should be learning from in any case. The best that can be hoped for is that you are never too far out of touch with those people who are the innovators – becoming a 'fast follower'!

However, it is not all doom and gloom for companies – they need not be reduced to chasing ever-more elusive consumers. Qualitative research can enable clients to become truly innovative – to be proactive rather than reactive; to get ahead of 'where consumers are at'. Research, however, needs to re-examine some of its core assumptions in order to do this. Before we consider the way forward, we first need to pause again and examine some of the problems which conventional qualitative research encounters in attempting to spark and grow innovative ideas.

THE ROLE FOR QUALITATIVE RESEARCH

The problems with 'traditional qualitative research'

Searching for reliability

One of the positive things about qualitative research as a profession in the UK is that we have never stopped trying to improve our procedures. We are not perfect yet, but we have spent years, for example, improving our procedures for recruiting respondents. A lot of effort goes into ensuring that they are indeed a true representation of a particular market. But why do we do this? Because we struggle to gain greater *validity*; we're searching for ever greater reliability in our understanding of consumers. Research has always aspired to bring information (that can be relied upon) back across 'the gap' from the consumer into the company. If, after all, clients are making major decisions based on the findings of qualitative research, they need to know that this information is something that can be trusted. Much effort has been spent on ensuring 'dependability' – representative samples, recruitment procedures, content analysis, 'neutral' moderation styles are the result of the quest for *reliable information*.

At its more enlightened, in addition to providing reliable information, conventional qualitative research aims to bring insights and understanding back from the consumer into the company. Here we see more 'modern' approaches: much more 'active' moderation styles in place of 'neutral' questioning; a willingness to interpret data, moving on and away from reportage; the use of more searching techniques to investigate consumers' perceptions and attitudes. This represents a much more dynamic and constructive approach, which builds for our clients a more sophisticated/ developed understanding of the consumer's perspective.

The information paradigm

Yet even in its more evolved, advanced forms this type of qualitative research has remained essentially within a basic 'information' paradigm; it has remained preoccupied with bringing 'the findings' (whether 'information' or 'understanding') back from the consumer/market into the company. The very language, the terminology that it uses to describe research remains evocative of a Victorian scientific expedition: we *do fieldwork*, we *sample markets*, we *build models*, we *segment consumers*, we produce our *findings*. It goes out to the market to look for the answers. It has been a one-way street, from the consumer back to the client. For all the improvements in our ability to explain consumers' perceptions to the client, qualitative research has been much less concerned with carrying the client-side reality out to the consumer. 'What's important to the client' has remained very much secondary to 'What's important to the consumer' in determining how we go about interacting with our research respondents.

Advances in qualitative research have clearly been of great benefit to client companies; hence the continued strong growth of research in recent decades. The trouble when it comes to gaining innovation is that, even though we have become 'better at understanding consumers', such an understanding is inevitably rooted in the past. All people make sense of new things in the light of their experience, and in research their reactions to new ideas are necessarily filtered through their previous experiences. We all do it, otherwise we would go mad – one simply cannot keep changing the way one thinks about the world every time a piece of new information comes along, so we fit it into the existing pattern. Life is more comfortable like that: it means that you can continue to function without reappraising everything, all the time. So it is with brands, products and companies examined in qualitative research studies: anyone who is involved in commissioning or conducting research knows it takes *a lot* to get people to re-frame their perceptions and embrace anything which is fundamentally different from the status quo.

Templating

Consumers will work to fit new thoughts about a brand or company into the pattern with which they are familiar – I call this 'templating' – and it is a fundamentally dangerous tendency for research which is trying to develop new thinking. Even if research attempts to 'explore the future', it is a future this is inevitably predicated on the past if we remain within a conventional information/understanding model.

'Templating' also means that it is considerably harder for qualitative research to deal with innovative ideas based around large, long-established, familiar brands than with 'blue sky' NPD, where ideas are developed without any brand baggage to act as a template against which to fit the new thoughts. Why should people jump to change the way they think about familiar brands they have known all their lives? Brands like Persil/Cadbury's/

Kellogg's have always been around; they are rich with meaning for consumers. They are known, familiar, reliable. So what do people do with new thoughts about such brands? They resist them. Or they whittle them down until they fit the template (or at least until they can be accommodated). This is why research is forever struggling to overcome consumers' comfort zones – are they just uncomfortable with a new idea (which might be a real recommendation for innovation) or does the idea *really* stink? I think that 'templating' is the primary reason why qualitative research is seen as so conservative among the creative communities: they see their formative, delicate ideas being subjected to the insensitive verdicts of consumers who have little involvement or awareness of 'what the idea is trying to do'. In the early stages of development, we should not be seeking consumers' *permission* for new initiatives, we should be enlisting their *help* as a development resource. Their evaluation should come later, once the ideas have become more clearly framed.

Of course, the past *is* important in understanding how things are, and how things could be in the future. Indeed, it is probably our most useful predictor of future behaviour – but only if we remain within the current template. The past is a major handicap if we are trying to build something genuinely new. In research which aims to assist innovation, we are trying to *create* and *exploit* discontinuities; we will not do this by looking at what consumers have to tell us, and bringing that back across the gap – no matter how clever we are. A research philosophy which is all about looking at consumers, listening to them and asking their opinion is still concerned with bringing understanding from the consumers' reality across the great divide to those on the client-side. It is always likely to struggle in helping to establish truly innovative ideas.

Looking backwards

Thus, consumers' perceptions are inevitably backward-looking. They have not been to the brainstorming meetings that produced the development routes; they were not party to the creative brief for the advertising – even the best qualitative researcher, with a full toolkit of projective techniques, can still only get out what is in there. We can certainly find out 'what people didn't know they knew', but what happens if the requirement to change is driven by something that is invisible to the consumer? Or irrelevant? What if we are asking for consumers' input into the development of something that has not yet happened? We cannot expect our research respondents to magically understand the corporate issues driving the initiative.

To illustrate with an example, Mercedes-Benz was faced with an interesting task in deciding how to market the A-Class; while the car is a technological *tour de force* it is a much smaller car than previously seen from the marque, and, in appearance, certainly does not fit the Mercedes template. Mercedes owners and owners of competitors' cars were all happy to keep the brand within its existing identity – as a manufacturer of sleek, luxury ('Diplomat') cars. This is despite the fact that from the company's perspective, this is likely to represent an ever-shrinking niche within the global car market, and ultimately comprises a losing strategic position against more broadly based competitors. Consumers, of course, were little concerned with the strategic validity of the marque into the next century: they love the idea of Mercedes, they're comfortable with what it means, which values it stands for; they don't want the brand to change, thank you very much. Unsurprisingly for one of the strongest brands in the world, they believe they 'know' Mercedes. The A-Class was certainly a radical departure from this template. Conventional research struggled against comfort zones and strong resistance to the idea of Mercedes launching such a small and inexpensive car: it just didn't feel like a 'proper Mercedes'. By working *with* consumers, the company was able to build an enduring positioning platform for the model, based on its highly innovative, radical design, drawing from and contributing back into the marque's reputation for technological and engineering leadership.

Isolation of the client and the consumer

Consequently, we shuffle back and forth between two groups which each have limited perspectives: our clients, and their consumers. Each group on either side of the gap has an absolutely integral impact on the success or failure of any new initiative; both are entirely interdependent. Yet we keep both isolated from each other. We take the brief from the client and carry it to the consumer – who has probably not given two seconds' serious thought prior to solemnly expressing a 'verdict '.

Let us take consumers first. They are the ones with the biggest problem: they are expected to walk in off the street and, on request and without prior thought, provide profound insights into our clients' business for them. We then think about what the consumer has proclaimed and present this back in our findings to the client. It is a tall order.

Don't forget your clients either. They might talk smarter but they can be just as limited in their perspective. Centralised, remote management means that not only are clients distant from their consumers but they are becoming ever more afraid of actually meeting their customers. They are aware of their consumers' critical importance, yet feel 'removed', separate from them. And don't forget that they are driven by their own internal agendas: politics, norms, career development, budgeting, which will all have an impact on how they will view research.

Within this framework, even developmental qualitative research projects tend to be driven by 'one-sided' thinking. They are tasked with either 'finding out what the consumer wants or seeks, and then bringing it to the clients to see if they can do it' or 'finding out what the client wants to do and carrying it to the consumer to see how we can get the consumers to buy it'. Neither scenario represents the best approach for sparking innovation. Very little effort is made to carry an understanding of the client-side realities to consumers (other than lip-service), and consumers remain insulated from the client's agenda and the factors driving the initiative. So, irrespective of whether the project is corporate- or market-driven, 'the gap' is maintained.

The 90-minute group

Finally, as researchers, we are expected to work our miracles with consumers in a single (usually 90-minute) step. But life, unfortunately, is nothing like a focus group: in the real world, people do not make instant judgments about new ideas; they do not feel it necessary to justify or explain their views to a group of strangers; they are not expected to take up positions on the spur of the moment. While group discussions have proven invaluable in reaching fresh insights and understandings about 'the way things are', they have much greater difficulty in exploring the – often uncomfortable, half-formed, difficult – seeds of really different, innovative ideas. People need to take time to get used to new ideas, to rethink their realities, to relax, play, feel confident, get brave. Eight strangers, in a viewing facility, talking about something they have never thought too hard about before, is stacking the odds somewhat against ourselves! It is a testament to researchers' skills that we get such insightful understanding out of this environment.

Commoditisation

Research which works in this way is struggling against increasing commoditisation; we are all using pretty much the same toolkits now, despite attempts to brand them differently. Research agencies are becoming more interchangeable. Claims that one company has better, more or different ways of talking to consumers are no longer credible; the key differentials are the interpretive abilities of the individual researchers. Clients have known this for a long time, which is why they always endeavour to buy individuals rather than companies. There is, however, a fundamental weakness in this single point of contact – even the most skilled researchers will filter their findings through their own 'realities'. The approach I discuss below has the ambition of establishing multiple points of contact between the company and its market (and indeed across all the groups comprising what I will call the 'brand community'). Just as Velcro's strength comes from the combined force of hundreds of tiny, individually frail connections, so brands can lock themselves securely into their communities in order to ensure that they move forward boldly, with the support of their key audiences. The brands which achieve this will be best positioned to innovate successfully. Qualitative research can take a primary role in creating and managing this happy state of affairs – it can 'velcro' together the disparate constituencies of a brand's community. The following section of this chapter discusses how.

How 'research' can spark and support innovation

A new approach

Strictly speaking, the research approach outlined here is not research at all, in the literal sense. My dictionary defines research as 'the systematic investigation into and study of materials, sources etc., in order to establish facts and reach new conclusions'. This would be anathema to innovation; we are most unlikely to produce a radically new idea from a 'systematic investigation'. We should not be going out *looking for an answer* but *building a solution*, with the involvement of those on either side of the great divide between those on the 'client side' and those on the 'market side'. Research and innovation are not natural companions – at least the kind of conventional research I have outlined above is unlikely to provide the kind of impetus we require to drive forward innovation.

We can, however, use research *skills* to spark creativity and to build and foster an innovation culture within our clients' businesses. To do this, we need to leave behind a number of conventions that we take for granted in orthodox qualitative research.

New 'conventions'

- We need to work very hard indeed to get the right 'sample' of consumers; but these will certainly *not* be a representative sample of the marketplace.
- Indeed, we need to move away from a singular focus on the *consumer*, and instead adopt a mentality in which the range of groups comprising the brand community are of potentially equal importance. The spark may easily come from someone making the product, selling the product, distributing the product, as well as those using the product.
- We should stop trying to keep the different parts of the brand community separate. Not only could any one of these groups provide the spark to innovation, but when they are working together to *negotiate the future*, we gain a synergistic benefit from drawing together each of the groups which will have an integral effect on the potential success of any new initiative. In effect, we can close the gaps, both between those client-side and those market-side, but also between the various groupings throughout the business. Brands often have a huge hinterland of producers, administrators,

distributors and retailers – this is a fearsomely powerful resource to combine on a joint task force with consumers.

- If we are working to innovate, we should drop our concerns with the validity/reliability of the thinking – i.e. stop thinking 'data'; instead think 'possibilities'.
- We should not restrict ourselves to speaking to people only once.
- We should try to avoid talking to people in environments which are divorced from the realities of the brand – why not take consumers into the factory, or let them spend the day in a shop before coming along to the research session, or take those working in R&D into consumers' homes, and then run integrated discussions?
- We should try to avoid working to the marketing function only within our clients' companies.

Research to inspire

I have discussed how innovation is in danger of moving away from companies and further into the province of the consumer, with companies resigned to playing 'catch-up'. Traditional research has aspired to be cleverer at looking at consumers by gaining insights and then carrying these back to our client. Research aspired to *understand*. In order to spark innovation, it needs to aspire to *inspire*. Instead of trying to discover the answers, qualitative research can literally facilitate the process through which progress is achieved.

To do this, qualitative research must adopt a very different approach. It needs to move away from the information/understanding model and towards a *task* paradigm. It should not be about 'bringing the findings back' but 'bringing the brand community together'. This means giving at least as much attention to those on the client-side as on the market-side: we need to create a shared agenda which recognises both the internal and external issues. It also means that probably the first person who needs to be 'researched' is the client.

Cracking problems

The broader community is often ignored by traditional qualitative research, with its determined focus on *understanding the market*. Instead of 'finding out what consumers think' about new ideas, we should create procedures through which clients and their consumers can 'crack the problem' together.

In a nutshell, qualitative research can close the gaps within the brand community and create a climate and methodology to *negotiate progress*.

PRACTICALITIES AND CASE HISTORIES

Nuts and bolts

- *Start off by 'researching' the client.* Conduct individual in-depth interviews to establish the client-side realities, drivers, ambitions, agendas.

- *Move from an information paradigm (or even an understanding paradigm) to a task approach.* Brief all participants on the aims of the project and make sure that the full range of viewpoints across the community are communicated to each group. Consumers need briefing too. They need to know about the company and the requirements for innovation or the scope of the opportunity we are trying to exploit, just as much as clients need to learn about the consumer, if they are going to work together effectively across the great divide. We need to establish a working dialogue across the brand community, getting people to interact directly on a shared task, and working constructively towards agreed aims.

- *Establish a small, multidisciplinary 'core team'.* This may be drawn from various client-side groups (perhaps production, administration, finance, retail in addition to marketing, advertising, design, R&D). Gain a commitment from this team to become active participants throughout the programme.

- *Build rapport and enthusiasm over time.* Groups get braver and bolder after a while; they work better once they have settled down. 'Instant breakthroughs' are an enticing promise, but sadly, my experience is that innovation does not normally happen like that.

- *Choose those who are going to be best for the job.* With regard to consumers, do not choose participants on the basis of demographics, usage or even attitudes but on personalities, aptitudes, ways of thinking, styles of interacting. These consumers are likely to be intensely curious people – buzzy, 'have a go' types. They are likely to be people who actively enjoy and seek out high levels of change in their lives, but they should not be clones of one another – it is important to get the chemistry and energy of the group right. Some may be perceptive, some energetic, some humorous, some 'lateral', some good at listening to other people's ideas and accelerating them forward. The best teams always have a mix of personalities and abilities. How one chooses to identify and recruit these 'golden consumers' is a matter of personal preference. Experience has taught me, however, that it is extremely difficult to recruit directly into a dialogue programme (in a single step), no matter how carefully or imaginatively the recruitment questionnaire has been framed. So much depends upon 'what they are like in a group', their chemistry with other participants and indeed with the researcher. Increasingly, I invite only those respondents whom I have met in previous research projects.

- *Only allow enthusiastic appropriate clients to be directly involved in the programme.* Anyone from the client-side can observe the programme, but just as we are choosing consumers who will be 'right for the job', so we should ensure that we have only the right kinds of client personnel participating.

- *Encourage clients to work with consumers.* Literally, *en-courage* them, help them to be braver, to get involved, to disclose their ambitions and fears. Why are people in client companies so afraid of sitting down and working with their consumers? Consumers are generally extremely understanding and positive towards those working for a brand, even if they are critical of the brand itself. Once they have experienced the benefits of this kind of interactive 'research', most clients cannot get enough of it. The first step can be very difficult to take, however. It is interesting to note that clients tend to need much more coaching on 'how to work with their consumers' than consumers need support in working with those on the client-side.

- *Make a clear distinction between the generation of new ideas, their subsequent development, and their evaluation.* Each calls for very different climates, techniques and participants. The cardinal rule of brainstorming – separate out the generation of ideas from their evaluation – is extremely valuable here: too often, research is expected to evaluate ideas as it is developing them. 'Sparking new thinking' calls for a very different approach to creating an ongoing innovation culture within an organisation. If we are working at an early stage, seeking new ideas, we need to have energetic, fun, lively sessions – ideally in a stimulating environment – in order to achieve a strong 'jump start' to a programme. *Hunting possibilities* is the keynote here: we are searching for the maximum number of possible ideas, with little regard for how 'right' they might eventually prove to be. If we are at the later 'development' stage, we need to get clients and consumers working together to ensure that both 'market' and 'corporate' agendas are satisfied as the initiative progresses. The people who are most valuable for this stage are likely to be different from the stars of the jump start stage; the climate is less playful, more considered, concerned with practicalities; the climate more 'thoughtful' than 'fizzy and energetic'. More traditional qualitative approaches are best able to deliver an evaluation – gauging the worth of the ideas against key practical criteria.

- *Become the pivotal figure in the building of strong brand communities.* Researchers are perfectly placed to do this. The strongest communities in society are those which share common beliefs and aims; those whose members pull together in unison. The strongest *brand* communities are just the same. With the very strongest of brands everyone 'knows' what they stand for, what is right and wrong for the brand, where the brand can and cannot go. There are constant processes of renegotiation and agreement between everybody connected with the brand. Qualitative researchers have the perfect skill-set to manage this process.

- *Develop specific methodology.* A range of different approaches, branded as 'brain banks', 'super groups', 'ideas workshops', 'sequential recycling', 'dialogue teams', 'breakthroughs', have already been developed by leading practitioners in this field. They have used different terminology and branding, but all these methods involve a shift from using research to *find out* about the consumer to using research as a means of managing clients and consumers *working together* in order to move forward together.

THE EXPERIENCE OF STEPHEN WELLS

Consumer workshops

The sorts of interactive projects I have been running for the past 15 years or so have typically lasted for around one-and-a-half days and involve a couple of extended groups among target consumers with creative team sessions sandwiched in between. Usually called a 'consumer workshop', such a session culminates in planning to commit the team to action, with defined timings and agreed responsibilities. The teams usually march off to the sound of gunfire and do as they have promised. Such projects tend to be hugely rewarding in terms of the quantity and quality of output and its speed of production, but most valuable of all is the energising of the company team: the process makes people curious to learn more and to generate better, more radical ideas. It makes them braver. Company people draw encouragement from what they sense. They become both more sensate, and sensory, managers.

Such developments are an essential antidote to an increasing tendency for company personnel to be apprehensive about encounters with consumers – when 'the gap', as described by David, becomes a gulf. They can feel nervously compelled to *'talk' to consumers*. Indeed, I once had to reassure a brand manager that he didn't need to take a 'deck of acetates' with him when he went on an accompanied shopping expedition!

Direct and informal contact with consumers

Having gained the confidence, through careful training and practice (led by qualitative researchers), to listen to consumers in 'formal' research, company people can then undertake a wide range of more direct and informal consumer contacts. In order to obtain the most powerful learnings from such encounters, these need to be carefully planned and controlled, with formal feedback sessions. These are often facilitated by qualitative researchers, so that the team truly feels that *'none of us is as smart as all of us'* (Japanese proverb). With a common consumer focus, ideas and possibilities take over from information and process; the MBIs (Masters of Business Intuition) start to ease out the MBAs. The energy of the ever-increasing rate of consumer change can be harnessed to build brands. Ignoring it is likely to prove disastrous.

Olivio

I have seen the raw energy of consumer change, once recognised and harnessed, lead to some telling innovations. For example, the dramatic shift over the past couple of years in consumers' definition of 'health', from a negatively defined absence of symptoms and an overriding concern to know what's bad for me, to a recognition that happiness is inextricably linked to healthiness, so that body and soul cannot be separated. People now strive for a state of well-being, and to worry less. This profound shift in consumer values was picked up at an early stage by the Olivio brand/agency team who had enjoyed, at best, only a modestly successful launch of the brand on a relatively rational olive oil/monosaturates proposition. Their adoption of a 'Mediterranean well-being' platform has transformed the brand and made it a runaway success in an area notorious for rampant consumer apathy.

Vaseline Intensive Care

This shift in people's definition of 'health', to a position where it co-exists in a virtuous circle with a notion of well-being, has also had implications for the marketing of brands outside the food and drink sector: for example, in skin care, where Vaseline Intensive Care is now positioned far more positively than in the past when its role was that of an antidote to dry skin. Highly memorable advertising for this brand now focuses on the sensory joys of freshly moisturised skin – of the user sensing that gently firmed skin is not only healthy, but also indicative of a happy, healthy state of mind.

Oxo

Years ago, in the very early 1980s, I undertook an experimental research project designed to explore a hypothesis emerging from other work under-taken at the time: namely, that family life in Britain had changed funda-mentally at around the time when Margaret Thatcher became prime minister.

The notion was that people were indeed getting 'on their bikes' and competing, and in doing so manifested their individuality, and that this, in turn, had profound implications for family structure and dynamics. The outcome of a long series of interactive consumer / management sessions was the mould-breaking, and eventually hugely popular, 'Oxo family' campaign which featured family life in the raw. *EastEnders* followed later! For the Oxo/JWT team, seeing and listening to consumers was believing, and this classic campaign ran for 16 years until it too became a victim of inevitable social change.

Guinness

In the alcoholic drinks market, the growth of Guinness in the UK over the past 15 years is rooted in a simple, yet profound consumer insight also gained in the early Thatcher years: namely, that the power of individualism could be harnessed by Guinness. The famous Rutger Hauer advertising campaign was the result, and the brand evolved from flat hat, Woodbine and whippet imagery to a brand sought after by younger thinking, 'clever' drinkers. And sales grew.

CONCLUSIONS

Innovation is based on achieving simple yet profound insights: a step on from simply having consumer understanding, and requiring company people to have genuine empathy with consumers. This, in turn, requires the right environment to be established in order to facilitate the intense listening necessary. All the insights referred to in this chapter were gained when company teams watched extended group discussions in which people were given plenty of opportunities to express themselves emotionally – so that they themselves became fascinated by the topic and wanted to explore more. Afterwards the watchers shared their insights in a disciplined way with the moderator of the groups and were then so moved that they acted.

The stakes are high; the empathy felt by organisations with consumers needs to be both accurate and genuine, 'the gap' non-existent. Qualitative researchers have a key role to play in expediting this by providing a common focus for discovery and development while celebrating the role of the different perspectives of what has been termed 'the brand community'.

In order to undertake this role effectively, qualitative researchers need to become less obsessional about reliability and process ... because life moves on, quicker than ever before; and so any claimed precision usually turns out to be somewhat spurious in practice. Perhaps we should all learn to enjoy our work more and to agonise less – just as we have learned to redefine 'health'.

Let's relax, and use our skills more to help people shape their futures rather than slavishly seek to provide an understanding of what's already happened. After all, that's how science is evolving. Failing this, can't we just be part of the creative process, facilitating discovery where discovery is: 'Seeing what everyone has seen and thinking what no-one has thought' (Anon.).

KEY IDEAS

- The worlds of consumers and companies are diverging and this has profound implications for innovation and change.
- Consumers are increasingly enjoying diversity, uncertainty and unpredictability, and their use of brands reflects their multi-dimensional lives.
- Consumers are now equal players in the marketing game, not mere recipients.
- Conversely, marketing companies are aiming, for cost and ease of marketing purposes, to make brands universal and single-minded – 'megaphone marketing'. All this means a widening gap between consumers and companies with many brands falling out of touch with their audiences.
- Companies need to get ahead of consumers if they are to become truly innovative.
- Conventional qualitative research is ill-placed for this task as it is too concerned with information, inevitably based on the past not the future. In addition, it keeps the client and consumer apart.
- A new approach is required using research skills but based on new assumptions and conventions regarding sampling, methodology and locations.
- Research needs to inspire, not just to understand, in order to foster innovation.
- A task-led approach to qualitative research based on a multidisciplinary core team alongside curious, buzzy consumers will enable the company to generate and develop really new ideas under the leadership of a talented qualitative researcher.

REFERENCES

Hagel III, J. & Armstrong, A.G. (1997) *Net Gain*. Harvard Business School Press, Cambridge, MA.

Tofler, A. (1973) *Future Shock*. Pan Books, London.

FURTHER READING

Dru, J-M. (1996) *Disruption*. John Wiley & Sons.

Foster, J. (1996) *How to Get Ideas*. Berrett-Koehler, London.

Gleick, J. (1999) *Faster*. Little, Brown & Co.

Gordon, S. (1999) *Permission Marketing*. Simon & Schuster, New York.

Kelly, K. (1998) *New Rules for the New Economy*. Fourth Estate.

Michalko, M. (1991) *Thinkertoys. A handbook for Business Creativity*. Ten Speed Press, London.

Morgan, A. (1999) *Eating the Big Fish*. John Wiley & Sons, London.

Steel, J. (1998) *Truth, Lies and Advertising*. John Wiley & Sons, London.

Chapter 14

International Qualitative Research

Peter Cooper
CRAM International

Editor's introduction

International qualitative research is not an 'industry' in the same way as advertising or social policy. However, it is probably the growing segment of qualitative research and now a multi-billion-dollar industry. Given the clear move towards globalisation in almost all the industries covered in this book, the role of international qualitative research cannot be ignored. The issues raised in this chapter, while predominantly focused on the commercial world, will impact relatively soon on research into such diverse areas as politics, broadcasting, media planning and potentially even the arts and religion.

This chapter explores the growth of internationalism in its various models, so setting the context for the need for international research. It explores in detail the special role for qualitative research internationally, in particular considering the importance of and theory behind analysis and interpretation. Peter Cooper explores the issues from the international stance, raising specific issues within that area. The theories discussed are illuminating and extremely useful when interpreting international problems.

The Practicalities section of the chapter is relatively lengthy as the reasons for methodological differences are considered in some depth. The issues for the future impact both on domestic and international research.

Peter Cooper writes as one of the pre-eminent practitioners and thinkers in qualitative research today and I think that this chapter is a valuable and highly stimulating read for those operating in both the international and also the domestic markets.

THE CONTEXT: THE GROWTH OF INTERNATIONALISM

International organisations

As we enter the new millennium a profound change is taking place in modern industrial and commercial organisations as they come to terms with the complex and challenging problems of developing their businesses into truly global concerns. Previously, many European companies had developed as international businesses during times when their home country had overseas colonies, and communications were of course much slower than they are today. Not surprisingly, they had organised themselves as multinationals with a centralised head office in the home country that set overall financial strategy, with a multitude of highly autonomous operating companies spread around the world. These companies had the major advantage that they were very sensitive to local needs.

As American and Japanese companies went global they had no colonial heritage to rely on and, because they were somewhat later into the game, they could capitalise upon much improved communication systems. In this context, their preferred model for globalising their companies was one that exercised far greater central control of products and knowledge. They were consequently less responsive to local requirements, but did enjoy the benefits of scale from producing and marketing the same product over large geographical areas.

A new model

Now we are seeing the emergence of a new organisational paradigm for internationalised businesses – the transnational – that has been designed to allow the benefits of local sensitivity and mass-production scale to be simultaneously enjoyed. Companies such as Unilever, ABB and Glaxo Wellcome, which have adopted this new model, view themselves as complex global networks with their various national companies as nodes within this network. The role of each node can vary, and each is defined in such a way that it can contribute to the total corporate knowledge pool which is then aware of local needs, while simultaneously being able to reap the benefits of scale by tailoring products to these local needs from common product platforms produced in large (often regional) manufacturing centres.

Managing knowledge

The new challenge that these transnational corporations have had to meet is that of managing knowledge within the transnational network, a process which encompasses not only collecting data from around the world but also processing, storing, disseminating and, most critically, ensuring that it is acted upon both rapidly and accurately. These changing needs have impacted profoundly upon market research as it too has had to face up to the changing needs of taking itself into the international arena. In particular, the qualitative aspect of the industry has experienced a paradigm shift of its own, reflecting these new corporate needs. Speed, sharing, and the exchange of qualitative data in a form that is rapidly decimated have become more critical to meet the needs of transnational organisations.

This major change in emphasis from local to global marketing warrants further discussion.

Globalism

Globalisation is critical when we consider the increasing power of multinationals, international branding, global communications, common or overlapping media.

The benefits to marketing are clear:

- Common development of brands
- Economies of scale in advertising, packaging and promotion
- Central organisation
- Common management language and disciplines

But there are also many other benefits of globalisation; for example, free trade agreements (GATT), international law, human rights movements, global environmental initiatives, and universal scientific and technological discourse. These point to a general shift towards homogenisation and integration, and erosion of local differences. This is inevitable and desirable in that all people share certain basic needs and have rights to higher standards of living, health, education, and access to goods.

From this global perspective there is a clear requirement to look for commonalties in consumer experiences. This is the main thrust of international qualitative research in view of the undeniable shift to global marketing.

Localism

The risk of course is a loss of local nuances and competitive edge. Nationalism, regionalism and devolution are also increasing as people come to value their differences.

Hence the resurgence of 'localism'. There is a recognisable effect worldwide of rejecting 'globalism' as 'artificial sameness', 'imposed global needs' and 'marketing imperialism'. This is especially obvious in developing markets. Consumers in Eastern Europe, South East Asia, China, India and Latin America often reject sheer 'Westernisation' (or 'Westoxification' as it has been called) in favour of local product qualities and local images. Within industrialised markets, too, there are marked shifts towards national identity and devolution, attaching value to local brands.

We still live in a world of nation states, which emphasise local cultural differences and national identity. In spite of the shift towards globalism and economies of scale, there is pressure to preserve local differences in relation to:

- Language, religion, upbringing and moral values
- Traditions, myths, values, symbols
- Continuity between generations
- Shared memories of major local events, history and common destiny
- Local foods, tastes, palate and customs
- Local media, stars, presenters and role models

From this local perspective, we need to be equally able to identify the unique properties of local markets. Localism requires us to reveal all the 'stuff' of local everyday experience. Much of this is really only known and accessible to locals; hence they need to be given freedom to express their local knowledge and passion.

Particular product areas where a balance between global and local is required are everyday life: eating, drinking, cleaning, shopping, savings and financial management, i.e. areas where there are both global trends and local traditional behaviours. Hence the blend, or 'glocalisation' as it has been called, of local expressions with global ideas. Many big international brands work in this way. It is worth noting that there are actually very few truly global brands (e.g. Coke, Pepsi, McDonald's, KFC), that market themselves in identical ways in all their markets. Most adapt global concepts to local expression.

Transculturalism

In contrast to sheer globalism or localism, new syntheses are now apparent. This new synthesis – transculturalism – combines elements of the local and global, but it also brings something new:

- The 'complex prism' of contemporary culture
- Weaving together local traditions and international values
- Combining local identity with international diversity

It is the so-called transcultural 'third culture', the rapid exchange and flow of goods, people, information, knowledge and images on a global scale – the 'ethnoscapes', 'needscapes', 'technoscapes', 'finanscapes', 'mediascapes' and 'ideoscapes' characteristic of modern global culture. Typical examples are in the fields of technology, communications and the internet, where new consumer cultures are developing at a rapid rate, especially among young people but increasingly in all consumer sectors.

Transculturalism is also bringing about a new breed of professionals – international lawyers, corporate tax accountants, marketing executives, management consultants, architects, film and video executives, journalists – and qualitative market researchers. The role of the international qualitative researcher is cosmopolitan, neither local expert nor stranger.

THE ROLE FOR QUALITATIVE RESEARCH

The objectives of qualitative research

International qualitative research deals with many of the same issues as local qualitative research but in different markets. The objectives are deceptively similar to those in local markets, i.e. to identify:

- Consumer needs, met and unmet
- Brand attitudes
- Consumer segmentations
- Responses to advertising, naming, packaging
- New product ideas
- Potential concepts and executions

However, the questions posed are different: Will my concepts travel? Is a global campaign possible? Can a campaign be adapted to local needs through local executions? Or will it need different concepts? Is what is happening in the West a forerunner of things to come in developing markets? Or will they develop differently? Are developing markets leap-frogging the West?

In fact as we shall see, the answer to many of these questions is 'Yes'. Concepts do travel in spite of local differences; developments in the West are guidelines for what is happening in the rest of the world. Markets are more similar than they appear at first sight. It is also the case that developing markets do 'leap-frog', creating their own special consumer needs. And there is an undeniable shift to 'global' marketing in spite of 'local' counter reactions. What is more interesting is the development of 'multiculturalism', new cultures and new ways of thinking.

The main differences between international and local qualitative research are that international qualitative research looks for synergy in consumer needs and motivations; real similarities and, where possible, for common platforms, without losing sight of critical differences where they do exist. It is this process of contrast, comparison and integration that holds the secret of excellence in international qualitative research.

International business therefore looks to international qualitative research to provide more than an in-depth understanding of consumers; it seeks a total understanding at global, regional and local levels simultaneously. In practice this means international qualitative research must:

- Get close to consumers in different markets, to relate and empathise with their idiosyncrasies. International markets are not just remote geographically, but culturally.
- Understand the social, religious and cultural context of consumer behaviour, what using a brand really means in that culture.
- Describe as a result the full core 'essences' of brands in context and around the world, what they mean and stand for in consumers' minds.
- Identify what causes these beliefs and images, how consumers in difficult markets interpret naming, packaging, advertising and all other aspects of the marketing mix. What errors are made, how things work, or don't.
- Above all, to understand change since change is the keynote of modern society.

In meeting international business needs, effective international qualitative research provides a compelling competitive edge in the global context. It helps international business understand the highly competitive marketplace of world trade, how to consolidate its brands and adapt them to changing consumer needs, goals and aspirations. It protects and develops brands and points up new opportunities.

But there is something else. International qualitative research challenges management by the contrasts and comparisons that are made. Its very diagnostic and insightful nature helps international management review their ways of thinking. It opens their eyes. It can therefore provoke fundamental reassessment of what products, brands and communication are all about, well beyond 'sheer' data. It may be a 'sniff' of change, an insight, a special incisive quote, on the basis of which new visions of brands and opportunities arise. This can, of course, be true of any qualitative research, but in the international context it is even more rewarding because of the huge opportunities out there, and the disastrous global consequences of getting it wrong.

The analysis and interpretation of international qualitative research

We need robust models of consumer behaviour to analyse qualitative data. Different models of qualitative analysis are necessary to take into account the variations in consumer behaviour, according to the economic development of a culture. The analysis of consumers in developed and developing markets is quite different. Here we look at some of the models and results from international qualitative research, with segmentation and consumer dynamics as our starting points.

(a) Segmentation

Segmentation can be undertaken from various perspectives: demographic, economic, political. In qualitative research we normally look for psychosocial segmentations, and differences between consumers in terms of upbringing, personality and attitude – for example, contrasts between:

- 'Inner' and 'outer' worlds
- Male and female principles
- Reality – testing vs. fantasy
- Control vs. play
- Social conformity vs. non-conformity
- Regressive vs. progressive
- Dependence vs. independence

Social change

In terms of social change, social milieux provide a basis for segmentation. Social milieux are the bundle of everyday life experiences, symbols and values that go to make one milieu recognisably different from another, in what brands they own, their aesthetics, and how they relate to advertising, brands, politics and so on. Milieux tend to vary by class and attitudes to change (Figure 1).

Patterns like this occur in most developed markets. They are found in Europe, the US, Japan, and also South East Asian markets; they therefore represent a sound basis for comparing and contrasting responses from different milieux, within and across markets. The impressions are that there are more similarities between markets in the milieux on the right which are more subject to similar global media, influence, and greater differences in the milieux on the left where local culture is more influential.

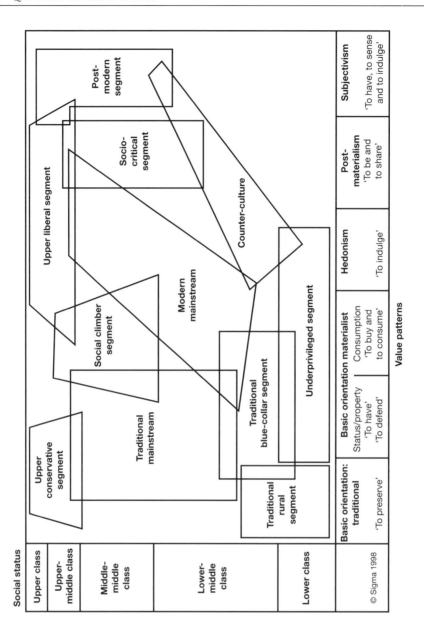

Source: Ueltzhöffer, J. and Ascheberg, C. (1999) Transactional consumer cultures and social milieus. *Journal of Market Research Society*, 41(1), pp. 47–60.

Figure 1 Transnational consumer cultures (© Sigma).

Individualism and collectivism

When we compare Western countries with other cultures, we find substantial variance, notably in terms of 'Individualism' and 'Collectivism', which pervade all aspects of thought and behaviour. The primary cultural distinctions are:

Individualism/Western	*Collectivism/non-Western*
Nuclear family	Extended family
Self or immediate family	Blood/kinship/work groups
Use of 'I' and 'Me'	Think in terms of 'us', 'we'
Beliefs in competition, challenge	Beliefs in harmony, co-operation
Self-expression	Avoid confrontation
Personal responsibility	Shared responsibility
Independence	Interdependence
Doing one's 'own thing'	Public self and 'face'
Resent authority	Respect for authority
Control by 'guilt' and conscience	Control by 'shame' and 'loss of face'

These account for many differences in decision-making, brand choice, adoption and diffusion of brands, brand image, and responses to advertising content and styles. They also show up in behaviour in groups, verbal expression, disagreement or acquiescence, responses to projective and elicitation techniques, and the role of the moderator.

Taking a global perspective, the influence of individualism and collectivism on different markets varies by economic development (Figure 2). There

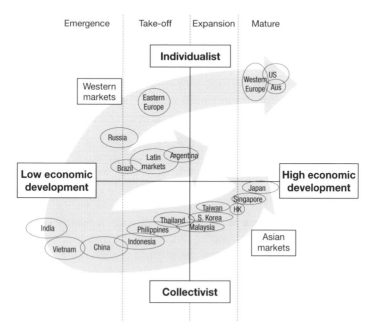

Figure 2 Global market dynamics (© CRAM International).

Table 1

Stage of economic development	Cultures based on:	
	Individualism	Collectivism
Mature	Western Europe, US, Australia	Japan Singapore
Developing	Eastern and Central Europe Russia India	South East Asia China

Source: Goodyear (1996)

are two main streams – Western Individualism and Asian Collectivism. Between these two, Latin America exhibits a mix of individualist and collective values depending on the product category and context.

These are therefore distinct marketing environments. In each, the process of qualitative data collection and analysis of consumer motivations requires adaptation to the stages of economic development and the prevailing priorities of individualism and collectivism (Table 1).

However, within developing markets there are subsectors in the collective stream which strongly identify with Western individualistic values. There are clear signs of shifts towards 'Individualism' among young people, higher classes, urban dwellers and women, who want their voices to be heard. For example, the main drivers of the Asian young are:

● Aspiration towards money, materialism, to be rich and successful, high standards of living, enjoying life.
● Hard work, beliefs in the future, striving, forward-looking.
● Display of success through branded goods – status symbols, showing off.
● Internationalism – travel, media, Western orientation, use of English, MTV, films.

But they are still Asian 'inside': family-oriented, valuing respect, social acceptability and conformity. Many young Asians may seem Western in their behaviour, appearance and attitudes. Like their Western counterparts, they enjoy fun, brands, excitement, spending money, modern technology and international contact. They like to think of themselves as 'individuals', selecting the best of international and local images. But inside they are deeply traditional, valuing home, savings and moral values. As they themselves put it, 'I'm Western at the weekends but Japanese during the week', 'I dress Euro but my soul is Malay', 'I select the best of the West and throw the rest away'. Such developing consumers therefore lead a 'schizophrenic' life, torn between modern media and youth values and national identity.

Branding and advertising are profoundly affected by individualism and collectivism, and where people are in these quadrants. For example:

- *Western individualistic branding* tends to encourage personal choice, style and character through brands. Role models demonstrate uniqueness and originality, standing out from the crowd, the understatement of wealth, and environmental concerns.
- *Collectivist branding* on the other hand emphasises trust, confidence and security in popular, famous brand names and corporations; imitation and emulation of group role models; peer approval; and rapid adoption; displays of wealth, success and achievement, and confidence in technology.

To use Asian advertising as a specific example, it uses more collectivist themes than Western advertising. For instance, Western consumers respond better to individual self-expression in brand advertising. There is more segmentation of brands in product categories, whereas in Asia consumers opt for advertising which shows collective relationships, respect and moral values. Asian reactions are also more literal than symbolic since they are, as may be expected, at early stages of advertising literacy: ads are taken to mean what they say or show; interpretations are relatively superficial; consumers are not disposed to search out hidden meanings. Presenters are important as a source of authority; perceived popularity is part of the appeal.

(b) Consumer dynamics

To put these segmentations and shifts into a global picture, consumer dynamics typically vary between the 'everyday' (or 'ordinary') and the 'special' (or 'enhanced') on the one hand, and the 'traditional' (or 'established') and the 'modern' (or 'progressive') on the other. We can therefore create a dynamic social change model (Figure 3).

- The major dynamic is the trend towards upgraded products that moves consumers from Quadrant 1 to Quadrant 3.
- Those with restricted incomes, particularly the young, upgrade from Quadrant 1 to Quadrant 2 and then, if they can, on to Quadrant 3.
- Quadrant 4 is the traditional aspiration category which contains products and brands that are appropriate for upgrades on special occasions and other celebratory events. However, limited income means that this quadrant is only occasionally visited by most people.

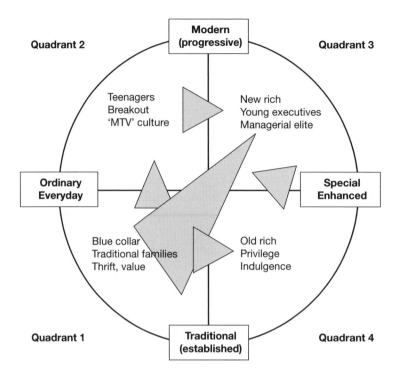

Figure 3 Consumer dynamics (© CRAM International).

- In many Western markets the focus of aspiration is now shifting away from pure Quadrant 3 to a balance of Quadrant 3 and 4 values. This is driven by an emergent idealisation of the past and disillusion with the benefits of modern technology.

During the course of their lives most consumers (60–70%) in developing markets like China, India, Indonesia or Brazil are obliged to live in Quadrant 1, as we see in Figure 4. The ways that differences are expressed are shown in Figure 5 in terms of dress, behaviour, values and role models.

Ethnicisation of the West

While all this is going on in developing markets, we must not forget the 'ethnicisation' of the West. Western values are undergoing radical change as the West reassesses the benefits of individualism, technology and capitalism in favour of harmony, social responsibility and traditional values. These are now manifest in contemporary Western advertising styles and messages.

Many changes in the West are inspired by Asian values. It is not just Asian products – cars, electronics, food, design and so on – that are being imported,

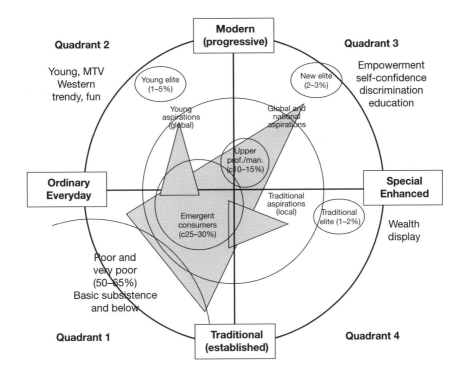

Figure 4 Global social change: economic milieux in developing markets
(© CRAM International).

but the values that go with them. Western aesthetics, philosophy, religion and culture are themselves being steadily transformed. Therefore, in looking into the Asian (and other) minds, we find benefits for understanding our own.

THE PRACTICALITIES OF INTERNATIONAL QUALITATIVE RESEARCH

The need for consistency

In spite of the growing confidence in international qualitative research, there is variability in methods, analysis and interpretation around the world because:

- Abilities of local moderators vary widely.
- There are variations in how groups are recruited, how long they last, what constitutes 'a group'.

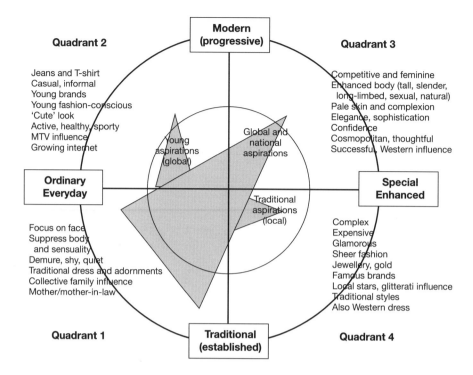

Figure 5 How differences are expressed (© CRAM International).

- Standards of recruitment vary.
- There is variable knowledge and use of projective techniques.
- Considerable differences exist in analytic frameworks for interpreting and presenting data.

Many leading buyers have made the point that for international marketing to succeed there must be consistency in research. Otherwise, there is a lack of confidence, wasted management time, conflicting interpretations, or worse, a repression to 'gut feel' or intuition in the absence of reliable data, which can lead to expensive mistakes.

Hence the importance of systematising international qualitative research by exercising control over how research is conducted and interpreted. Controlling this upgrades the quality, value and reputation of qualitative research locally and internationally.

The steps required for conducting a successful international qualitative study are as follows.

(1) International organisation

There are two strategies: one is working with a central multinational agency, which offers qualitative research at its local offices; the other is selecting independent local specialist agencies. The benefits of the former are greater control of administrative systems and standardisation, and the benefits of going to specialists are that quality may be higher. In either case, shared understanding with the local moderators is critical.

My own preference is for independent local agencies with which we have worked on the basis of many studies, and developed a shared understanding and common language for briefing, undertaking, and analysing qualitative research. We can therefore reach the highest creative common factors demanded by international qualitative research rather than risk the lowest common denominator.

(2) Research design

'Hands-on' approach to international fieldwork is critical. International qualitative executives must either undertake work themselves or observe (and 'police' if necessary) local agencies. From the beginning to the end of an international project continuous contact is essential.

The maintenance of client objectives is key. A clear statement of purpose, sample, method and content analysis is required at the outset from which we can build shared understanding, and excitement as the findings unfold.

(3) Content analyses

Content analyses are based upon the methods, topic guide and results, organised in a systematic and comparable manner. For some extensive international studies a regional or global debriefing of local moderators is beneficial to the commissioning agency prior to the formal debrief. The advantages are that local moderators can exchange views with their peers and listen to what other cultures say, especially in the context of client observers.

The European–American divide

The likelihood of consistent and reliable comparison is greater where there are broad agreements on how to investigate branding and advertising, sharing the basic constructs described above. This is more evident within Europe and the US, which share common traditions in marketing and training in qualitative research, although there are noteworthy differences between European and US practice:

Europe	*US*
More open-ended	Deeper interpretation
Groups often smaller in numbers and longer in duration	Detailed topic guides
	Groups often larger and fixed (two-hour) duration
More use of projectives	More direct questioning
Deeper interpretation	More direct interpretation

These reflect differences in philosophy and attitudes to marketing and advertising, in particular the mechanistic, 'logico-positivist' approach traditionally associated with US corporate thinking about brands and consumers, and the more organic, 'phenomenological' or 'humanistic' approach of European companies. This is changing as US companies recognise the importance of brand relationships and emotional values in the products and brands they offer, and conversely as Euro companies acknowledge the importance of product benefits and value. Nevertheless, deep differences in approach exist:

Europe	*US*
Holistic	Linear
Symbolic	Measurable
Complex	Assertive
Rapport	Control

Within European countries there are also differences in the attitudes to and practice of qualitative research. UK qualitative research, influenced by the US, is relatively pragmatic in outlook. French qualitative research has traditionally been deeper, indeed it has been at the forefront of work on imagination, fantasy and meaning, largely through the inspiration of French semiology and structuralism; writers like Saussure, Lévi-Strauss, Barthes and so on, have had important influence on French methodology and analysis. In the 1970s French qualitative researchers were using art-forms like collage and montage as forms of consumer expression which are now part of the Anglo-Saxon 'kit-bag'. German qualitative research, on the other hand, is more influenced by 'everyday life' phenomenology, requiring detailed examination of people's everyday experience and how this is reflected in behaviour, attitudes, lifestyles, and so on.

When we consider comparisons between these Western industrialised countries and developing markets, the gaps in culture and accepted interaction in qualitative interviewing become wider, thus introducing further variability in the conduct and interpretation of qualitative research. These differences also affect behaviour in groups, and in particular respondents' willingness to express themselves, disagree with one another and to criticise stimuli, as noted earlier.

Qualitative imperialism

Qualitative research therefore needs to adapt to different cultures, in spite of the benefits of standardisation. Otherwise we see a sort of 'qualitative imperialism' whereby what works in one part of the world becomes imposed on another. Research in Asia, Central and Eastern Europe, the Middle East or Africa are good cases in point. Although we need harmonisation and comparability, qualitative research in these markets cannot just assume Western practices. The recruitment of respondents, the nature of the interview, styles and questions asked need to be adapted to local conventions to ensure respondent co-operation. Above all, analysis needs to be based upon understanding of the local context, as well as the global perspective.

There are of course other factors which clearly require their own control and standardisation: sampling frames, group recruitment, administration, location, training, instructions to respondents, stimuli formats, probing and discussion techniques, back-checking, translation, timing and debriefing.

Globalism is undeniable. A preferable term is systemisation. It is a matter of obtaining the optimum balance between the benefits of standardisation and the risks of blandness. Done well, systemisation can achieve the peaks of performance.

METHODOLOGICAL APPROACHES

(1) Focus groups, or group discussions, are efficient methods of data collection around the world, largely because the group is a standard form of human intercourse. However, they have serious limitations. Bringing together a group of people unknown to one another is artificial and inhibiting, especially in cultures based on collectivist principles. People in these cultures do not want to meet people whom they do not know; hence some of these formalities may need to be relaxed. If not, there is a risk of artificiality and superficiality.

(2) Extended groups, creative sessions, consumer workshops, or ECGs™ (extended creativity groups) have special value for understanding the basics of a cross-cultural category. ECGs are longer sessions: three to four hours' duration designed to include extensive projective and elicitation techniques. They provide time for exhaustive, in-depth analyses, and collecting rich and expressive material. Participants can often be usefully screened to be creative and articulate; screening needs

to be adapted to the local culture – not just how many things can you do with a household brick or paper-clip, but how many things you can do with a single chopstick!

(3) Individual in-depth interviews are of course basic to qualitative research. Nevertheless, there are problems with them. First, the skills required to undertake truly in-depth interviewing are rare. Second, they are not as controllable as groups, nor can they be so readily observed when in-home. For these reasons they are less widely employed than they perhaps should be.

(4) Other qualitative methods that work effectively across cultures are:
   • family groups for studying cross-cultural child upbringing and 'pester power', family styles, and joint decision-making;
   • duos, friendship pairs, couples;
   • mini-groups with sectors which have shared experiences or responsibilities;
   • interviews with local 'experts';
   • groups made up of the local community.

(5) Laddering is a useful approach in international qualitative research. It is usually based on some 40 to 80 individual interviews in a given market to identify key triggers in choosing a particular product or brand within a particular category. The process of laddering is, first, to identify the most important attribute differences between products, brands or ads, and second, to 'ladder these up' to find the benefits and values they lead to. The interviewer works with variants of the probe '…and why is that important to you?', repeating the responses to find the means–end chain of associations inside consumers' minds. This generates detailed data on attributes, benefits and values that can give insights for initiating global concepts and executions.

Two further aids to group interviewing play useful parts:

(1) *Video-conferencing* Watching groups from a remote location. Theoretically this cuts down on travel and on occasion can make for efficient reporting.

(2) *Online groups* Recruiting and conducting groups at a prearranged and private 'chat room'. Contact is made with 'connected' generations, precise transcripts are available and clients too can intervene. However, the risks of deceit are well-known. There is also a 'Luddite' reaction – the traditional cues to body language are not available, you don't 'see' the respondents – although these objections are scarcely relevant for studying virtual realities. The vehicle of the viewing theatre gives way to the computer screen.

In applying all these qualitative methods, client involvement in the interviewing process is highly desirable, to attend or watch groups and individual interviews where practical. Clearly, caution is required to avoid wrong or over-quick conclusions from a single group or interview, but the benefits of client involvement in the data collection process usually outweigh these. More and more management have a sympathy with qualitative research: it helps them make contact with their consumers and to buy into the qualitative process.

This can be especially important in developing and emerging markets, where local management often come from richer strata or the same pool of universities and are very remote from their consumers; this of course can also apply to research agencies which sometimes find it difficult to make contact or form relationships with 'lower' levels or castes than themselves.

Projective and elicitation techniques

Projective and elicitation techniques are both sources of creativity and insight, and systematisation globally:

(1) Providing 'permission' to express feelings by switching to the emotional, or 'right brain' mode. In groups, this occurs through exchange of feelings or images: one person responds and this acts as a catalyst to others.

(2) Projecting private and unconscious beliefs and feelings on to unstructured material. This is the formal application of projective techniques, familiar in Rorschach inkblots or TAT pictures described earlier. It is a way of bypassing the conscious mind and gaining access to unconscious processes.

It should be added that in a group, projective tasks can be done individually and then shared with the group. This allows individual data to be inspected independently afterwards.

East versus West

Projective techniques are in fact based on the Western concept of repression, i.e. that some behaviours are unacceptable to the conscious mind or society, and therefore the thoughts behind them have to be consigned to the unconscious. Hence the role of projective techniques is to encourage consumers to express their private and unconscious guilt, aspirations and inner, 'free' wishes or feelings. In non-Western cultures, individual feelings are often denied in favour of the social order, respect, 'face', obligation and denial of emotion. Consequently, the main use of projective techniques in these cultures is to elicit emotional expression and 'get behind the mask' of conformity.

In practice, both processes work across cultures by:

- Encouraging emotional as well as rational reactions
- Providing non-verbal and verbal means of communication
- Giving permission to express novel ideas
- Allowing fantasy, idiosyncrasy and originality
- Reducing social constraints and censorship
- Encouraging group sharing and 'opening up'

The question is: Which techniques work best for international qualitative research? A very wide number of verbal and non-verbal projective and elicitation techniques exist: free association, picture completion, sentence completion, collages, analogies and metaphors, personalisation, role-playing, planetariums, obituaries, mock-selling, passing on ideas, mime, masks, guided dreams, magic wands, psycho-drawing, clay, creative writing, gaming, photo-sort, fables, folklore, heroes, etc.

Individual researchers in different countries also have their own favourites. Some rely heavily on projectives; others make scarce use of them. In many underdeveloped countries there is ignorance of their purpose and use.

Projective and elicitation techniques provide a basis for standardisation and comparison. The benefits of standardising projective and elicitation techniques are that they are systematic tasks for respondents to perform, which can underpin the normal process of probing and following up reactions. Thus they reduce moderator variability and permit direct comparisons between results from different countries.

The key criteria, therefore, for selecting projective and elicitation techniques for standardising cross-cultural international qualitative research are:

(1) *Relevance,* i.e. which methods most effectively address the marketing issues being tested.
(2) *Culture-free,* i.e. which methods 'travel' across all cultures, and work in Western and non-Western cultures, in different languages, with unsophisticated as well as sophisticated consumers.
(3) *Ease of application,* i.e. can be used economically, without occupying excess time, or demanding special skills on the part of moderators or respondents.

From worldwide experience we find the following techniques satisfy these three criteria:

- Collages
- Picture completions
- Analogies
- Psychodrawings
- Personalisation
- Guided dreams

These techniques vary in their projective depth and in their elicitation use for creating group interaction and building between respondents.

They can be used with equal confidence in Westernised cultures (e.g. US, EC, Australia), and in countries under the influence of different cultural value systems (Confucian, Muslim, Buddhist, Shinto, etc.). They can be used in different languages, and local moderators feel comfortable with them, given proper training and elaboration of their purposes, and how to interpret the results.

This is not to say that other techniques do not have their specific uses (e.g. photo-sorts of standard faces or other symbols to identify user imagery, planetariums to explore the 'worlds' of products and brands (often a short cut for collages), and so on).

The general points, however, are as follows:

(1) Projection is essential to understanding consumer motivations and inhibitions. Without it we are forced to rely on what the consumer chooses to tell us, and the limitations of asking, which are subject to all the problems of access, communication and embarrassment described.
(2) These techniques also have elicitation or enabling value around the world. They help respondents open up, relate and build upon what other people say, express and feel.
(3) The outputs are not just literal but are symptoms of the complex human mind in different cultures. They should never be presented literally. Instead, the international qualitative researcher should employ them to interpret and analyse and, where appropriate, illustrate the local and global consumer mind.

Ethnographic methods

Ethnography, otherwise known as naturalistic or contextual research, has its origins in social anthropology, using culture as its organising principle. Methods are a mix of observation and interviewing. Typical examples are:

- Observation of shopping behaviour, either as a participant or observer. Shoppers may be asked to articulate their behaviour and thought processes as they shop (protocol analysis), followed by an interview in which the decision processes are re-enacted.

- Video records of product usage, in home, at leisure, at work, and so on.
- 'Day in the life of' videos and photos, including shots of people's favourite objects, their homes, decor, etc.
- Collections of local artefacts, including cultural icons, famous local advertising, personal lists, diaries, etc.

Ethnology enters people's everyday lives in as naturalistic a way as possible. Compared to focus groups, ethnography has been described as 'like moving from black and white to colour'. The intensity and intimacy of the smells, textures, tastes, heat, sounds, movements and muscular strain are all brought to life to enrich levels of understanding.

Much of this is simply taken for granted in local cultures and not readily expressed in interviewing; it just 'feels right' to members of the local culture. Since culture is deeper than language, interviewing only gives an approximate and blurred view of the experiences that people have in their culture. Observation can help go deeper and illustrate real, everyday life. Interviews with local informed opinion (e.g. sociologists, psychologists, journalists, local style leaders and others whose opinions and influence bear upon consumer behaviour) help this interpretation.

Ethnography helps overcome the 'limitations of asking' in conventional qualitative research, especially in international qualitative research, i.e. the gaps, distortions and downright subterfuge between what consumers say they do and what they actually do in the real world.

The benefits of ethnography to the international qualitative researcher are that it supplements groups or in-depths with local realities. Ethnography is much more important than sheer observation, valuable as that is; it also aids comprehension of symbol and idea generation through studies of urban and rural life. For example, studies of health, hygiene or eating behaviour would not be complete without understanding the roles of local nutritionists, doctors, nurses, and even priests and shamans in some cultures.

The practice of ethnography therefore has many benefits, but it also has limitations. Ethnographic methods take time and patience, and are costly. Many hours of videotaping require extensive resources to edit into a simple compelling film. Nevertheless, the gasps of interest from the client audience as they discover, 'Is that what they do with our products!', are justified in NPD and idea-generation products.

Semiotics

Semiotics (from the Greek 'semeion') is the study of signs. These signs, words, symbols, icons, have two different levels of meaning which interact with one another.

(1) The literal, what consumers read and see, and of which they are usually conscious.
(2) The underlying, symbolic, connotative meaning, which may be unconscious.

Internationally, semiotic analyses are of special value because the language of signs is buried deep in the culture. Behind these often stand local myths and values. At the same time there are universal signs or archetypes emanating out of the collective conscious of mankind, and increasing global signs deriving from global media which can be detected across cultures. Semiotics assists in identifying and decoding these signs.

The analysis of advertising is the major application. All ads are impregnated with meanings, some literal and some symbolic. Full meanings are rarely grasped at the moments of perception. Typically they are registered fleetingly, and consumers use visual–verbal 'shorthand' to recognise, classify and relate to them. But it is the deeper, symbolic, signified meanings of ads that work more powerfully – motivating, reinforcing and making sense of the world out there. These deeper meanings are conveyed by content, analogies, style, gaze, colours, music, words, etc. The language of advertising is living, and hence new signs and meanings are continually evolving to obtain competitive edge. Furthermore, ads do not just 'do things' to consumers; consumers 'do things' to ads, use them, corrupt them, apply them to their lives.

To make an international semiotic analysis:

(1) We need to collect a broad range of ads in the local culture, not just for the product/brand investigated, and to analyse these for the underlying connotative meanings of the various signs, symbols and styles used.

(2) The set of meanings should not just be what the ad is saying, but what it is not saying. Binary opposites help the analytic process. Of particular value is understanding what the brand 'transformation' signs or rhetorics are (e.g. science, realism, fantasy, authority, control, order, humanity, status, achievement, tradition, change, etc.).

(3) This analysis will then generate a set of hypotheses about how advertising works in the culture, i.e. the 'advertising ideology'. These hypotheses can then inform the qualitative interviewing process, providing interviewers with insights into signs and symptoms to look for in consumer responses, enriching the quality of the data and subsequent analysis.

Semiotics is also useful for drawing up standardised collections of visual images that work across cultures, based upon different moods, emotions and values, such as parenting styles, gatekeeping, feeding, pleasure, indulgence, individualism, collectivism, etc., and the brand transformations listed above. In these ways, international qualitative research assembles 'image banks' for evaluating positions.

THE FUTURE ODYSSEY

International qualitative research is now a multi-billion dollar industry which plays a major part in international product and brand development. However, the odyssey of international qualitative research – for that is what it most certainly is – is not just a matter of business value. There is also a passion in international qualitative research for understanding the changing consumer worldwide, exploring the labyrinths of culture and seeing the global consumer mind unfold.

Qualitative thinking over the past few decades has had a profound effect upon marketing and the market research industry as a whole. It has been largely responsible for the paradigm shift in marketing and social thought that is now so important to marketing in understanding consumers, brands, advertising and the changing world around us.

Qualitative research has its own peculiar roots in humanistic, phenomenological and relativistic philosophies. It embraces dynamic psychology, social psychology and social anthropology, and, for international qualitative research in particular, the disciplines of ethnography, linguistics, semiotics, history, politics and semiology. It is therefore eclectic and wide-ranging. It confronts marketing and social policy-making with a different view of the consumer. It draws attention to the conflicts, segmentations and uncertainties as consumers face the future. It points up how brands and consumers can find new visions.

This is not to say that all is well. There is much qualitative research that still hangs on the positivist model or is little more than investigative journalism. In some markets the term 'focus group' has become synonymous with mere 'sound bites'. The media also offer 'research' of a qualitative nature around the world in the form of phone-ins, chat rooms, and debates described as 'research'. Much of this may benefit the democratic process, but we need to be careful about the abuse of 'qualitative' methods.

The need for professional institutions

All of this calls for the further development of professional institutions to represent international qualitative research. We require a register of qualified international qualitative researchers. We need to build up the body of international qualitative theory and practice which stands on the three grand pillars of qualitative research – motivational research, ethnography and semiotics. We need to set out more programmes of education for ourselves and for users. We need to get the 'hygiene' factors of sampling and recruitment firmly under control, not just in the West but in developing markets as well. Above all, we need to demonstrate the commercial benefits and applications of qualitative research.

Celebrating qualitative–quantitative differences

There are of course profound differences between qualitative and quantitative research in the nature of knowledge and how to collect it. This applies equally in the international environment. Rather than minimise these differences, my view is that we should celebrate them for the complementary values they provide. Quantitative research depends largely upon objective tests of sample size and criteria drawn from the physical sciences to demonstrate its reliability and validity.

Trustworthiness

Qualitative research also needs objective criteria to validate itself and encourage 'trustworthiness' in its processes, results and conclusions, instead of relying on 'depth' and 'insight'.

There are three tests of 'trustworthiness' uniquely applicable to qualitative research, as we have seen.

(1) *Models of consumer behaviour*. Qualitative findings should be related to broadly accepted models of cross-cultural human behaviour and indeed build them. Qualitative research is not merely a set of anecdotes or reportage.
(2) *Social context*. They should be based upon demonstrating understanding of the cultures on which the data are based. The 'thick' and 'deep' aspects of consumer behaviour need to be made available to us.
(3) *Transparency*. Assumptions, processes and agendas should be explicit, and open to inspection and criticism, for the practicable and actionable world in which qualitative research lives.

With these criteria in mind, qualitative research can reach strong, firm and actionable conclusions. Warnings about sample size, so much a feature of past qualitative studies, or beliefs that qualitative research is merely a precursor to quantification dissolve because modern international qualitative work is well-grounded in human and cultural understanding.

We can then look forward with confidence to the future of international qualitative research. Heavy demands will be placed on it and international marketing in the future. We can expect concerns, even neuroses, from global management as they struggle with the increasing power of consumers and the complexities of the twenty-first century world. International qualitative research as a living, evolving, adaptive process is ideally suited to its role as partner, guide and source of consumer understanding.

KEY IDEAS

- For economic and political reasons many organisations are increasingly multinational in approach.
- International organisations need to consider such issues as how well a concept might travel, whether globalisation is possible and whether the East always follow the West.
- A balance must be sought between localism and globalism, and a new model, transnationalism, is evolving which allows for the joint benefits of local sensitivity and mass production scale.
- Speed, sharing and the exchange of data have become more critical to meet the needs of transnational organisations.
- International qualitative research must provide a total understanding of consumers at global, regional and local levels simultaneously.
- Social milieux (bundles of everyday life experiences, symbols and values) are a useful means of segmentation. In particular, they illustrate the difference between those milieux which value Individualism (primarily the West) versus Collectivism (primarily the East).
- Even within the Collective stream there are those, primarily the young and affluent, who have incorporated some aspects of individualism into their lifestyle and attitudes.
- Similarly, the ethnicisation of the West is a factor, as Asian values, not just products, are increasingly imported.
- For international marketing to succeed there must be more consistency in research approach without resorting to qualitative imperialism where what works in one region is imposed on another.

FURTHER READING

Bartlett, C. & Ghoshal, S. (1998) *Managing Across Borders*. Century / Arrow Press, London.

Cooper, P. (1987) The new qualitative technology, in *ESOMAR Market Research Monographs*, Vol. 2. Sampson, P. (ed). Amsterdam: ESOMAR.

Cooper, P. (1997) Western at the weekends. *ADMAP*, Issue 377, October.

ESOMAR Handbook of Market and Opinion Research (1998) Ed. McDonald, C., Vangelder, P. See especially chapters by M. Goodyear on qualitative research and L. Caller on multinational research.

Fournier, S. (1998) Consumers and their brands: developing relationship theory in consumer research. *Journal of Consumer Research*, 24, March, pp 343–373.

Journal of the Market Research Society (1999) Special Issue on Qualitative Research for the 21st Century, guest ed. P. Cooper, Vol. 41, No 1, January. See articles by T. Hanby on branding, J. Pawle on international qualitative research from the client perspective, J. Ueltzhöffer and C. Aschenberg on transactional consumer cultures and social milieus, and H. Mariampolski on ethnology.

Kapferer, J-N. (1997) *Strategic Brand Management.* The Free Press, New York.

Index